METAPHOR

A Musical Dimension

Edited by

JAMIE C. KASSLER

Gordon and Breach Publishers

Metaphor

Musicology: A Book Series

Edited by **Hans Lenneberg**, The University of Chicago, Illinois

This book is part of a series. The publisher will accept continuation orders which may be cancelled at any time and which provide for automatic billing and shipping of each title in the series upon publication. Please write for details.

Editor's Preface

Metaphor has often been regarded as a rhetorical device, marginal to language as a whole, in which a figurative word is substituted for a literal one. Since about the 1960s, however, some writers have argued that this view both misunderstands the nature of metaphor and greatly underestimates its significance for language. These writers hold that metaphor does not operate at the level of the word or sign, but at the level of discourse; that metaphor is a syntactically deviant usage which establishes a novel connection within the terms of discourse; that when considered in the unfolding of discourse, metaphor is the very process whereby new meanings are created. More recently, the thesis has been propounded that metaphor is not a figurative departure from a base line of linguistic reference. Rather, metaphor actually transforms the referential dimension of language, creating new modes of representing or describing reality. Such a thesis, which rejects the structuralist or post-structuralist notion that a text is an expression of discourse in general, implies that a text is a specific *artifact* of discourse, produced as a result of *creative activity* that shapes discourse into a particular configuration.

Since musical texts tend to be disregarded in the philosophical literature on metaphor, the purpose of this volume is to provide illustrations of different kinds of metaphor—cognitive and rhetorical, past and present, Western and non-Western—in which the unifying focus is music and musical activity. This was not the original aim of the authors of the papers, whose work had its origin in a Symposium of the International Musicological Society held in Melbourne from 18 August to 2 September 1988, one of the main themes of which was analogy. All papers have been rewritten (and in one case, a completely new paper submitted) so as to bring out more clearly the dimension or dimensions of metaphor treated. It was then left to the editor to group the papers in order to emphasize certain other dimensions which might otherwise be obscure. Although readers may peruse the contents of this volume in any order, the following rationale underlies the sequence of papers as printed.

The first five papers focus on cognitive metaphors, since the authors explore the relation between language and such cognitive processes as listening to music (Guck and Taylor) and composing music (Sichardt, Baron and Debly). The paper by Leppert contains two different metaphors. On the one hand, there is a cognitive metaphor in which the author examines the relations between language and the process of 'reading' a painting. On the other hand, the author's 'reading' of the painting is a rhetorical metaphor, since he aims to transform our way of 'seeing' through the power of Marxian criticism. Transformative power is the focus of the four papers by Samuel, Becker, Turner and Shiloah, in which music and musical activity are metaphors for the unification of entire communities of for the healing of individuals within communities. The next two papers treat the process of theory construction by examining the texts of two writers who use extended metaphors to produce, respectively, a theory of human character (Kassler) and a theory of music (Cumming). In the last paper, by Pont, we are reminded that analogy has limits and, consequently, that not only the artifacts of analogy, which include metaphors, but also the process itself require critical assessment.

Publication of these papers would not have been possible without the foresight and energy of Margaret Kartomi, who was the motivating force behind the 1988 Symposium and its success. The editor is also indebted to Peter Platt for his continuing encouragement of the kinds of explorations that the papers in this volume represent. In preparing the papers for publication, the editor's task was eased and made pleasant by the cheerful cooperation of the authors and by the creative cooking and computer expertise of Michael Kassler.

J.C.K.
McMahons Point, N.S.W.
January 1991

Introduction to the Series

The Gordon and Breach Musicology series, a companion to the *Journal of Musicological Research,* covers a creative range of musical topics, from historical and theoretical subjects to social and philosophical studies. Volumes thus far published show the extent of this broad spectrum, from *Music and Its Social Meanings, Musical Life in Poland,* and *Witnesses* and *Scholars: Studies in Musical Biography* to *Music-Cultures in Contact: Convergences and Collisions.* This editors also welcome interdisciplinary studies, ethnomusicological works and performance analyses. With this series, it is our aim to expand the field and definition of musical exploration and research.

Introduction to the Series

Metaphor

A Musical Dimension

Edited by

Jamie C. Kassler

Gordon and Breach Publishers

Australia • Austria • Belgium • France • Germany • India • Japan • Malaysia •
Netherlands • Russia • Singapore • Switzerland • Thailand • United Kingdom • United States

Published under license by Gordon and Breach Science Publishers S.A.

Gordon and Breach Science Publishers S.A.
Postfach
4004 Basel
Switzerland

Originally published in 1991 as volume1 of the Currency Press series *Australian Studies in the History, Philosophy and Social Studies of Music.*

British Library Cataloguing in Publication Data

Metaphor: A Musical Dimension. - New ed. -
(Musicology: A Book Series, ISSN 0275-5866;
Vol. 15)
  I. Kassler, Jamie Croy II. Series
  781.8

  ISBN 2-88449-136-8

Contents

METAPHOR — A MUSICAL DIMENSION

METAPHOR

A Musical Dimension

Edited by
JAMIE.C.KASSLER

CURRENCY PRESS • SYDNEY

First published in 1991
by Currency Press Pty Ltd
330 Oxford Street
Paddington, NSW 2021
Australia

National Library of Australia Cataloguing-in-publication data.

Metaphor — A musical dimension.

Bibliography.
Includes index.
ISBN 0 86819 301 1.
ISBN 0 86819 277 5 (pbk.).

1. Musicology — Australia. I. Kassler, Jamie Croy.
II. International Musicological Society. Symposium
(1988 : Melbourne, Vic.). (Series : Australian
studies in the history, philosophy and social
studies of music.)

780

Typeset by Deadline Typesetting Ltd, New Zealand
Printed by Colorcraft, Hong Kong

Contents

Two Types of Metaphoric Transfer
Marion A. Guck   1

Understanding Style: Wölfflin's Principles of Art Applied to Music
Morris Taylor   13

Music as a Sight in the Production of Music's Meaning
Richard Leppert   69

Music and Shamanic Power in the Gesar Epic
Geoffrey Samuel   89

The Javanese Court Bedhaya Dance as a Tantric Analogy
Judith Becker   109

Belian as a Symbol of Cosmic Reunification
Ashley Turner   121

Musical Modes and the Medical Dimension: The Arabic Sources (c.900–c.1600)
Amnon Shiloah   147

Man a la Mode: or Reinterpreting the Book of Nature from a Musical Point of View
Jamie C. Kassler   160

Analogy in Leonard B. Meyer's Theory of Musical Meaning
Naomi Cumming   177

Foreword

This book launches a new series of monographs entitled *Australian Studies in the History, Philosophy and Social Studies of Music.*

The initial volumes in this series will consist mainly of papers presented at the Symposium of the International Musicological Society (SIMS '88) and Festival of Music, which were held in Melbourne during Australia's Bicentennial year, 1988. The symposium which was attended by four hundred delegates from around the world, dealt with themes of analogy in musicological method, cultural interaction through music, and music since c.1960. This event, whose major sponsor was Monash University, was hosted by the Musicological Society of Australia and the International Council for Traditional Music. The event was made possible through the generous support of many funding bodies and cultural organisations which either directly supported parts of the programme or provided delegates' travel costs. Publishing subvention was provided for the initial volumes by SIMS '88 and for the first volume by the Alfred S. White Music Bequest Limited, Sydney.

Margaret J. Kartomi
General Editor

Editor's Preface

Metaphor has often been regarded as a rhetorical device, marginal to language as a whole, in which a figurative word is substituted for a literal one. Since about the 1960s, however, some writers have argued that this view both misunderstands the nature of metaphor and greatly underestimates its significance for language. These writers hold that metaphor does not operate at the level of the word or sign, but at the level of discourse; that metaphor is a syntactically deviant usage which establishes a novel connection within the terms of discourse; that when considered in the unfolding of discourse, metaphor is the very process whereby new meanings are created. More recently, the thesis has been propounded that metaphor is not a figurative departure from a baseline of linguistic reference. Rather, metaphor actually transforms the referential dimension of language, creating new modes of representing or describing reality. Such a thesis, which rejects the structuralist or post-structuralist notion that a text is an expression of discourse in general, implies that a text is a specific *artifact* of discourse, produced as a result of *creative activity* that shapes discourse into a particular configuration.

Since musical texts tend to be disregarded in the philosophical literature on metaphor, the purpose of this volume is to provide illustrations of different kinds of metaphor—cognitive and rhetorical, past and present, western and non-western—in which the unifying focus is music and musical activity. This was not the original aim of the authors of the papers, whose work had its origin in a Symposium of the International Musicological Society held in Melbourne from 18 August to 2 September 1988, one of the main themes of which was analogy. All papers have been rewritten (and in one case, a completely new paper submitted) so as to bring out more clearly the dimension or dimensions of metaphor treated. It was then left to the editor to group the papers in order to emphasize certain other dimensions which might otherwise remain obscure. Although readers may peruse the contents of this volume in any order, the following rationale underlies the sequence of papers as printed.

The first five papers focus on cognitive metaphors, since the authors explore the relation between language and such cognitive processes as listening to music (Guck and Taylor) and composing music (Sichardt, Baron and Debly). The paper by Leppert contains two different metaphors. On the one hand, there is a cognitive metaphor in which the author examines the relations between language and the process of 'reading' a painting. On the other hand, the author's 'reading' of the painting is a rhetorical metaphor, since he aims to transform our way of 'seeing' through the power of Marxian criticism. Transformative power is the focus of the four papers by Samuel, Becker, Turner and Shiloah, in which music and musical activity are metaphors for the unification of entire communities or for the healing of individuals within communities. The next two papers treat the process of theory construction by examining the texts of two writers who use extended metaphors to produce, respectively, a theory of human character (Kassler) and a theory of music (Cumming). In the last paper, by Pont, we are reminded that analogy has limits and, consequently, that not only the artifacts of analogy, which include metaphors, but also the process itself require critical assessment.

Publication of these papers would not have been possible without the foresight and energy of Margaret Kartomi, who was the motivating force behind the 1988 Symposium and its success. The editor is also indebted to Peter Platt for his continuing encouragement of the kinds of explorations that the papers in this volume represent. In preparing the papers for publication, the editor's task was eased and made pleasant by the cheerful cooperation of the authors and by the creative cooking and computer expertise of Michael Kassler.

J.C.K.
McMahons Point, N.S.W.
January 1991

Two Types of Metaphoric Transfer

Marion A. Guck

Abstract

Music theorists in the United States have examined how theoretical and analytical statements ought to be framed. Less formal discourse, e.g., metaphoric descriptions, has been disregarded. However, since even Western music's technical vocabulary is rooted in metaphor, its contribution to musical discourse requires examination. In a study of metaphor's role, a musician, conversing about Chopin's Prelude in B Minor, Opus 28, No. 6, proposed that an arching line stretched over the whole piece. This suggested a detailed musical analysis in terms of three perspectives: brief melodic arch shapes, gestural-emotional phrase arches and a piece-spanning narrative curve. Reflection on the technical and metaphoric aspects of the analysis reveal several attributes of the arch image and of metaphoric descriptions in general. Two modes of analogical thinking are identified: direct comparison of single features in two different conceptual domains (comparative metaphor) and interpretation of a complex of features in one domain as similar to the structure of such a complex in a second domain (ascriptive metaphor). The author argues that if music is expressive of other experience, it is because of similarity of conceptual structure.

Introduction

When Milton Babbitt raised questions of 'the nature and limits' of musical discourse (1961, 1965, 1971), music theorists in the United States took his assertion, that music theory must meet the same standards of cognitive clarity or rigor as the sciences, as a restrictive endorsement of scientific-style language. Though nothing that he said can be claimed to proscribe any style of description so long as reasons can be given for assertions, the theory community adopted scientific-appearing formulation as the standard for legitimate musical discourse. Thus, certain styles of less formal theoretic and descriptive discourse, such as metaphoric description, that are of significant value in at least such practical contexts as teaching and coaching performers, came to be dismissed.

In fact, however, even the legitimate technical vocabulary of Western music is rooted in metaphor, and the metaphoric roots are often still in evidence. For example, the notion of space is so pervasively and deeply embedded in the language of musical discourse, and of musical thought, that if we wish to speak of music, we must speak in spatial terms. Thus, in tonal music lines rise and fall in registral space, and the root identifies a chord with a pitch at the bottom of its third stack. Though these notions are thought literally true of music, their sources are metaphoric; and the remnants of those sources are still discernible: such technical terms are *music-literal*.

The notion of musical movement is almost equally pervasive. We resort to it, and to notions of change, to connect musical objects and to describe their succession. Thus, pitch sequences are transformed into lines moving through the space defined by pitch location, responding to tendencies perceived as inherent in the pitch and chord relations. Some of these terms, too, are music-literal, but most retain an overtly metaphorical resonance, even in musical discourse.

It seems essential to consider how we do—in fact, how we must—resort to metaphoric language (and to analogical thinking) to describe music in order to discover what it contributes to musical discourse and to musical understanding.

To study the role of metaphoric and underlying analogical thinking in musical discourse, a circumscribed situation was developed—loosely speaking, an experiment—that attempted to duplicate some relatively informal contexts in which music is discussed principally in metaphoric terms, so that the contribution of such description would be exposed for examination. Three groups of musicians (students in an introductory tonal analysis class, students in composition and graduate students in musicology) were asked to converse about Chopin's *Prelude in B Minor*, Opus 28, No. 6 [*see* Plate 1] and, in particular, to focus their conversation on measure 11, beat 3 to measure 12, the beginning of beat 2. Initially, they were not provided with a score but were played Maurizio Pollini's performance (Deutsche Grammophon 2530 550) of the passage, of the phrase that includes the passage (ending with the passage) and of the whole piece.

Though in the absence of scores even musicians rely less on technical description, conversants were asked to discuss the piece in non-technical terms. Since common-language terminology for musical sounds (words like 'loud') is very limited, the resulting conversation naturally turned to metaphor. In order to investigate the relation between metaphoric description and musical structure, conversants were, after a period of time, given scores, played the piece again and asked what about the piece's

Plate 1: F. Chopin, *Prelude in B Minor*, Op. 28, No. 6 (New York: Dover)

structure had suggested the non-technical descriptions they had proposed. These conversations were transcribed and analyzed.[1]

One of the graduate students in musicology proposed the metaphor of an arch to describe the general (in addition to the particular) shape of the melodic line over the course of the whole piece, with the passage cited seen as the top of the arch. The group's brief comments on the subject eventually suggested to me a detailed analysis of the *Prelude*, which is presented below.

I imagine the *Prelude* as two-measure arching melodies nested within phrase-length arches in turn nested within a single piece arch. The relatively literal spatial notion of melodic arch shape leads me on to the movements of arching gestures and, then, beyond these, to the rise and fall of mood and to a narrative curve. The interaction of image and musical structure at each level illuminates immediate and compelling features of the piece, and the interactions among the different arch interpretations and their analyses yield both a dynamic analysis of the Prelude and a wealth of information about the imagery of musical description, which I will go on to examine.

1. The Image of an Arch

1.1. Analysis

As the *Prelude* opens, the left-hand melody sweeps up through arpeggiating sixteenth notes to hover on D, drawn out by its lower neighbour in languorous quarter-dotted eighth-sixteenth. A lingering three eighth-note fall through the same arpeggio closes in sedate steps. The sheer registral span makes an arch of the melody's contour; and the progressive lengthening of sweep, hover and lingering fall make it graceful. Dynamics, too, swell and shrink as the line rises and falls.

Melodic arching underlies each of the piece's two phrases as well. The first phrase rises as the sixteenth-note sweeps propel the line from D that touches the right-hand chords in m. 1, through F sharp that intrudes on the chord space in m. 3, to G, the apex of the melody, in the midst of the right hand's chord space in m. 5. Each arpeggio broadens the line's span and increases the line's intensity. The simple, clear i-VI progression, opening diatonic tonal space and brightening from minor to major, inclines toward a rising mood.

As the phrase continues, sweeping ascents are complemented by a single, incrementally articulated decline (mm. 5-8). Sixteenth notes are forgotten in the falling quarter-and eighth-note steps. The mood falls as the music turns away from the diatonic G-major chord to chromatic diminished-seventh sonorities. More tellingly, despite the greatly increased rate of chord succession, the progression stalls on vii and then V, entangled with frustratingly interstitial VI's and i's. Even the lift afforded by the soprano's escape upward to F sharp is obliterated by its sixteenth-note rush down to be captured in the cadence.

The left hand falls the final steps to regain the level of the opening (m. 9), but the rise of the new phrase is curtailed by elimination of the second B-minor arch. At the same time, the voice-leading rise is at first delayed by repeating m. 9's D in m. 11; then, it accelerates when E follows immediately and climbs directly to F natural. The dotted eighth-sixteenth that impelled earlier lower neighbours forward is replaced by broad eighths that impede the rise of the line, drawing attention to the climaxing harmonic tritone. Its resolution in mid-arch to the sixth, C natural-E, conclusively moves beyond G into the relatively remote tonal region of the Neapolitan. With resolution into the Neapolitan, the ascent of the phrase and of the piece conclude together. The apex and fall of the phrase are also the apex and decline of the piece.

At the apex the left hand plays through the expansiveness engendered by all the earlier upward sweeps when, having dropped to C (m. 13), it wells up through its broadest arpeggio twice without an intervening descent (more later). But the repeated surging upward to E begin to call for further decisive progressive movement, and the arpeggios seem to have forgotten how to continue the melodic line. When they fail (m. 14), the climax is revealed to contain the seeds of its own destruction. E continues to hover, now requiring resolution; the right-hand soprano reverses mm. 11-12's B-C to C-B; and the chord dissolves. The descent of the arch has already begun.

The decline of the piece (and second phrase) exaggerates the downward mood-swing of the first phrase. A slow step up and rushing stepwise fall, heard earlier when the right-hand's melodic escape was forestalled in m. 7, now replaces the left- hand sweeps (m. 15). The lowering mood recurs with the diminished-seventh chords, and irresolution is enhanced by waffling between the dominant and tonic that stretches out through the repeated melodic figure. The right hand no longer ascends from B but alternates restlessly with A sharp below it. The music is stuck, aimlessly retracing familiar ground until the sixteenths fall further to the cadence (m. 18). But it is deceptive, and the soprano delays the chord at that, so it all has to be done again.

Instead of 'decisive progressive movement', the piece meanders somewhere in the dominant, dissipating the energy of the first half's sweeps. It declines to a dimly recalled echo (mm. 22-26) of the opening measures, the accompanying chords stripped down to an increasingly feeble third. The promise of the piece's rise is undermined and, thwarted, the piece withers away.

1.2. Interpretation

In the *Prelude* arch shape—abstracted from the material features of arches as a line ascending to curve toward a focus of structural tensions and curving again to descend—models the pitch aspect of the left hand's two-measure melodic arches as a linear contour. It is most convincing over this short span, because the music can be taken in as a single continuous event and converted into a single continuous object, almost as if it were not presented over a span of time at all but in a single instant, the moment required to take in the shape of a real arch. Because arch shape depends on music-literal ascent and descent, it is possible to describe pitch relatively precisely and objectively by claiming that a given melody is an arch. Because arches are typically symmetrical, the claim points, as well, to the temporal symmetries and dynamic complementation perceived in this piece; but, already, this suggests that there is more to a melodic arch than what meets the metaphoric eye.

Arching shape can also be glimpsed in the emphasis on repeatedly ascending or descending lines over longer spans and on middleground voice-leading arcs. However, because the former do not form a continuous line but rather generalize a directional emphasis, and the latter is a slow, intermittent, gentle curve, a greater imaginative effort must be made to convert them into an arch shape: if they are heard as archlike, it is under the influence of the foreground arches. Something else must make vivid the continuity of line, and something more must be made of the piece than a projection of pitch contour alone.

Of course, 'something more' is already there in the *Prelude*, and it is the guide to 'something else'. From the beginning, I described the lines rising and falling; just above, I described how an arch's line ascends, focuses and curves. *Movement* infuses both the moment I try to describe them. It might be like the movement of a ball thrown in the air, or the movement of an observing eye or of the arm that threw the ball. Consider the gesture of the arm.

To hear arching movement, one most likely recalls, subliminally, memories that incorporate the fine, continuous adjustments in muscle tensions needed to produce the smooth gesture: the initial impetus that increasingly opposes gravity as the arm rises, stretching to the point of fullest extension, then decreasing tension as the arm yields to gravity. In the gesture, rise and fall are also converted into increase and decrease of effort and tension. In fact, the notion of increase-and-decrease has already been introduced through the melodic arch's swelling dynamics. The conversion superimposes a metaphorical reinterpretation on the music literal, and the resulting description is more deeply metaphoric.

The notion of gesture is most clearly discernible in the phrase-length arches. Though music-literal ascent and descent are still evident in the phrase's melodic contour, its line is not brief enough to convert into an instantaneously perceived shape, like the left-hand melodic arches. The timespan of the phrase is more appropriate to sensing movement through the shape as it unfolds through the mediation of the foreground figures.

This sense is not conveyed just by the interpretation of conventional pitch relations. Sweeping ascent and lingering fall are conveyed through durations, through the gradual widening of arpeggios contrasted with laborious steps and through the breadth of a slow, brightening diatonic-harmonic rhythm opposed to a relatively fast chromaticism. Thus, the phrase's arch retains vestiges of its origin in shape, while it incorporates the movement and tension *qualities* of gesture.

However, these notions of sweeping and subsiding do not yet capture all the senses in which we might care to hear the phrase expand and contract. The opposition between broad, clear chord progression and constrained, entangled alternation suggest expansive, rising *moods* in opposition to exhausted, falling moods. The tensions and sensations of physical acts can be extended to the realm of feeling. Increases and decreases can be of emotional tension, and ups and downs can be of mood.

On the model of the phrase and melodic arches, the whole *Prelude* can be heard as a single arch. It, too, emphasizes ascent followed by descent, but this alone is an inadequate explanation. In addition to music-literal shape the single arch draws on the figurative senses of movement and tension embodied in gesture and on their further figurative interpretation as mood, incorporating all in a depiction of human (inter-) actions: the piece's arch is a *narrative curve* (a notion that is figurative even in its home domain). A narrative curve is usually thought of as the presentation of a situation that, through some exploration, development or complication, arises to a confrontation, culmination or climax. This crisis initiates the untangling, resolution or simplification that leads to closure.[2]

The *Prelude* initiates a registral expansion in a primarily diatonic framework that turns into an inexplicable chromatic contraction; when expansion arises a second time, it continues on to climax at the furthest tonal remove;[3] but the climax fails, and its intensity drains aimlessly away until it arrives at a wasted form of its initial state. Thus, it can be heard as a narrative curve framed in terms of the piece's particular logic of aural interactions.

1.3. Reflections

An arch is a plain, even dull, image; but, once suggested, notions of arches worked their way into my hearing of the *Prelude*, began to proliferate and to direct my attention to more and more refined details of the music, while gathering those details into their conceptual nets. This is, of course, because the notion of an arch was just a starting point; denuded of its physical properties, it took on many forms and moved progressively deeper into figurative territory.

The role of the perceiver-promoter of a visual image like the arch shape is that of observer of an external object. Directly observable features of the image are correlated with directly observable features of the musical work. Each feature may undergo metaphoric reinterpretation as even music-literal terms do, but each is directly perceivable in both domains.

A gestural arch unites the external, visible movement with internal, therefore private, physical experience. The visible movement incorporates arch shape and, thus, arch shape's musical correlates. It also incorporates directly observable aspects of the sound, like duration, that correlate with such features as rate of movement. However, these and other audible features also suggest how it feels to move through a particular gesture: whether muscles feel tight, whether great exertion is required. For example, at the top of the mm. 11-12 line, greater exertion is conveyed in part by eighth-note inching up a step and then a half step beyond the arpeggio's top note. Thus, gesture depends on both correlations between directly perceivable features and interpretation of the perceivable as quality of movement.

Apprehension of rising and falling moods requires an even more subtle interpretation of the directly observable features of the sound. There is no directly perceivable arch in this case and, even in its home domain, the notion of rise and fall is figurative. Scruton (1983) describes this process by analogy with our ability to interpret mental states in other people. External, physical gestures are taken in; and the perceiver, remembering what that complex of gestures feels like and what it means when he or she performs it, identifies the mood and reconstructs its progress from the physical symptoms. Similarly, one can take in the gestural interplay in a piece's sounds and correlate them with physical gestures, interpreting those gestures as if they were symptomatic of real moods in an individual. To clarify this last point, let me explore another image.

2. An Alternate Image

2.1. Urgency

One of the musicology graduate students discussing the *Prelude* made the claim that '[w]hat's so interesting about [m. 13] is that same harmony through the whole measure, and yet the urgency and the speeding up nonetheless, because of the repeated sixteenth thing, is really striking to the ear'. Urgency describes a situation that evokes strong feeling. Response to it typically takes the form of agitated activity that yet feels like it gets one nowhere. This conflict can cause anxiety, disorientation, and both intense focus of attention and a failure of concentration. The music conveys the response to urgency.

In m. 13 the pattern of melodic arches breaks when two ascending arpeggios immediately succeed each other. The pace is quickened by the occurrence of two sixteenth clusters without an intervening neighbour and descent (without, as the speaker noted, 'working out [the] momentum'). Exacerbating the faster pace is disorientation resulting from temporarily cutting $\frac{3}{4}$ to $\frac{2}{4}$. E is left hanging twice, melodically unfinished by a neighbour or fall of a third. But, contradicting this flurry of activity, the Neapolitan, introduced early (in the middle of a two-measure arch), stretches on for too long, stalling the harmonic progress.

Metaphorically, music-structural features exemplify the qualities of frantic movement associated with urgency: a faster rate of events, a disorienting metric shift, an unfinished line, yet unchanging harmony.[4] Thus, musical features are assimilated to qualities of human behaviour. As one might read the signals projected by an individual tearing around heedlessly, while talking on and on about getting nothing done and, entering into those movements, recall how one has felt, one can recognize the urgency behind the individual's activities. Similarly, by entering into their metaphoric portrayal in this piece, one thereby recognizes the urgency of the piece's activities. Thus, the passage can be interpreted as metaphoric movement or action interpreted as symptomatic of metaphoric emotion; the metaphoric emotion is thereby at a level of greater figurative remove than the symptomatic metaphoric movements. The speaker was so convinced that the piece possessed such qualities that she did not say 'urgency' is descriptive of the passage, she said the passage *is* urgent. Nor would she have been likely to recognize her description as metaphoric: it was true of the passage for her. I might even claim that she dealt with the piece as if it were a human being whose actions she was interpreting.[5]

Often *ascriptions* like urgency arise apparently acontextually in response to a complicated or striking point in a piece. However, as with urgency, such a claim can be interpreted only in light of its precise musical context: events can seem fast only in contrast with slower events; meter can be upset only if first set; a pattern can be left unfinished only if the finished version is known; and a harmonic rhythm that seems to stop suddenly requires an earlier, faster pace. While such metaphors focus attention on a single point, they are highly interactive in their structural sources.

Urgency, and metaphors like urgency, are more context dependent than metaphors like arch shape. Their virtue is the strength of their bond to a specific context. They distinguish precisely how the music's qualities are interacting at a particular point.

2.2. Ascription vs. Comparison

This difference in degree of context dependency partially distinguishes comparative from ascriptive metaphors. Roughly, a *comparative metaphor*, like arch shape, seems more straightforward, more like a technical term, in delimiting the relevant features of an analogy and, thus, implying, relatively clearly, its extension. The features so correlated are directly perceivable, even if they undergo metaphoric transformation in the process. An *ascriptive metaphor*, like urgency, is more evocative, less clearly limited. It promises a greater wealth of transference; however, the transference is not feature by feature but more like urgency's complex of interactive symptoms united in a single effect and requiring an imaginative leap to conjoin the image and the music. The heart of ascription is found in the fact that it is not the perceivable features themselves but what they allude to that is transferred.

Ascriptives need not be novel. Tension is a conventional ascriptive which, despite its ubiquitous use, has never achieved technical status in musical discourse. The inability to become literal (even music literal) also seems indicative of the nature of ascription. As with urgency, criteria for invoking tension cannot be generalized: its assertion depends on the particular way things proceed at a particular point in the progress of a piece—that is, it depends absolutely on interpretation of contextual particularities. If one takes the three types of arch as representative of three increasingly figurative levels of metaphor, progressing from shape through gesture to psychological state, then ascriptives seem to be characteristic of the most figurative level.[6]

3. Return to the Arch

3.1. Mutability

To the extent that 'arch' is a theoretical (or technical) term, it is because what is specified is clearly specified—the shape seen frontally—and what is omitted is equally clear. In this guise it is a comparative metaphor that can be applied without significant change of interpretation in many contexts. At the same time, it is not an ideal theoretical term, because it can have the unhappy tendency to undergo metaphoric transformation dependent on its context; and each transformation—based on interpretation of a complex of features that suggest a symmetry of increase and decrease, expansion and contraction, or some such 'shape'—endows it with new properties. In such circumstances it is an ascriptive metaphor, and the proliferation of interpretation cannot be controlled.

As a result, it inhabits the borders of technical discourse: sometimes it is legitimately based on music- literal spatial notions and is music-literal itself under those conditions; but it is not trustworthy, because it is able to take on metaphoric connotations and change its character for every piece it encounters. So its chameleonlike nature is a source of appeal that grants room for imaginative reconstruction in the presence of a particular piece and a source of distrust, since its particular appearance—its extension—cannot be depended on.

Perhaps there is another source of appeal as well. The capacity for the notion of arch shape to transform itself into almost any dynamic process that waxes and wanes over what we might care to perceive as equivalent timespans makes it archetypical, not only of music's temporal structure but also of temporal structures and experience in general. Arch forms are universally evident and connect any entity that can be so described to the archetype. But, to make the description of sound palpable, they must cease to be merely arches. The arch skeleton must be fleshed out in precise and vivid terms in order to convincingly depict a particular musical context: if anything, it must be much more thoroughly figurative in order to describe, exactly, the structure of a particular musical work.

Conclusion

A piece's sounds do not drift inertly in air. Just as they literally vibrate, I think that they become vibrant. Every minute aspect of the sound is directed toward projecting an entity that transcends its individual features. Each moment's experienced qualities are achieved through active interpretation of the particular ways in which the sound at that point is shaped with its variously prominent and recessive features. The experienced qualities are equally shaped by the shades of their particular relations to other moments, both immediately successive and recalled distant moments.

To really engage these compelling qualities of a piece, I embroil myself with imagery that is at least as figurative as gesture and, more likely, with images comparable in figurative complexity to emotional and intellectual states. They encapsulate the creative act of listening that greedily encompasses the manifold sounds and, by an imaginative leap, reifies their qualities as they influence and are influenced by the larger context. They distinguish each separate facet of the sound while assimilating all to the specific qualities of the whole. They are attuned to each event's intensity to compel attention, to its magnitude and weight, and to each moment's temporal focus, its degree of absorption in the present, its straining backward or its impulsion forward. They constantly direct me back to the piece. This is the point of drawing on metaphoric description—to facilitate an endlessly closer, more profound hearing of each musical work.

Notes

[1] A more detailed report of this study is found in Guck (1981a). Guck (1981b) interprets the analysis class's narrative about laboured breathing.
[2] This outline of narrative curve is similar to that more carefully elaborated in Todorov (1977: 108-19).
[3] *See* Pierce (1983) for a detailed discussion of climax as a point of structural extremity.
[4] *See* Goodman (1968) on exemplification.
[5] In addition to Scruton (1983: 77-100), *see* Cone (1974) and Maus (1988), who elaborate theories of musical works as evocations of human beings.
[6] Glenn Guhr, in a seminar at Washington University, Spring 1988, posited a yet more figurative level that detaches itself from linguistic elaboration almost immediately. For example, Kendall Walton once reported that Pablo Casals, in a master class, encouraged a student to play a passage 'like a rainbow'. Beyond some sense of playing a particularly glorious arc, it is difficult to know precisely what to *say* in further explanation.

References

BABBITT, M.
   1961   'Past and Present Concepts of the Nature and Limits of Music', *Congress Report of the International Musicological Society* (reprinted in Boretz and Cone 1972: 3-9)
   1965   'The Structure and Function of Musical Theory', *College Music Symposium* 5 (reprinted in Boretz and Cone 1972: 10-21)
   1971   'Contemporary Music Composition and Music Theory as Contemporary Intellectual History', in B. Brook, E. Downes and S. Van Solkema (eds), *Perspectives in Musicology*, New York: W.W. Norton, 151-84

BORETZ, B. and CONE, E.
   1972   *Perspectives in Contemporary Music Theory*, New York: W.W. Norton

CONE, E.
   1974   *The Composer's Voice*, Berkeley: University of California Press

GOODMAN, N.
   1968   *Languages of Art*, Indianapolis: Bobbs-Merrill

GUCK, M.
   1981a 'Metaphors in Musical Discourse: The Contribution of Imagery to Analysis', Ph.D. dissertation, University of Michigan (UM # 8125119)
   1981b 'Musical Images as Musical Thoughts: The Contribution of Metaphor to Analysis', *In Theory Only*, 5: 29-43

MAUS, F.
   1988   'Music as Drama', *Music Theory Spectrum*, 10: 56-73

PIERCE, A.
   1983   'Climax in Music', *In Theory Only*, 7: 3-30

SCRUTON, R.
   1983   *The Aesthetic Understanding*, London: Methuen

TODOROV, T.
   1977   *The Poetics of Prose*, Ithaca: Cornell University Press

Understanding Style: Wölfflin's Principles of Art Applied to Music

Morris Taylor

Abstract

Heinrich Wölfflin (1874-1945) postulated five principles to explain stylistic shifts in art, especially from Renaissance to Baroque. In this paper the author suggests that Wölfflin's five principles may be extended to account for stylistic shifts in music. To demonstrate how this may be done, he applies the principles to two style shifts, one in painting and one in music.

Introduction

The influence of Heinrich Wölfflin within the discipline of art history continues to this day, and many of his publications are still printed, translated and cited. Herbert Read summarizes Wölfflin's overall contribution to art history and criticism thus:

> When Heinrich Wölfflin died in 1945 at the age of eighty-one it could be said of him that he had found art criticism a subjective chaos and left it a science. . . . Wölfflin's great distinction is that he did perfect such a scientific method in art-historical criticism, and there is no art critic of importance after his time who has not, consciously or unconsciously, been influenced by him (1952: v).

Joan Hart similarly concludes that 'Wölfflin's descriptive, inductive method has become a standard procedure for art historians, because it provides a useful tool in understanding the primary essence of a work of art: what is given visually' (1981: 490-1). Luigi Salerno also credits Wölfflin with integrating 'cultural history, psychology, and a formal analysis into a historiographic system' (1963: 527). And in a major article written a decade after Wölfflin's death, Alfred Werner (1957) submits that Wölfflin's influence is still felt in theoretical discussions of music and literature, although he gives no clues as to the manner or no evidence as to the extent.

Born on 21 June 1864, in Wintertur, Switzerland, Wölfflin remained a bachelor until his death in 1945. He succeeded his mentor, the prominent Swiss historian Jacob Burckhardt, at the University of Basel; and subsequently, he held similar professorships at Berlin, Munich and Zurich. Neumeyer describes a personal impression of Wölfflin thus: 'His very entrance was stirring. Over six foot two inches tall, lean, with an impressive skull, a satyr's beard—everything in this beautiful human being was "*gestaltet*"' (1971: 33-4). According to Neumeyer, hundreds of auditors attended Wölfflin's lectures because his compelling manner and brilliantly analyzed illustrations made his lectures a theatrical experience.

Among Wölfflin's five major publications and scores of monographs, three books continue to exert influence on art historians and critics. His pioneering work, *Renaissance and Baroque* (1907), examines the nature of the stylistic shift which occurred between these two periods. His earlier and still popular book, *Classic Art* (1898), explains the author's critical theories about renaissance classicism. This generously illustrated volume analyzes painting, sculpture and architecture of the high Renaissance. It also discusses their formal content and ideals of beauty. His landmark book, titled in English, *Principles of Art History: The Problem of the Development of Style in Later Art* (1915), outlines most clearly the author's method of analyzing art works.

1. Wölfflin's Theory

In *Principles of Art History* (1915), Wölfflin postulated five contrasting pairs of concepts which define and compare stylistic development from the classic art of the Cinquecento to the baroque art of the Siecento. The five pairs of concepts are:

(1) Linear to painterly. 'Seeing by volumes and outlines isolates objects: for the painterly eye, they merge.'

(2) Plane to recession. 'Classic art reduces the parts of a total form to a sequence of planes, the Baroque emphasizes depth.'

(3) Closed to open form. 'In comparison with the loose form of the Baroque, Classic design may be taken as the form of closed composition.'

(4) Multiplicity to unity. 'In both styles unity is the chief aim, . . . but in the one case unity is achieved by a harmony of free parts, in the other, by a union of parts in a single theme, or by the subordination, to one unconditioned dominant, of all other elements.'

(5) Absolute clarity to the relative clarity. 'It is the special feature of the Classic age that did develop an ideal of perfect clarity which the fifteenth century only vaguely suspected, and which the seventeenth voluntarily sacrificed' (Wölfflin 1915: 14-6).

Wölfflin's paired concepts organize his observations about the progression from renaissance to baroque style. The systematic consideration of these concepts enables an art historian to distinguish salient characteristics of a style and to compare these observations with the style of other art works similarly analyzed. The musicologist, Curt Sachs, who began his career as an art historian, extended Wölfflin's principles of art history to a commonwealth of arts. According to Leo Schrade (1965: 6), 'With the gauge of Wölfflin's pairs in hand, Curt Sachs measured the musical style of the Baroque and found its characteristics to be identical with those of the style of the visual arts'.

In this paper I apply Wölfflin's principles to two style shifts, one in painting and one in music. First, I analyse comparatively *The Last Supper* as painted by Leonardo da Vinci and as painted by Tintoretto. Second, I provide a similar analysis of Schubert's *Piano Sonata in A Major*, Opus 120 and Schumann's *Faschingsschwank aus Wien*, Opus 26. By means of this parallel application of Wölfflin's principles, similarities become evident between one step in the succession of style in a visual art and a comparable step in the succession of style in an auditory art.

2. Applying the Theory to Painting

Leonardo da Vinci's *The Last Supper* painted in fresco (1495-1498) and Tintoretto's treatment in oil painting of the same subject matter a half-century later (1547) admirably exemplify the contrast between renaissance and baroque style (*see* Plates 1 and 2).

Wölfflin's first pair of concepts, linear to painterly, becomes readily apparent when the two paintings are compared. Leonardo's familiar presentation of *The Last Supper* in the Refectory of Santa Maria delle Grazie in Milan uses line as a path of vision. In this painting each of the disciples and Christ are isolated by line. The architectural setting is simply stated in a precise linear perspective with the vanishing point focusing attention on the head of Christ. Tintoretto's presentation of *The Last Supper* from Santa Giorgio Maggiore in Venice only partially describes the edges of people and objects. This work illustrates the gestural aspect of paint application and the consequent blurring of some edges.

Wölfflin's second pair of concepts, plane to recession, deals with a formal organization of three dimensional space within a two dimensional picture plane. In Leonardo's painting the table occupies the foreground, the figures reside in the middle ground and the room ends with a distant prospect forming the background. This controlled space parallels the picture plane. Tintoretto paints with exaggerated recession. The space he suggests is less controlled and more active than Leonardo's. Tintoretto sets the objects and figures on diagonals. His spaces are ambiguous and do not end at the picture frame.

In the third pair of concepts Wölfflin describes two observable attitudes

Plate 1: Leonardo *L'ultima cena*
Plate 2: Tintoretto *L'ultima cena*

towards formal organization as closed to open. In Leonardo's painting the symmetrical organization unifies the form. Two groups of three disciples each carry the energy of the inquiry, 'Lord, is it I?' towards the central figure of Christ. The only curved line in the architecture calls attention to the silhouetted head of Christ whose outstretched hands form a stable isosceles triangle. In Tintoretto's painting no such closed and balanced form exists. Rather Tintoretto's formal organization is asymmetrical. He arranges the twelve disciples in an undulating grouping about the table. Twisting, turning, turbulent figures move about the room. Phantom-like angels emerge from indefinitely defined space.

In the fourth pair of concepts, multiplicity to unity, Wölfflin further defines the difference between these two paintings. The viewer can see how in the late sixteenth-century work Leonardo maintains a certain independence for each person while the figures together make up the unity of the whole. In the mid-seventeenth century painting the viewer may observe how Tintoretto unifies the figures, in spite of their activity, into the single dramatic theme. Both artists aim for unity. The former artist achieves unity by the principle of adding comparatively independent parts. The latter artist achieves unity by the principle of multiplying parts which are dependent upon each other. The renaissance quietude and the baroque energy stem from these contrasting attitudes towards style and form.

The fifth pair of concepts, absolute to relative clarity, grow out of the first pair of concepts, linear to painterly. The renaissance artists developed an ideal of perfect clarity which the baroque artists voluntarily gave up. In Leonardo's painting the pervading light source from the upper left sifts gently over the figures; while in Tintoretto's painting the flickering light source from the flaming lamp harshly highlights certain persons and objects.

3. Applying the Theory to Music

By analogy, the underlying principles of Wölfflin's analytic techniques might be expected to apply to shifts of style in music history, for example, from the classic to the romantic periods in music. Such an expectation implies a correspondence between the visual arts of the high Renaissance and the music of the classic period and, likewise, between the visual arts of the baroque period and the music of the romantic period. This implication seems consonant with the theory of art cycles as postulated by Curt Sachs in his book *The Commonwealth of Art* (1946: 314-89).

The following comparison of a well-known piano composition by Schubert with a somewhat similar one by Schumann serves to illustrate the application of Wölfflin's theory to music. Franz Schubert composed his *Piano Sonata in A Major*, Opus Posthumous 120 (D 644), in 1818.[1] Robert Schumann wrote the *Faschingsschwank aus Wien*, Opus 26, only twenty years later in 1838.[2] During these two decades romanticism overtook classicism as the dominant trend. An application of Wölfflin's analytic techniques focuses attention on important points of style which develop within this short time span.

Wölfflin's first principle, linear to painterly, specifies the relative limitation which line places upon space. In music the comparable concept specifies the relative limitation which cadence places upon phrase and period organization. In the art of painting, line, adjacent colors and juxtaposed values divide two dimensional space into sections which are more or less defined. In the art of music, articulation, rests and cadences divide the musical utterances into phrase groupings which are more or less defined. Schubert shows his phrases by solid cadences and often a rest. Schumann in his sonata-like work still depends on cadences; however, shorter units combine into longer units propelling the listener forward. The second movement entitled 'Romanze' exhibits this tendency. A relationship exists between the word 'painterly' as used by painters and the word 'pianistic' as used by pianists. Schubert composes chamber music which sounds well on the piano. Schumann effectively exploits the sonorities of the instrument including the use of pedals. It would be easier to adapt Schubert's piano sonata for a chamber orchestra than it would be to transform the pianistic conceptions of Schumann to the orchestra. (Perhaps, this fact underlies the charge brought against Schumann as a weak orchestrator.)

Wölfflin's second principle deals with plane to recession. No such physical or representational dimensions exist in music; however, musical texture creates a similar allusion of the predictable or the changeable. Schubert's piano writing exhibits creativity by producing characteristic textures which permeate the movement. Schumann displays a greater variety of texture and articulation. How the pianist controls the damper pedal affects the listener's perception of texture also.

The third principle, closed to open, compares the relatively formal design of the classicist with the comparatively loose form of the romanticist. Like the majority of classic models, Schubert organizes his phrases in multiples of two or four measures with occasional exceptions. Schumann uses regular periods also, but there are notable exceptions. In the opening of the 'Intermezzo', the fourth movement of Opus 26, Schumann answers the first phrase of 8 bars by a second phrase of 7 bars. Each of Schubert's movements exhibits a more symmetrical concept of form than do the comparable movements of Schumann's composition. Compare, for example, the sonata-allegro movements—the straightforward first of Schubert with the headlong last of Schumann.

The fourth principle, multiplicity to unity, suggests that a classic composition consists of comparatively independent parts. A non-classic work achieves harmony by a union of a single idea or by making a principal idea dominant. Schubert's sonata appears near the close of the classic era and exhibits some characteristics of nineteenth-century romanticism. This composition offers many themes and accompanying ideas which serenely cohere within a classic model of sonata form. Schumann's composition in five movements roughly parallels the form of a sonata. The first movement modifies the classic rondo form (ABA'CADAEFACoda). The second movement, 'Romanze', spins a short, enigmatic melody. The third rather strictly presents a short scherzo in the usual form. The fourth energetically expresses musical passion in the free form of an intermezzo. And the last movement presents Schumann's fiery romanticism within the framework of an adapted sonata-allegro form. These observations on multiplicity and unity become manifest in the performance style. When performing Schubert's work, pianists breathe at phrase endings, making each segment an important part of the whole. But when playing Schumann's composition, pianists feel an onward impulse soaring towards the dynamic climaxes in spite of the phrases and cadences.

The fifth principle, absolute to relative clarity, deals with the plastic feeling of the sections to the whole. Various musical elements such as dynamics, register, articulation, orchestration and acoustics contribute to the relative clearness of the sound. In Schubert's *Sonata in A Major*, Opus 120, the transparent harmonic language, the skillful use of the piano's registers and the rather uniform and thin texture contribute to a sense of clarity. By contrast, in Schumann's *Faschingsschwank*, Opus 26, more pungent non-harmonic tones, more distant key relationships, more dense textures and more frequent use of the damper pedal contribute to a relatively unclear sound.

Both art viewers and music listeners react to absolute versus relative clarity. A painting in classic style invites the observer to relate clearly de-fined segments into a formally balanced and unified expression. A musical composition in classic style enjoins the listener to correlate separate phrases into a well-organized formal design. Likewise, a romantic painting usually impresses the viewer with an overwhelming drama or a solitary poetic idea. A romantic musical composition impels the listener to move forward with the emotional tide, to sustain a delicate mood or to alternate between these two modes of expression.

Conclusion

Wölfflin's five principles succinctly express the differences in style between renaissance and baroque painting. Art historians have long recognized the usefulness of these principles as a tool for investigating and explaining style shifts in art. As I have hoped to demonstrate, the same five principles also facilitate comparisons between music of the classic and romantic periods. The understandings gained by applying Wölfflin's five principles of art to the auditory experience enhance listeners' enjoyment of music and facilitate their learning about musical style. The same principles provide music historians with a method for investigating and explaining style shifts in music as well as for making comparisons between the arts.

Parallel analyses of visual and musical arts promote interest and increase comprehension of style in classroom presentations. A direct and easily understood set of principles for comparing style aids professors teaching arts and humanities courses to utilize classroom time efficiently and effectively. Through the comparative study of various arts, young performers, including conductors, more quickly develop maturity of musical expression. And students of human culture find delight in parallel study of visual and auditory arts.

Comparative studies between the arts demand clearly expressed principles for comparison. Since Wölfflin's principles meet this criterion, they provide possibilities for interpreting the interface between the visual and the auditory arts.

Notes

[1] (Score) F. Schubert, *Piano Sonatas I* (München: G. Henle Verlag, 1961); (disc) F. Schubert, Sonatas for Piano, complete. Performed by Kempff. Deutsche Grammophone 423496-2 GX7.

[2] (Score) R. Schumann, *Piano Works III* (München: G. Henle Verlag, 1959); (disc) R. Schumann, Faschingsschwank aus Wien, Op. 26. Performed by Michelangeli. Melodram CD-28019.

Acknowledgments

The illustrations are credit Alinari/Art Resource: Plate 1 (11090 Anderson) Leonardo, *L'ultima cena*, Milano, Chiesa di S. Maria delle Grazie; Plate 2 (13581 Anderson) Tintoretto, *L'ultima cena*, Venezia, S. Giorgio Maggiore.

References

HART, Joan
    1981   *Heinrich Wölfflin: An Intellectual Biography,* Ann Arbor: University Microfilms International
NEUMEYER, Alfred
    1971   'Four Art Historians Remembered: Wölfflin, Goldschmidt, Warburg, Berenson', *Art Journal,* 31: 33-4 and 80
READ, Herbert
    1952   'Introduction' (*see* Wölfflin 1889)
SACHS, Curt
    1946   *The Commonwealth of Art,* New York: W.W. Norton
SALERNO, Luigi
    1963   'Historiography', *Encyclopedia of World Art,* New York: McGraw Hill Book Co, vol. 8
SCHRADE, Leo
    1965   'Curt Sachs as Historian', *The Commonwealth of Music,* ed. Gustave Reese and Rose Brandel, New York: The Free Press

WERNER, Alfred
1957   'New Perspectives on the Old Masters', *Art Yearbook*, 1: 79
WÖLFFLIN, Heinrich
1889   *Classic Art: An Introduction to the Italian Renaissance*, tr.
       Peter and Linda Murray, Oxford: Phaidon Press Ltd., 1952
1915   *Principles of Art History: The Problem of the Development of
       Style in Later Art*, tr. M.D. Hottinger, London: Bell c.1932
1907   *Renaissance and Baroque*, tr. Kathrin Simon, New York:
       Cornell University Press 1966

Convergence and Divergence: The Interdependence of Poetical and Musical Structures in Atonal and Early Twelve-Tone Works by Arnold Schoenberg

Martina Sichardt

Abstract

The examination of the word-tone relationship in Schoenberg begins with a case featuring the divergence of both levels. However, through perceiving the aesthetic difference involved, access is gained to a deeper level of Schoenberg's manner of textual setting, in fact of Schoenberg's compositional thinking altogether. The divergence initially established leads to the recognition of a convergence at a higher level. (The results are summarized at the close of the article.[1])

Introduction

In his creative development Arnold Schoenberg—more than virtually any other composer before him—forged ahead into new and previously unknown realms of musical expression. At least two of the decisive turning points in his creative life resulted from the inspiration received from the poetic work of a particular poet. The 'decisive influence' of the poetry of Richard Dehmel upon his 'musical development' was commented upon later by Schoenberg himself: 'Because of them [the poems of Dehmel] I was compelled for the first time to search for a new lyrical tone in music'.[2] Then, later, in the case of the Stefan George settings, *Das Buch der hängenden Gärten*, Schoenberg broke 'all the barriers to the aesthetic values of the past': 'In the "*George-Lieder*" I was able to achieve for the first time an expressive and formal ideal, which I had envisaged for years'.[3]

The poetry too of Ludwig Pfau had had a similar significance for Schoenberg as a young composer.[4]

The close of the flourishing of German song composition, coinciding approximately with World War I, marks simultaneously the end of the very important role which German poetry exercised upon Schoenberg's creative work. In 1917 the unfinished oratorio, *Die Jakobsleiter*, originally conceived as the principal work rounding off this period in his development, was based upon a text of his own. The extraordinary importance which the setting of texts had generally represented for Schoenberg's compositional development receded after *Die Jakobsleiter* for a long period of time. After years of silence, Schoenberg's creative regeneration from 1923 witnessed not merely a new method of musical composition— the twelve-tone method—but also an initial rejection of textual settings in favour of purely instrumental works (the Opus Numbers 23 to 26). An exception exists, however, in the case of the Sonnet of Petrarch (4th movement) in the *Serenade* Opus 24, an early twelve-tone work, composed between 1920 and 1923, scored for seven instruments (clarinet, bass clarinet, mandoline, guitar, violin, viola, violoncello) and baritone voice.

1. Two Types of Text Setting

The Sonnet of the *Serenade* is taken from the *Canzoniere* of Petrarch, a collection of canzonas and sonnets dating from the year 1350. Here Petrarch celebrates his love for Laura: the happiness of their meeting, his doubts, his certainty of her returned love and his lamentations over her death. Schoenberg had first set poems of Petrarch to music in 1904, in the *Six Orchestral Songs* Opus 8, Numbers 4, 5 and 6, the texts of which were also taken from the *Canzoniere*.[5]

Dümling (1981: 17) has attempted to explain Schoenberg's selection of the poetry of Petrarch at this time by referring to the occurrence of Petrarch's 600th birthday and to the renaissance cult of the time. Neumann finds more deep-seated reasons for the selection of the lyrics of both Petrarch and George, both of which are related to key works in Schoenberg's development:

> Stylistic elevation, *genus grande*. . . . Stylistic elevation aims at artificiality, at the transformation of all elements of reality into the artificial. Its characteristics are indirectness, refinement, symbolization. The same may also be fittingly said of the poems of Petrarch and of George. Both are the product of a similar striving for stylization. . . . (1978: 144).

The grammatical and linguistic archaisms of the German translation of Petrarch in Schoenberg's possession, the work of Ludwig Tieck's contemporary, Karl Förster, may have encouraged this particular manner of reception.[6] However, Neumann's astute observations do not quite suffice in explaining Schoenberg's selection of the Sonnet in the *Serenade*. Petrarch's poetry, with its glowing and, quoting Neumann (1978: 144), 'ecstatically figurative language restrained in the strict form of the sonnet', seems hardly fitting to the character of the *Serenade*, a character established in the other movements and certainly not in keeping with the plucked-tremolo sound of the mandoline. The orchestral colourings and the rich musical language of the Petrarch settings in the *Six Orchestral Songs* Opus 8 fit much more closely the style of the texts. Thus, another reason must have existed for Schoenberg's selection of the Sonnet. There must have been something in this Sonnet which, on the one hand, enabled Schoenberg to conceive the entire movement in a single act of inspiration (Little Sketch Book IV, Sk. 824-827) and, on the other hand, made it possible for him to disregard the aesthetic discrepancy between the character of the Sonnet and the *Serenade*. The underlying reason for the selection of this text may be brought to light by an examination of its content and its manner of musical setting.

Let us begin by considering the question of the Sonnet's structure and content. Two differing levels of lyrical self-reflection exist in the Sonnet: the two quatrains depict complaint and accusation on account of the loved one's rejection; the following terzets express this pain again, but now in the form of a metaphysical image. Underlying the words (lines 9 and 10) '*Die Seele . . . trennt sich von mir, und, ihrer Haft entkommen . . .*' [My soul . . . severs itself from me and, escapes its confinement . . .] is the idea that the body is the 'prison' of the soul, an image of ancient origin passed on through Plato and known presumably to Petrarch through the *Somnium Scipionis* of Cicero. The immortality of the soul was a conviction shared by both Petrarch and Schoenberg (*see* Schoenberg's *Requiem* in Schoenberg 1926: 32-3). If we compare the Sonnet of Petrarch with Schoenberg's principal poetic work of some years earlier, *Die Jakobsleiter*, we notice, in addition to this fundamental agreement, that they also share a similar manner of presentation. The contrasting of the material and spiritual realms, as in the division between the quatrains and terzets of the Sonnet, is also found in much larger dimensions in *Die Jakobsleiter*. In *Die Jakobsleiter* the description of the ascent of the soul is distinguished from the vision of the *Himmelswelten* [heavenly worlds], in which space and time no longer exist. This breach—in structure and content—between both sections is essential. The text already contains an indication of the intended contrast between these two 'worlds' in the following remark: 'the music proceeds over into the character of the new scenes'.[7]

In returning again to the Sonnet, we will consider how this polarity is reflected in the particular setting of the text. From the outset an obvious external difference is to be seen between the first and second parts. In the case of the two quatrains, the setting of a line of text requires on the whole two to three bars of vocal line, corresponding more or less to what Schoenberg later termed a phrase—that which one can sing in a single taken breath (Schoenberg 1979: 13). In the terzet, however, a sung line requires four to eight bars. The vocal line of the second part is also differentiated from that of the first through virtually uninterrupted melodic continuity. Here the few occurring pauses function sooner as compositionally-conceived breathing spaces than as indicators of divisions between inner segments. A lyrical conception of the voice part is thus confined primarily to the second part, while in the first its contours reflect above all the melodic shapes of spoken prose, thus approximating the style of the dramatic recitative.[8]

This differentiation of tendency between a more prose-like and a more melismatic shaping of the vocal line is also confirmed by a glance at the sketches of the Sonnet. The definitive version of the vocal line, which (as has already been said) represents the initial step in the compositional process and which serves as the framework of the movement as a whole, was preceded by two earlier versions. The declamatory style characteristic of the first part of the Sonnet may be seen to be progressively apparent in the evolution from the first to the third versions. Here is the first line of text in all three versions:

Example 1

In principle the accentuation of a syllable can be implemented in two different ways: either by an increase of duration or by a new pitch level arrived at by a leap. We are able to recognize a tendency running through the first to third versions towards the accentuation of ever more syllables in one or the other way, so that finally in the last version all five accents of the *Endecasillabo*—the rhymed five-foot iambus with feminine ending—are accentuated. The vocal line receives its dramatic-expressive character through wide-ranging alternations of pitch, which encompass already an octave and a sixth (G - e' flat) in the first phrase. In the second part of the Sonnet, on the other hand, a progressive tendency towards a song-like quality may also be recognized:

Example 2

The clumsier and more prosaic first version is superseded, despite the maintainance of a syllabic style, by a more singable melismatic design. The tendency towards expansion, towards calm, also directs the re-conception of the last line (bar 73ff.):

Example 3

The tendency we observed in the Sonnet towards a contrasting of two types of textual setting had already served Schoenberg as a structural principle in the song, *Herzgewächse* Opus 10, composed in 1911 (based upon a text by Maurice Maeterlinck). The recitative-like declamatory shaping of the vocal line in bars 1 to 15, approaching in style the *Sprechstimme* or *Sprechgesang* of *Pierrot Lunaire*, is transformed in the second half of the song into a vocal line of widely sweeping melismatic contours (bars 16-30).[9] Similarly, in *Die Jakobsleiter*, the 'character of the new scenes' (referred to above) is not only to be recognized through a new characteristic quality of sound, the result of a specific manner of orchestration and the utilization of choirs placed behind the scenes and in elevated positions, but also through a manner of text-setting which differs completely from that preceding. Here, with the exception of a few brief choral entries in a prose-like declamatory style, only the broadly sweeping melismas of the voice of the *Seele* [soul] are to be heard, which become 'pure' song through being relinquished of all textual connections (*see* Ex. 4). In the first part of *Die Jakobsleiter*, however, the recitative-declamatory style is largely predominant, although differentiated through passages of *Sprechgesang* character and expressly 'sung' episodes of prosaic-recitative design.[10] The semantic difference of both types of setting is also evident in Schoenberg's 'Drama with Music', *Die glückliche Hand* (1909-1913), without involving there a dualistic form.

2. Identity of Word: The Symbol *fliegt* [flying]

In the consideration of the Sonnet our attention was drawn repeatedly to

Die Jakobsleiter. Therefore, it would be legitimate to look for further analogies between both works. These are in fact to be found. The second half of Petrarch's Sonnet possesses symbols relevant to the ideas underlying *Die Jakobsleiter*. The sphere of *Seele*, referred to in the second part of the Sonnet, establishes (as has been shown) a general relationship to bars 565ff. of *Die Jakobsleiter*. There exists, however, a literal correspondence between the Sonnet and the text of *Die Jakobsleiter*, embodied by the word *fliegt* [flying] (line 11). It may be accepted without a moment of doubt that this word evoked in Schoenberg's mind an association to the central section of *Die Jakobsleiter: 'er fliegt - Ich fliege - Der selige Traum erfüllt sich: fliegen! Weiter! Weiter! Zum Ziel - Oh -'* [he flies - I am flying - The blissful dream is being fulfilled: flight! Further! Further! Towards the ultimate destination! - Oh -] (bar 556ff.). At this point, however, the transition over into the 'character of the new scenes' occurs, to the *Himmelswelten*, or heavenly worlds, situated at the centre of *Die Jakobsleiter* (according to its original conception). Schoenberg's self-admitted inclination to allow the sound of individual words inspire him rather than the total content of a poem is well known (Schoenberg 1976: 5). This inclination suggests that it was the association aroused in Schoenberg's mind by the word *fliegt* of Petrarch's Sonnet to the particular context of *Die Jakobsleiter* which consequently inspired him to set the poem to music.

The relationship of the Sonnet and *Die Jakobsleiter* is attested to further by the date of the Sonnet's conception. The sketches for the Sonnet are to be found notated in the same sketch book (the Little Sketch Book IV, as used in 1922-1923) which also contains the sketches for the second part of *Die Jakobsleiter*. The assumption expressed earlier, that Schoenberg's selection of the Sonnet must have had deeper reasons than merely its stylized language, has thus been confirmed at several levels.

3. Semantic Function of the *Klangfläche*

The analysis of the instrumental accompaniment of the Sonnet setting, ignored until now, will indicate its affiliation to the period of the so-called *Weltanschauungsmusik*, as coined by Stephan (1974: 276-8); that is, music expressive of an all-encompassing philosophical understanding or vision of the world. According to Stephan, the epoch of the *Weltanschauungsmusik* in Schoenberg's oeuvre broadly covers the span from 1908 to 1917, a period in which he undertook to present a summary view of all artistic achievement and basic questions of human existence. This period— to which *Die glückliche Hand, Herzgewächse*, and the *Four Songs for Voice and Orchestra* belong as well as those sections of the *Second Chamber Symphony* composed before 1916—reaches its culmination in the text of *Die Jakobsleiter*, the composition of which was broken off for non-personal reasons in 1917 after more than 600 bars had been completed.

144

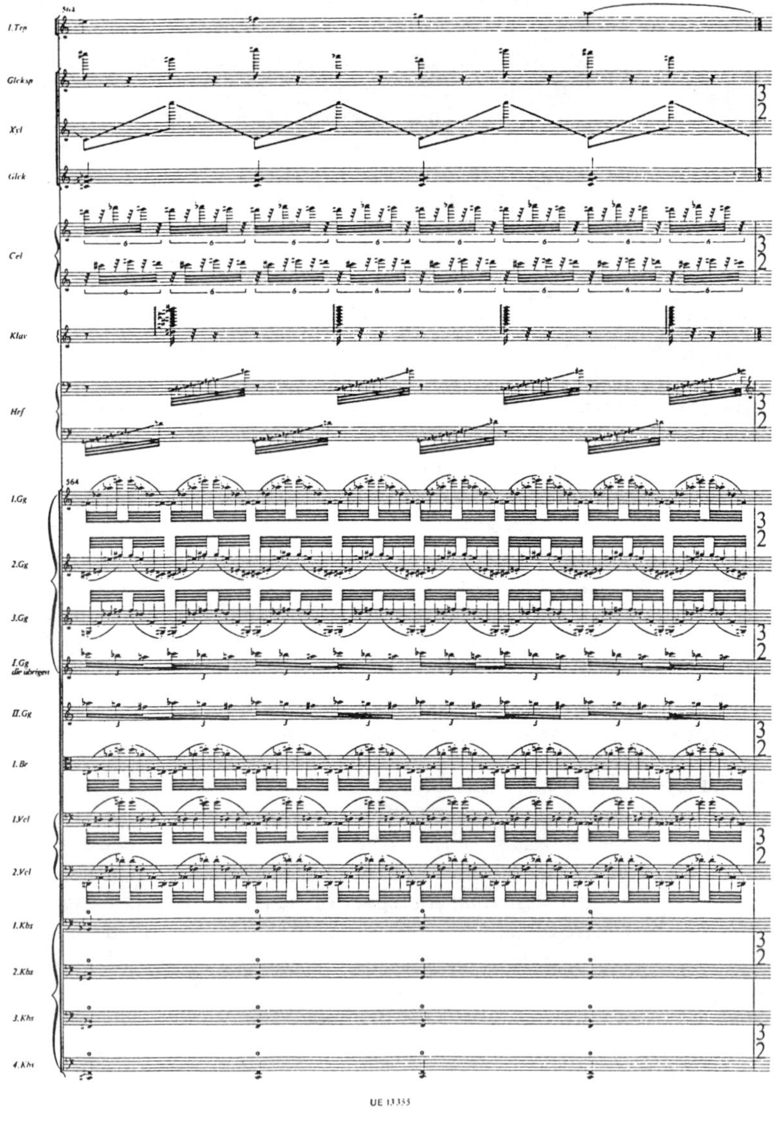
564
I.Trp
Glcksp
Xyl
Glck
Cel
Klav
Hrf
1.Gg
2.Gg
3.Gg
I.Gg die übrigen
II.Gg
1.Br
1.Vcl
2.Vcl
1.Kbs
2.Kbs
3.Kbs
4.Kbs

UE 13355

Example 4: *Die Jakobsleiter*: transition into the 'character of the new scenes', bars 564ff. [© 1974 by Belmont Music Publishers, rev. edn. © 1980. Used by permission]

In the Sonnet the setting of the word *Seele* (bars 41-43) is accompanied
by a sonorous ostinato effect, a *Klangfläche* which Adorno once perti-
nently described as a 'continuo involving a jingling, plucked, highly
coloured, but non-sustained and, accordingly, non-atmospheric accompaniment system' (1982: 343).

Example 5

Here a clarinet duet underlies an ostinato in the mandoline and the viola (with
the latter being expressively marked 'springing bow' so as to fit the character
of the mandoline). The setting of the word *fliegt* is already emphasized in the
first conception of the movement (Little Sketch Book IV, Sk. 826): the e' flat
(in bar 51), highly placed for the baritone voice, is marked '*(subito) PPP*'.

Example 6

The accompaniment comprises, on the one hand, an animated sonorous foundation involving guitar and bass clarinet, then bass clarinet, viola and cello and, on the other hand, lines with extensive intervallic leaps, reminiscent of the melismas in the passages relating to the *Seele* passage in *Die Jakobsleiter*.

The *Klangfläche* is of particular importance in Schoenberg's atonal works as a medium of formal organization. Mauser (1982: 98ff.) differentiates between three types of compositional zones [*Satzzonen*]—momentary formal segments—in his analysis of *Erwartung* Opus 17: the athematic zone, the thematic zone and the tone-layered or *Klangflächen*-zone. He defines this last variety of zone—the only one of the three which need interest us here and which in the following I will refer to simply as *Klangfläche*—as a compositional zone based upon a (mostly) mobile ostinato or a pedal-note foundation. The manner of setting of the word *Seele* in the Sonnet of the *Serenade* fits this variety of zone, whereas the word *fliegt* fits better with that of the thematic variety. The *Klangfläche*, typified by states of inherent movement within an outward framing concept, is distinguished by its overall static dimensions, by its being outside of the process of time. In *Erwartung*, according to Mauser (1982: 95-101), this gesture of pausing is of dramaturgical significance, as these *Klangfläche* mostly occur in the company of images of nature, which themselves represent static moments in the dramatic course of events. Common to all occurrences of this third variety of compositional zone, *Klangfläche*, which are to be found mainly in the atonal works, is their quality of being beyond time.[11]

The *Klangfläche*, it is to be observed, is often given a quite specific colouring. This is found in its purest form in the song, *Herzgewächse* Opus 20, with its instrumentation of only celesta, harp and harmonium. The caesura in the treatment of the vocal line in this song—the abandonment of the recitative-declamatory character after bar 16 in order to go over into 'pure' song—has already been described. This treatment of the voice finds its equivalent in the accompaniment. The recitative section, athematic in conception, is followed in the second section by a *Klangfläche*, which functions not only as an effective contrast but also to lift the words of the text into 'higher' regions through a quality of timelessness. The treatment of the voice corresponds with the dissolution of the process of time, which—no longer bound by normal feelings and sensitivity—appears to drift over from another unearthly world. The sound of the extended tones in highest soprano register—c''', e''' flat, f''', marked quadruple piano over the full length of a bar—is scarcely reminiscent any longer of human song but possesses an inherently etherial quality.

The symbolic figures of speech in the second part of the Maeterlinck poem—*weißer Mondesglanz* [white glow of the moon], *Kristall* [crystal], *richtet sich empor* [stretching itself upwards]—hit home in regard to

Schoenberg's imaginative idea of an etherial sonority and were in fact the underlying reason for his setting of this poem to music.

The semantic connotation of the shimmering instrumental *Klangfläche* is subjected in *Die glückliche Hand* to an alteration which already looks ahead to *Die Jakobsleiter*. At bar 97 a *Klangfläche* appears, the instrumentation of which corresponds to that of the moonlit night in *Erwartung* as well as *Kristall* in *Herzgewächse*. A stage direction of Schoenberg's at this point states: '*Ein Gedanke scheint in ihm zu werden*' [An idea seems to take on shape in his mind]. Implied is the 'idea' which precedes the artist's act of creation. This important direction refers back to the words of the opening chorus: '*Du, der das überirdische in dir hast. . . .*' [You, who carry the celestial within yourself]. At the central point of *Die Jakobsleiter*, where the transition into the 'character of the new scenes' occurs (bars 563-564), this instrumental combination again returns with the same connotation. In *Die Jakobsleiter*, envisaged by Schoenberg as the principal work in the period of the *Weltanschauungsmusik*, the *Klangfläche* achieves—in association with the shimmering instrumentation and the 'etherial' song— a semantic connection to the celestial, which allows this work (although remaining only a fragment) to appear as the climax of the period of the *Weltanschauungsmusik*.

In the Sonnet of the *Serenade*, composed five years after the first part of *Die Jakobsleiter*, we find the remnants of the *Klangfläche*: its characteristic instrumentation and a reminiscence of the 'etherial' song with a high e' flat in the voice part (on the word *fliegt*).[12]

Conclusion

The consideration of the Sonnet from the *Serenade* Opus 24 has shown that the poetic structure of this particular Sonnet of Petrarch aroused associations in Schoenberg's mind with the formal structure of earlier works. The structure of Petrarch's Sonnet encouraged: (1) the polarization of two differing types of language settings which are applied in a form-constituting way; (2) the direct association to works of an earlier period through the identity of word; and (3) the utilization of the *Klangfläche*, the semantic connection of which to the word *Seele* refers back to the by-gone era of the *Weltanschauungsmusik*.

The poetic structure of Petrarch's Sonnet induced the composer to continue at a subterranean level a manner of composition belonging to a past compositional period. In other words, in the selection of this text Schoenberg reveals a continued although perhaps only unconscious spiritual attachment to the idea of the *Weltanschauungsmusik*. This is remarkable when one considers that a greater gap is hardly to be imagined than that between the works belonging to the period of the *Weltanschauungsmusik*, bound as they were to the idea of art as religion, extending beyond the confines of art, conceived for enormous dimensions although never completed, and those of the early nineteen-twenties, cleansed as they are of all such pretention and approaching the practical music-making style of functional music.

(Translated by Lewis Wickes)

Notes

1 An expanded treatment of this subject-matter is to be found in my forthcoming book, *Die Entstehung der Zwölftonmethode Arnold Schönbergs*, Schott/Mainz (in press).

2 '*Durch sie war ich zum erstenmal genötigt, einen neuen Ton in der Lyrik zu suchen*', letter to Dehmel, December 13, 1912 (Birke 1958: 282).

3 '*Mit den "Liedern nach George" ist es mir zum erstenmal gelungen, einem Ausdrucks- und Formideal näherzukommen, das mir seit Jahren vorschwebt. . . . Nun ich aber diese Bahn endgültig betreten habe, bin ich mir bewußt, alle Schranken einer vergangenen Ästhetik durchbrochen zu haben. . . .*' (Reich 1968: 71).

4 From the years 1893-1896 there exist eleven songs based upon texts of Pfau, as well as three song fragments and one fragment for chorus and orchestra (*see* Arnold Schoenberg, *Sämtliche Werke*, 2A and B, Mainz 1966ff, and *ibid.*, 18 B, in press).

5 Two musical fragments based upon Sonnets of Petrarch (Nos. 116 and 214) also belong to this same period (*see* Arnold Schoenberg, *Sämtliche Werke*, 3B, Mainz 1981, No. 116, p. 259, and *ibid.*, 2B, ed. Christian Martin Schmidt, forthcoming, No. 214). The source of Schoenberg's Petrarch settings is Francesco Petrarca, *Die Sonette*, übersetzt und mit erläuternden Anmerkungen vessehen von Karl Förster, Reclam, Leipzig, undated. Schoenberg's personal copy of this book is to be found in his estate now housed in the Schoenberg Institute, Los Angeles (Maegaard 1972: 19).

6 Regarding Schoenberg's prose interpretation of the interlocking syntax of the lines 5 to 8, see Maegaard (1972: 105).

7 '*Sofort nach diesem langgezogenen 'Oh' --- geht die Musik in den Ton der neuen Szenen über*', *Die Jakobsleiter* (Schoenberg 1926: 48).

8 It is to be noted that the caesura between the two styles of textual setting does not correspond exactly with the poetic caesura (as between quatrains and terzets). The basic underlying structural conception is occasionally overlaid by moments of detail, even in fact contradicted by an inspired setting of individual words making use of characteristic forms of tone-painting (for instance, *Ruhe*, and *brüllend wie ein Leu*).

9 Regarding the dualism of form in Schoenberg's *Herzgewächse, see also* Ruf (1984: 257-273), and Hough (1983: 197-221).

10 Here too the basic structure is broken at certain points, such as in the part of *Der Berufene* and in choral sections, for example, in bars 105ff.

11 *See* Op. 10, 16, 17, 18, 20, 21, 22 and *Die Jakobsleiter*.

[12] It is to be noted that varieties of *Klangfläche* also occur in the Sonnet, the design of which are subservient to the demands of tone-painting (as for instance, *brüllend wie ein Leu*, and *matt bekümmert Wesen*).

Acknowledgments

The author wishes to thank the following for permission to reproduce the musical examples: Mr Lawrence Schoenberg; Prof. Dr Hans W. Sikorski; and Universal Edition A. G. (for Belmont Music Publishers).

References

ADORNO, Theodor W.
    1982 'Über einige Arbeiten Arnold Schönbergs', *Impromptus* (in: *Gesammelte Schriften*, 17, ed. Rolf Tiedemann), Frankfurt
BIRKE, Joachim
    1958 'Richard Dehmel und Arnold Schönberg. Ein Briefwechsel', *Die Musikforschung*, 11: 279-85
DÜMLING, Albrecht
    1981 *Die fremden Klänge der hängenden Gärten. Die öffentliche Einsamkeit der Neuen Musik am Beispiel von Arnold Schönberg und Stefan George*, München
HOUGH, Bonny
    1983 'Schoenberg's *Herzgewächse* and the *Blaue Reiter* Almanac', *Journal of the Arnold Schoenberg Institute*, 7: 197-221
MAEGAARD, Jan
    1972 *Studien zur Entwicklung des dodekaphonen Satzes bei Arnold Schönberg*, I, Copenhagen
MAUSER, Siegfried
    1982 *Das expressionistische Musiktheater der Wiener Schule*, Regensburg
NEUMANN, Peter Horst
    1978 'Schönberg, George, Petrarca. Zur Textwahl von Opus 8 bis Opus 24', *Bericht über den 1. Kongreß der Internationalen Schönberg-Gesellschaft*, ed. Rudolf Stephan, Wien: 140-6
REICH, Willi
    1968 *Arnold Schönberg oder Der konservative Revolutionär*, Wien/Frankfurt/Zürich
RUF, Wolfgang
    1984 'Arnold Schönbergs Lied *Herzgewächse*', *Archiv für Musikwissenschaft*, 41: 257-73
SCHOENBERG, Arnold
    1926 *Texte*, Wien
    1976 'Das Verhältnis zum Text', *Gesammelte Schriften*, I, ed. Ivan Vojteck, Frankfurt am M.

1979 *Grundlagen der musikalischen Komposition*, A, ed., Rudolf
       Stephan, Wien
STEPHAN, Rudolf
1974 'Schönberg als Symphoniker', *Österreichische Musikzeit-
       schrift*, 29: 267-78

Meaning in the Music of Charles Ives
Carol K. Baron

Abstract

Charles Edward Ives (1874-1954) created literary material relevant to his music. A comparison of related musical and extramusical forms shows that Ives composed analogues for life experiences in his music which frequently shape the formal design and even the language of his music. These analogues consist of different kinds of experiences whose extramusical meanings are an inherent aspect of a critical and aesthetic appreciation of this music.

Introduction

In the music of Charles Ives messages beyond those conveyed by the abstract relationships of sound are communicated to the listener. These messages are intended to accompany the sounds of the music and endow the music with meaning. Such meaning is integral to the musical conceptions—the formulation of the sound abstractions themselves. Therefore, Ives worked with both musical and extramusical ideas, creating and utilizing musical and extramusical structures as analogues when both were needed to fulfill his purposes.

The expression and appropriateness of extramusical dimensions apparently were basic concerns to Ives throughout his career. The following recollection, in his memos, of a conversation with a poet during his college days, is indicative of Ives's early interest in this aesthetic issue: 'He quite agreed with me that music could "proclaim" any part of the human experience' (1972: 61). Towards the end of his composing career, Ives accompanied the *Concord Sonata* with an entire book, *Essays Before A Sonata*; meaning in music is the subject of the first chapter. In the opening statement of this chapter, he clearly articulated anxiety about his musical aesthetics:

> How far is anyone justified . . . in expressing or trying to express in terms of music (in sounds, if you like) the value of anything material, moral, intellectual or spiritual which is usually expressed in terms other than music? . . . Can it be done by anything short of an act of mesmerism on the part of the composer or an act of kindness on the part of the listener (1961: 3)?

Ives then questioned the value of the 'extreme materializing of music' and of

> . . . the theory that music is the language of emotions and *only* that. . . . Does not this theory tend to limit music to programs?—a limitation as bad for music itself, for its wholesome progress, as a diet of program music is bad for the listener's ability to digest anything beyond the sensuous or physical-emotional.[1]

He called for the word 'emotion' to be interpreted 'in a deeper sense—which may be a feeling influenced by some experience, perhaps of a spiritual nature, in the expression of which the intellect has some part'. His definition of program music took on a broader meaning when he asked:

> Is not all music program music? Is not pure music, so called, representative in its essences? . . . Do all inspirational images, states, conditions, or whatever they may be truly called, have for a dominant part, if not for source, some actual experience in life or of the social relation? To think that they do not—always at least—would be a relief. But as we are trying to consider music made and heard by human beings (and not by birds or angels), it seems difficult to suppose that even subconscious images can be separated from some human experience. . . . Here is a program!—conscious or subconscious, what does it matter (1961: 4, 6-7)?

Thus, Ives resolved his anxiety about immediate aesthetic concerns, reaffirming a commitment to a mimetic and programmatic art.[2]

The amount of programmatic content in Ives's music is noteworthy. I have already pointed out that an entire book, *Essays Before A Sonata*, accompanies the *Concord Sonata*. Additionally, Ives gave programmatic titles to pieces and to movements; he made extensive marginal notes on the manuscripts; and although not literary or programmatic in the usual sense, the popular musical material Ives frequently uses carries associative values. Not least, Ives's memos, compiled between 1931 and 1934 by rewriting and expanding old notes and adding new material, are the single major source about his music and his career.[3] These memos contain important information about specific works as well as about Ives's musical ideas in general.

The extramusical elements serve various functions in the music. They determine the individualized and unique forms of Ives's musical motives, formal designs, notation and musical language. The pitch organizations and rhythmic conceptions result from the interaction of Ives's innovative musical ideas and the extramusical subject matter he portrays. Analytical methods that postulate consistency, organicism or coherence in the abstract musical language alone will lead to misunderstanding Ives's aesthetic intentions and his music; the assumptions of schools of normative and formalist analysis and criticism have therefore been largely inadequate in their encounters with Ives's work. Organicism in Ives's music, to use one example, is found in the relevance of the specific musical experience to its meaning.

In this paper I relate the musical to the extramusical ideas in order to clarify and interpret the meanings expressed by notation, texture, rhythm, motives, procedures and tonal language of the musical structures. In particular, I examine the way in which Ives conveys sensory images, humor, literary ideas and parody in four works: 'Hallowe'en', a work for string quartet and piano, from *Three Outdoor Scenes*; 'Putnam's Camp', the second movement of *Three Places in New England*; 'Thoreau', the third movement of *Piano Sonata No. 2, 'Concord, Mass., 1840-1860'* (*i.e.*, the *Concord Sonata*); and the *3-Page Sonata*. These four works span most of Ives's mature creative period—the decade from 1905 through approximately 1915—and represent a cross-section of his instrumental genres. In their use of images derived from America's New England states and Ives's remembrances of childhood activities, they also represent the composer's ties to the places where he was born, raised, educated and, later, a resident.

1. Sensory Images

In his program for 'Hallowe'en', Ives describes the sensory, kinetic and affective dimensions of the subject:

> The . . . little piece is but a take-off of a Halloween party and bonfires— the elfishness of the little boys throwing wood on the fire, etc. etc.—it may not be a good joke, [but] the joke of it is: if it isn't a joke, it isn't anything. . . . In this piece, I wanted to get, in a way, the sense and sound of a bonfire, outdoors in the night, growing bigger and brighter . . . (1972: 90-1).

The musical depiction of the bonfire occurs in a motive written for string quartet, in which the rising and descending lines of scale passages, broken into short phrases by octave displacements, changes in direction and occasional rests represent the rising and falling of licking flames, as shown in Example 1.

Although Ives referred to the 'sound of a bonfire', he made no attempt to imitate, in music, the crackling sounds of fire. Instead, he found analogies between different sensations and media. He transferred the dimensions of size—big and small—and space—high and low—from the sensory experiences of sight to those of sound. 'Bigger' is transformed to registrally higher as well as dynamically louder. Intensity values also are transferred from sight sensations to hearing sensations in an analogy between 'brighter' and 'louder'. The visually kinetic complexity of flames—the texture of fire—is captured in the musical texture of two paired canons.

Ex. 1: 'Hallowe'en', from *Three Outdoor Scenes*, mm. 1-4 of string quartet parts [© 1949 by Bomart Music Publications; reprinted by permission]

Composed for first violin/viola and second violin/cello, the canons retain strict imitation; even inserted rests—leaving out single notes—do not disturb the pitch contours of the paired lines.

    Ives's musical image for fire has an impressive precedent. It is similar to one composed by J. S. Bach in *Cantata 101,* in which *Deines eifers Flammen* ('your flames of anger'), the *locus topicus*, is depicted by sharply angular scale passages, in canon from measure 5, shown in Example 2.

2. Humor

Humor plays a large role in much of Ives's music, and 'Hallowe'en' is an example of Ives's composing this affect. To a degree, the humor is a consequence of the subject of the music. More significantly, in this work it takes the form of musical punning—an intellectual activity requiring a shared frame-of-reference in any medium. Ives's program clarifies and interprets some of the jokes and suggests the existence of others for those listeners who either are not predisposed to this musical affect or lack the necessary frame-of-reference—the complacent concert-goers Ives abhorred ('even Herbert Hoover could get it, and the average listener always gets it').

    After describing the subject of 'Hallowe'en', Ives made his first suggestion of a joke in a parenthetical statement: '(and at the end, the take-

Ex. 2: J. S. Bach, *Cantata 101*, 4th movement, mm. 1-8

off of the regular coda of a proper opera, heard down the street from the band stand).' The music's ending is also parenthetical: it consists of repeated root position C major triads, unrelated to the preceding music, followed by a parallel triadic ascent from C major to E flat major—a passage containing all twelve tones. The triadic configuration as well as the specific triads are linguistically irrelevant and parenthetical—a joke. The repeated major chords are a metaphor for the opera's coda; to understand the sarcasm in the metaphor, we need to know that a 'proper' opera is one that Ives would not have approved.

Ives's allusions to the musical puns in 'Hallowe'en' are formulated in a defensive response to criticism from the prominent conductor/educator, Albert Stoessel, who read through the work in 1934 during the period Ives was putting his memos together. In one of the memos Ives wrote:

In spite of the subject matter, this was one of the most carefully worked out (technically speaking), and one of the best pieces (from the standpoint of workmanship) that I've ever done. The four strings play in four different and closely related keys, each line strictly diatonic. Then it is canonic, not only in tones, but in phrases, accents, and durations or spaces. I happened to get exactly the effect I had in mind, which is the only ([or] at least an important) function of good workmanship. Allie S. [referring to the conductor] made some criticism implying that the workmanship was poor—the "four keys at once" didn't seem nice to him (1972: 91).

A pun is implied in Ives's description of different and closely related keys and diatonicism. As used in this piece, these concepts have meanings that contradict how they were generally understood. The strictly diatonic keys of each line are related by consecutive half-steps: B, C, D flat and D. The double meaning of a pun exists in the context of this combination of musical relationships: the so-called diatonic keys imply a contradictory, linguistically-atonal milieu.

Another pun is developed notationally. It points to a humorous kind of pitch organization, dependent on the visual structure of the staff and clefs. The relationship between notes placed on the staff using the G clef and those placed on the staff using the alto C clef is a transposition of one half-step or its complement of eleven half-steps. By pairing the C major scale passages of the first violin using G clef and the D flat major passages of the viola using the alto C clef, the pitch notation for these two keys is visually identical in canon. Similarly, the relationships between notes placed on the staff using the G clef and those placed on the staff using the F clef is a transposition of three half-steps or its complement of nine half-steps. By pairing B major for the second violin in G clef and D major for the cello in F clef, the pitch notation is again visually identical, sometimes simply displaced by the octave. Punning in notation is an example of Ives's sensitivity to the meanings inherent in this parameter of musical thought.

3. Literary Ideas

In 'Putnam's Camp', measures 67 through 81 (score letters H through I, 2d measure) represent conflicting protagonists. In his program Ives described the protagonists as part of a child's dream about an historic event memorialized in a small park in Redding, Connecticut. In the dream the protagonists are a group of mutinous soldiers breaking camp and a tall woman with a sorrowful face, reminiscent of the 'Goddess of Liberty'. The woman pleads with 'the soldiers not to forget their "cause" and the great sacrifices they have made for it'. But the soldiers do not heed the woman's pleas.

The musical elements are molded to portray this dramatic confrontation. Independent musical configurations, using contrasting motives and bi-tempi, are set in polyphonic layers. The motive of the woman is a lyrical melody, that of the soldiers is a march rhythm without a melody, as seen in Example 3.

Ex. 3: 'Putnam's Camp', from *Three Places in New England* (1st edn., 1935), mm. 74-78 [© 1935 Mercury Music Inc.; used by permission of the publisher]

With both motives sharing a 4/4 meter, the relationship of the bi-tempi is the ratio 4 to 3. The measure with the faster tempo has a whole note in the space of a dotted-half note in the slower tempo; therefore, rhythmic values in the faster tempo are three-quarters as long as the same rhythmic values in the slower tempo.

Literary ideas occur also in the *Concord Sonata*, the four movements of which correspond to four chapters in *Essays Before A Sonata*. Both works portray Emerson, The Alcotts, Thoreau and Hawthorne, all associated with 'the spirit of transcendentalism that is associated in the minds of many with Concord, Mass.' (1961: xxv). The two works were most likely conceived at approximately the same time as part of the compositional process. Motivic successions, reiterated motives and their variations share associations in the musical and literary media transformed one to the other. Hence, the musical designs have no relationship to conventional formal structures.

In 'Thoreau' the musical motives follow Ives's literary depiction of Thoreau's thoughts on one 'autumn day'. The ideas develop synchronously in the unambiguous program provided at the end of Chapter 5 and in the music. The character of the motives can be associated with the moods and images in the text. Motivic development concretizes the extramusical ideas, evoking and conveying meanings through complex musical relationships: some motives appear only once; others are repeated many times, intertwining, overlapping, intruding on other motives in developing and varying relationships.

The relationship of idea complexes and thematic linking can be demonstrated in the first two sentences of the program and the opening musical section, shown in Example 4.

Significant images/motives are introduced which recur throughout the movement: 'a shadow of a thought at first, colored by the mist and haze over the pond. . . . But this is momentary—the beauty of the day moves him to a certain restlessness—to aspirations more specific' (1961: 67). The arabic numerals in Example 4 mark the musical motives. Number 1, the 'mist and haze', consists of rising arpeggios. Number 2, a 'shadow of a thought', in two parts, emerges from the three statements of the mist motive. Its first statement begins with a spiral, using a set with four consecutive half steps. Its second statement (from the middle of the second system where B flat is in the top voice) begins with an opening descending interval-3 cycle, a configuration traditionally described as a diminished triad. Number 3, the 'restlessness' motive, is a small, wedge-like figure. Its harmonic reference is the whole-tone subcollection G sharp, B flat, C, D. Through the mist and haze, the shadow-thoughts emerge, at first tentatively, incompletely. The process is interrupted by 'restlessness', first in small spurts, and then is overcome by 'restlessness'.

Ives preceded his characterizations of Thoreau in the program— restlessness is but one of his qualities—with commentary providing

Ex. 4: 'Thoreau', from the *Concord Sonata*, p. 59, 1st three systems [© 1947 by Associated Music Publishers; reprinted by permission]

information about the origination of the pitch structures underlying the Thoreau-identifying motives. Ives associated the whole-tone scale with the French and the Orient and all three with Thoreau. He established Thoreau's 'French connection' as follows: 'Besides what he [Thoreau] received from a native Unitarianism, a good part must have descended to him through his Huguenot blood from eighteenth-century French philosophy'. Ives then talks about Thoreau's study of Oriental texts, comparing it to the inappropriate use of Oriental ideas in some French music. In what is undoubtedly a criticism of Debussy, Ives writes: 'Strains from the Orient get the best of some modern French music, but not of Thoreau. He seems more interested *in* than influenced *by* Oriental philosophy'. Of course, Ives is also talking about himself when he then says: 'This is not the whole tone scale of the Orient but the scale of a Walden morning' (1961: 53).

Ives's whole-tone language is complex. The 'restlessness' motive—numbered 3 in Example 4—is one example of it, referring to subcollections of a whole-tone scale plus one to three added notes which provide chromatic elaboration. All motives portraying Thoreau refer to a whole-tone scale. Another example is the group of motives representing his 'eagerness', introduced subsequently. The whole-tone scale is a metaphor for Thoreau.

I will present one other example from 'Thoreau', showing how another literary idea is related to a musical one, again metaphorically. The following passage from the program, marking the first formal caesura, moves the thought progression to a new phase: 'As the mists rise, there comes a clearer thought, more traditional than the first—a meditation more calm' (1961: 67). In the music the idea of the 'more traditional thought' is expressed in a diatonically-implicated motive; it is shown in Example 5 after the tenuto and double bar, the parallelling musical caesura.

Ex. 5: 'Thoreau', from the *Concord Sonata*, p. 60, 2d system, 4th quarter, 2d eighth — 3d system, 2d quarter, 1st eighth [© 1947 by Associated Music Publishers; reprinted by permission]

The implication of diatonicism is composed into a passage that is cyclically organized; therefore, the syntax is not diatonic. The referential collection contains two major scales, C and F. This collection is used in the verticalities of the motive and in the implied simultaneity of the combined vertical/horizontal dimension. It is expressed as a 5/7 cycle, the traditionally-named 'cycle of 5ths'. A metaphor for tradition lies in the diatonic implications.

4. Parody

The program for the *3-Page Sonata* is about music. This work is therefore most unusual. It is a satire of eighteenth-century musical language and conventions composed in a totally innovative context. Ives perceived the music of the eighteenth century and music based on it—the nineteenth-century music he knew—to be the music of conventional concert audiences, academics and critics: it was the criterion by which they heard all subsequent music and the gauge by which they measured it.

In part, the *3-Page Sonata* is a tangible parody in music of a statement by the music critic, W.J. Henderson, who wrote:

It was deemed altogether fitting and, indeed, intellectually satisfying that Beethoven should be smugly patted on the back, Brahms viewed with lifted brows, and Wagner convicted of lunacy by persons who could not, while in the concert-room, detect a fantasia masquerading as an overture, nor a suite disguised as a symphony—nay, more, who could not tell when the composer dropped the elementary rhythm of the valse to take up that of the polonaise (1898: 3-4).[4]

Henderson's interest in, and knowledge of, the music of Beethoven, Brahms and Wagner were anathema to Ives's own interest in progressive musical techniques. In a memo Ives wrote a paraphrase of Henderson's statement, turning Henderson's criticism into a burlesque of itself: 'He has been able for many years to detect a fantasia masquerading as an overture, or a suite disguised as a symphony—nay more, he can now tell when the composer drops the elementary rhythm of the valse to take up that of the polonaise . . . (see Rollo's own book, pages 3 and 4)' (1972: 61).[5]

Ives's attack on the criticism of Henderson is integrated within the musical conception of the *3-Page Sonata*. The formal design of the first movement is a musical parody of Henderson's statement in which a fugal subject 'masquerades' as a first theme, and a second theme is 'disguised' as a fugal episode—the musical parody parallels the literary one in his memo. The outline below of the formal design shows the amalgam of fugal and sonata-allegro procedures in this uniquely-conceived work:

1st statement of the Fugal Complex (1st Theme)
Bridge
2d statement of the Fugal Complex, in diminution
Bridge
2d Theme/Episode
3d statement of the Fugal Complex, in inversion
Repeat sign
Bridge
New 'Octave Theme'
Bridge
2d Theme/Episode
Variation of New 'Octave Theme'
End Phrase

Examples 6, 7 and 8 contain the three statements of the fugal complexes. The opening statement of the fugal subject consists of the intervals of the B-A-C-H motive from J. S. Bach's *Kunst der Fuge*, accompanied by what are traditionally called 'parallel fourths'. It is shown in Example 6.

The subject appears in an irregular diminution in Example 7 and in inversion in Example 8.

The meaning of the formal design is implied both in the accompanying extramusical materials and in the procedures themselves. For example, the title of the work and the marginal notes on the manuscript denote a sonata; the instruction placed after the third fugal statement states: 'back to 1st Theme all nice Sonatas must have 1st Theme'. The term 'nice' associated with 'sonata' is always pejorative. In the music the 'second theme' first

Ex. 6: *3-Page Sonata* (unpubld. edn., ed. C. K. Baron, 1986) 1st movement, p. 3, 1st fugal complex [© 1949, 1975, 1986 Mercury Music Inc.; used by permission of the publisher]

Ex. 7: *3-Page Sonata* (unpubld. edn., ed. C. K. Baron, 1986) 1st movement, p. 3, 2d fugal complex [© 1949, 1975, 1986 Mercury Music Inc.; used by permission of the publisher]

appears as an episode between the second and third statements of the fugal complexes, as shown in the outline above. At the same time, the repeat of the first section after the double bar is a convention of sonata-allegro procedures. A form such as this one never existed before. The contradictions and distortions are composed deliberately. In this music form is a vehicle of meaning: the music has become the program, and the program has become the music.

Conclusion

In the various forms his literary contributions take, Ives has more or less defined the subject matter of most of his music, the sources of his

Ex. 8: *3-Page Sonata* (unpubld. edn., ed. C. K. Baron, 1986) 1st movement, p. 4, 3d fugal complex [© 1949, 1975, 1986 Mercury Music Inc.; used by permission of the publisher]

inspiration and how the music should be listened to. According to Dahlhaus, extramusical content is 'an ingredient of the musical work itself'. He goes on to make a generalization about program music that is relevant for perceiving the totality of Ives's aesthetics: 'If the subject specifies meanings for musical themes and motives, the opposite is equally valid: the broad significance and import of the subject is newly minted by musical themes and motives. Program music rests on the interdependence of its components' (1981: 59). I would add that the breadth of new, abstract musical ideas available to, and utilized by, Ives made the depiction of a wide variety of subjects and types of subjects possible and particularly vivid. I conclude, therefore, that Ives's music can only be understood and appreciated on its own terms. A theory of Ives's music, which embraces the programmatic, extramusical dimensions that are integral to its construction fosters such understanding and appreciation.

Notes

[1] Ives also quotes the following statement of Henry Sturt: 'The nearer we get to the mere expression of emotion as in the antics of boys who have been promised a holiday, the further we get away from art' (1961: 4; *see* Sturt 1902).

[2] However, a futurist ideal, which Ives nurtured for the intrinsic communicability of music, concluded his discussion of aesthetic issues: 'But we would rather believe that music is beyond any analogy to word language and that the time is coming, but not in our lifetime, when it will develop possibilities inconceivable now—a language so transcendent that its heights and depths will be common to all mankind' (1961: 8).

[3] Ives (1972: 25) called his memos a 'desultory scrapbook (= "memos"—not memoirs—no one but the President of a nice Bank or a Golf Club, or a dead Prime Minister, can write "memoirs")'. Perry, a scholar in

American studies, maintains that Ives was aware of his need to engage the listener in his 'thought-stream' because of the unusual nature of his musical vision. His literary writings provide what Perry calls 'carefully dropped clues to unravel his scheme throughout his work' (1974: 48).

[4] Henderson's book subsequently went through six editions and was reprinted in fifteen different years. Ives had a copy of the third edition, published in 1905, the year the *3-Page Sonata* was composed. Baron (1987) develops the evidence relating Ives's memo, numbered 5, to the *3-Page Sonata*.

[5] Rollo is the main character in a series of children's books by the Rev. Jacob Abbott (1803-1879). He became a symbol for Ives of literal-minded, unimaginative, pedantic people.

Acknowledgments

I wish to thank the following publishers for their permission to quote from works by Charles Ives: Associated Music Publishers for permission to quote from 'Thoreau' from the *Concord Sonata*; Mercury Music Inc. for permission to quote from the *3-Page Sonata* and 'Putnam's Camp' from *Three Places in New England*; and Music Associates of America, representing Boelke-Bomart/Mobart Music Publications, for permission to quote from 'Hallowe'en' from *Three Outdoor Scenes*.

References

BARON, Carol
    1987   'Ives On His Own Terms: An Explication, A Theory of Pitch Organization, and A New Critical Edition for the *3-Page Sonata*', Ph.D. dissertation, Ann Arbor. (UMI, #87-10,602)
DAHLHAUS, Carl
    1981   *Esthetics of Music*, tr. W. Austin, Cambridge: Cambridge University Press
HENDERSON, William James
    1898   *What Is Good Music?*, New York: C. Scribner's Sons
IVES, Charles E.
    1961   *Essays*, ed. H. Boatwright, New York: W.W. Norton
    1972   *Memos*, ed. J. Kirkpatrick, New York: W.W. Norton
PERRY, Rosalie Sandra
    1974   *Charles Ives and The American Mind*, Kent, Ohio: Kent State University Press
STURT, Henry
    1902   'Arts and Personality', *Personal Idealism*, ed. H. Sturt, London: Macmillan and Co.; New York: The Macmillan Co.

Social Commentary in the Music of Haydn's Goldoni Operas

Patricia Debly

Abstract

Carlo Goldoni (1707-1793), one of the leading Italian playwrights and librettists of the eighteenth-century, had his texts repeatedly set by various composers, Italian and non-Italian alike. Three of his librettos, Il mondo della luna *(The World of the Moon, 1750),* Lo speziale *(The Apothecary, 1751) and* Le pescatrici *(The Fisherwomen, 1752), were revised at Eszterháza for the opera ensemble conducted by Joseph Haydn (1732-1809). In this paper the author examines some of the ways in which Haydn created music as an analogue of the social commentary explicit in Goldoni's librettos. Her examination is based on the assumption that libretto and music reflect particular aspects of eighteenth-century society. Goldoni's text, the primary analogue, satirizes society's values and mores through unrealistic incidents in the plot and the shortcomings of its characters. Haydn's music, as the secondary analogue, underlines these aspects, since it contains elements that do not follow the regular formula patterns of the eighteenth-century classical style.*

Introduction

Like other eighteenth-century playwrights, Carlo Goldoni adhered to the eighteenth-century dictum that the purpose of the theatre was to please and to teach. In his *Mémoires*, for example, he wrote: 'Comedy, which is, or ought to be, a school for propriety, should only expose human weaknesses for the sake of correcting them' (1787/ 1926: 255). And in Act II, sc. i of his play, *Il teatro comico* (written in 1750), Goldoni had one of the characters, Anselmo, discuss the meaning of comedy: 'Comedy was created to correct vice and ridicule bad customs; when the ancient poets wrote comedies in this manner, the common people could participate because, seeing the copy of a character on stage, each found the original either in himself or in someone else' (1751/1969: 31). Steele summarizes the playwright's thoughts on how society and the theatre should be linked:

Goldoni wrote in the preface to the first collected edition of his works that the essential elements in his plays were "the two books on which I have meditated, and have never repented using: The World and The Theater." He claims to have learned, not from Aristotle and the erudite theorists, but from this equilibrium between the world and the theater. Of course, Goldoni used "the world" in a specific sense of time, place, and social reality. . . . In Goldoni's conception, "the world" was an essential element for the vitality of comedy. The variety of the world about us stimulated an examination of follies, vices, and defects "which are common to our age, and our Nation," and also provided the means by which "certain virtuous persons resist this corruption" (1981: 68-9).

Although Joseph Haydn did not know Goldoni personally, he would have had access to contemporary writings which criticized the *ancien régime* in its corrupt state (*see* Zeman 1976). While Haydn rarely revealed his innermost convictions and attitudes concerning people and society, there are a few brief reflections in his correspondence and London diaries. In a letter dated 6 July 1776 enclosing the requested autobiographical sketch for publication, Haydn concluded: 'my highest ambition is only that all the world regard me as the honest man I am. . . . [M]y sole wish is to offend neither my neighbour, nor my gracious Prince, nor above all our merciful God' (Landon 1976-80: ii/399). And in a letter of 1791 Haydn, writing about his sojourn in Britain, could overlook the jealousies of his peers and at the same time appreciate the positive response to himself and his music by the British audience: 'There is no doubt that many people in London are also envious of me, and I know almost all of them. . . . But they cannot harm me, for my credit with the common people has been firmly established for a long time. Apart from the professors, I am respected and loved by everyone' (Landon 1976-80: iii/105).

Haydn's philosophy of life can also be glimpsed from his involvement with Freemasonry. One of the few extant documents in this regard is a letter of application to the secretary of a Masonic lodge in Vienna. In the opening sentence Haydn expressed his respect for the movement and its doctrine: 'The highly advantageous impression which Freemasonry has made on me has long awakened in my breast the sincerest wish to become a member of the Order, with its humanitarian and wise principles' (Landon 1976-80: ii/504). When Haydn was accepted into the lodge in 1785, one of the brothers, as was the custom, wrote a speech for him, outlining the aims of the masonic movement, a movement to which Haydn would pledge allegiance:

I know of no more dignified, no more delightful concept, none where-in the upright man can find true happiness and real joy, than a society of noble human beings, each driven by the same thirst to drink from the spring of wisdom; who seek not to be parsimonious with the knowledge that is given them in the Temple of Truth, but on the contrary seek to share it with the others for the common good; a society in which neither the smile of fortune, nor the change of birth, reign, but in which the wisest and best are given the leadership; a society in which a shining enlightenment does not give rise to jealousy but rather is a source for emanation; where the manly handclasp is the sign of a heart expanded to much greatness, not the mask of a false friendship; where the clear-eyed lead the mistaken to the truth without rancour; where man may open his heart to man without having to fear prejudice, hate or intrigue. . . . (Landon 1976-80: ii/507).

With the aid of Goldoni's librettos, Haydn created music that enhanced the librettist's aim of pleasing and teaching. Even though his operas were to be performed for royalty, the critical social commentary of the librettos was left intact. The characters embody human traits (*e.g.*, greed for power and/or money, deceit, jealousy and dishonesty) and are placed in circumstances that enable them to illustrate negative qualities to their fullest advantage. In translating the librettist's aims into music, Haydn represented characters according to their social status and their particular personalities. He also allocated special treatment to certain plot situations.

Predicate Society	Primary Analogue Libretto	Secondary Analogue Music
marriage contracts and dowries	pun: '*donò*' and '*no*'; '*me l'ha detto*' and '*maledetto*'	tritone; harmony; constant changes of key
hypocrisy	explanation of the false image that people project	false recapitulation; harmonic resolutions
fraudulent relationship between the sexes	dialogue: flirtation and rejection	irony: man and and woman have same melodic phrase
	dialogue: disagreement	use of contrary motion in vocal and instrumental parts
plot	increase and decrease of dramatic tension	choice of tonal areas to increase and decrease musical tension

Figure 1: Summary of selected correspondences

Figure 1 presents a summary of correspondences which I have selected for examination in this paper. The first column, the predicate, is a particular aspect of society. The second column, the primary analogue, is the literary technique in the libretto by means of which Goldoni treats a particular social aspect. And the third column, the secondary analogue, lists the musical techniques by means of which Haydn deviates from common eighteenth-century musical style in order to emphasize the didactic message in the libretto.

1. Haydn's setting of *Lo speziale* and *Le pescatrici*

The earliest of Haydn's Goldoni operas, *Lo speziale* (1768), was written for the opening of the new opera house at Eszterháza. This opera needs only four singers (two sopranos and two tenors), with an orchestral accompaniment of two flutes, two oboes, bassoon, two horns, strings and harpsichord continuo. The original libretto had serious and comic characters; but because of the small opera troupe at Eszterháza, the serious characters were omitted. The textual means to accomplish this were quite simple, since the pair of lovers—the serious characters—did not interact with the others, the comic characters. Only a few minor changes, in addition to the omissions, had to be made to the revised libretto.

The plot can be summarized as follows: Sempronio, an apothecary, spends his days reading and fantasizing about faraway places. He is the guardian to a young girl, Grilletta, whom he secretly plans on marrying. Grilletta, however, is already being sought after by two other suitors, Mengone and Volpino. Mengone, in order to be near Grilletta, is Sempronio's apprentice. By the end of Act II, Grilletta, who is angry with Mengone, has agreed to marry Sempronio. Their marriage contract is drawn up by two notaries—none other than Mengone and Volpino in disguise! Act III commences with Volpino, dressed as a Turk, convincing Sempronio that to open a dispensary in Turkey will make the latter a rich man. In the process Sempronio gives Grilletta to the disguised Volpino to marry. Meanwhile, Mengone, also dressed as a Turk, and Grilletta outwit Volpino and fraudulently obtain Sempronio's blessing for their marriage.

This basic intermezzo plot of the old man attempting to win over the young girl (or vice versa) was crucial to Goldoni's argument, since it enabled him to comment upon the mannerisms of their social interaction. Although one finds references to the relationship between the sexes constantly throughout Goldoni's librettos, in *Lo speziale* character development and other topics of social commentary are limited to a few passing remarks and do not take on the larger dimensions that will be found in the librettos of Haydn's later operas. The music employs the characteristic elements of the *buffo* (comic) style: large leaps, unexpected harmonic resolutions, dotted rhythms, disjunct melodic lines and patter song. The second act finale in *Lo speziale*, which foreshadows Haydn's emerging operatic style, is an exception to the standard *buffo* style, for it represents Sempronio's gullible yet greedy character and the social practice of marriage contracts and dowries. In the eighteenth century the woman's dowry was crucial in securing a husband, who, if she was favourably matched, would be of a higher social standing. For the man, this would be a chance to fill his coffers, an opportunity not to be taken lightly, especially if he was an impoverished aristocrat.

The finale opens with the two rival suitors disguised as notaries ready to write the marriage contract for the guardian, Sempronio. In the process of the dictation, a number of puns are employed. When Sempronio states that he is going to receive Grilletta's dowry, we have the word '*donò*'. The notaries, who up until this point have been voicing the last part of each phrase, reinterpret it as '*no*', meaning they disagree (Example 1). In the

Example 1: *Lo speziale*, Act II Finale (1768, 1959: iii/148-9, mm. 27-30)

next sentence the notaries write '*à me*', referring not to Sempronio but to themselves. Sempronio then continues to defend himself by saying '*me l'ha detto*', meaning 'she told me that'; but the notaries reinterpret it by interchanging the vowel sounds to '*maledetto*', meaning 'cursed or damned'. The vocal lines reinforce the negative connotation by having the interval of a tritone separate Sempronio's last note, E, from the first note of the notaries, A sharp (Example 2).

Musically, the harmony progresses through a series of keys mainly using dominant and tonic chords. A German sixth chord is used for emphasis for the pun on '*no*', and a diminished seventh chord is employed for the pun on '*maledetto*'. By constantly shifting the tonal centre, the precarious nature of the situation is accentuated (Example 3). One could claim that Haydn's ingenious setting is merely within the comic context of the opera; but the strategic use of the German sixth and diminished seventh, along with a subtle musical humour in comparison to the more blatant *buffo* style, causes the audience not only to laugh at the situation but also to reflect upon the criticism aimed at the bourgeoisie. Accordingly, I would claim

Example 2: *Lo speziale*, Act II Finale (1768, 1959: iii/149, mm. 35-39)

that this setting demonstrates Haydn's deeper understanding of the libretto and his affinity to an enlightened concept of marriage as being more than a mere contractual agreement.

Le pescatrici, set to music by Haydn one year later, is based on a libretto that Goldoni wrote in 1752. The plot and characters belong to a different world from that of *Lo speziale*. The setting is an idealized rural location far from the city, in congruence with the contemporary literary trend of the *poesia arcadica*, which included shepherds or shepherdesses (or, in our case, fishermen) found in a rustic setting. The theme of 'natural man' who experiences natural emotions, particularly with regard to love, is explored here. The setting by Haydn evokes the pastoral elements through the use of the simple, folk-song-like melodies for the arias sung by the lower-class characters. The nobility's music is written in the style of *opera seria* with coloratura passages for the singer and full orchestra. Besides flirtations with their boyfriends, the fisherwomen's dialogue focuses on how they can elevate themselves socially. Haydn's music, at least the two-thirds that is extant, remains stylistically similar to *Lo speziale*.

2. Haydn's setting of *Il mondo della luna*

The last of Haydn's Goldoni operas, *Il mondo della luna*, was written in 1777, the year following the expansion of the operatic troupe at Eszterháza. The opera is scored for eleven singers (two sopranos, alto, two tenors, alto castrato, bass and four choral bass parts), with an orchestra of two flutes, two oboes, two bassoons, two horns, two trumpets, timpani,

Example 3: *Lo speziale*, Act II Finale

SEMPRONIO	A major	SEMPRONIO
Con la presente		With this
scrittura privata		confidential contract
resta accordata		the beautiful Grilletta
la bella Grilletta		agrees

VOLPINO, MENGONE   VOLPINO, MENGONE
Grilletta....   Grilletta....

SEMPRONIO   SEMPRONIO
...in matrimonio....   ...to enter into
                                          marriage....

VOLPINO   VOLPINO
...in ma....   ...to enter into mar....

MENGONE   F# minor   MENGONE
...trimonio....   ...riage....

SEMPRONIO   SEMPRONIO
...con il signore....   ...with this gentleman....

VOLPINO, MENGONE   VOLPINO, MENGONE
...signore....   ...gentleman....

SEMPRONIO   E major   SEMPRONIO
Sempronio.   Sempronio.

VOLPINO, MENGONE   VOLPINO, MENGONE
(ogun scrive il suo nome)   (each writes his own name)
Volpino...Menghino....   Volpino...Menghino....

SEMPRONIO   A major   SEMPRONIO
Sempronio. Scrivano   Sempronio. Write it
bene.   properly.

VOLPINO, MENGONE   B major   VOLPINO, MENGONE
...onio.   onio.

SEMPRONIO   SEMPRONIO
Lei promette di sposarlo.   She promises to wed him.

VOLPINO, MENGONE   VOLPINO, MENGONE
...arlo.   ...wed him.

SEMPRONIO   E major   SEMPRONIO
E con tale promissione....   And with this promise....

VOLPINO, MENGONE   E minor   VOLPINO, MENGONE
...one....   ...mise....

SEMPRONIO ...i suoi beni gli donò.	(German sixth)	SEMPRONIO ...I will give him the possessions that are due to him.
VOLPINO, MENGONE ...no....	(German sixth)	VOLPINO, MENGONE ...no....
SEMPRONIO Come no? Signori si. La suo dote vien a me.	E major	SEMPRONIO Why not? Yes, gentlemen. Her dowry belongs to me.
VOLPINO, MENGONE ...a me.		VOLPINO, MENGONE ...to me.
SEMPRONIO Ella stessa me l'ha detto.	E minor	SEMPRONIO She herself has told me that.
VOLPINO, MENGONE Maledetto.	B major	VOLPINO, MENGONE Cursed.
SEMPRONIO Siete sordi? Siete pazzi? Che maniera è questa qui?	E major	SEMPRONIO Are you deaf? Are you crazy? What kind of behaviour is this?
VOLPINO, MENGONE (La non vuol finir così.)		VOLPINO, MENGONE (This won't end like that.)

Example 3

strings and harpsichord continuo. It is only in the libretto to this opera that one finds constant references to contemporary society and its foibles. Like the other satirical fantasies that Goldoni wrote between 1750 and 1751, *Il mondo della luna* satirizes society's vices and, in a blatantly fantastic context, magnifies them 'far out of proportion, making a polemical point and achieving comic effect through the deliberate distortion of reality' (Emery 1985: 183-9). In *Il mondo della luna*, however, the real world is evoked not by a direct representation of life on earth but by presenting its supposed opposite, life on the moon.

The plot may be summarized as follows. Buonafede, a merchant, has two daughters, Clarice and Flaminia, whom he hopes to marry off advantageously. He himself plans on marrying the servant girl, Lisetta. But Ecclitico, an astrologer, loves Clarice; Ernesto, a cavalier, loves Flaminia; and Cecco, Ernesto's servant, loves Lisetta. Ecclitico shows Buonafede how delightful life on the moon is, and Buonafede is tricked into believing that he has been flown to the moon to live. On the moon, with Cecco as emperor, Buonafede is again outwitted by consenting to the triple marriage of Ecclitico-Clarice, Ernesto-Flaminia and Cecco-Lisetta. Buonafede eventually gives his blessing to the newlyweds, although he is angry at having been duped.

The libretto contains numerous examples of characters commenting about the inconsistencies of human nature and society at large. After the opening chorus Ecclitico reveals his basic philosophy about people: they can be made to believe anything, whether they are well educated or not. He gloats over the fact that being an imposter is in itself a great calling. The plot then continues with Ecclitico plying his trade as astrologer on the gullible Buonafede. Just as Buonafede is preparing to look through the telescope, Ecclitico states that men with fake telescopes cannot see the truth, just as men with their human eyes are blind to falsehoods. He then reflects on the folly of people: they assume they know others, just as they think they know themselves; but because they do not know themselves, they do not know others.

A pun on the word lunatic (*lunatico*) occurs at various times throughout the opera. In Italian the word can be used as an adjective for people belonging to the moon (the equivalent of the English 'lunar'), but it can also describe a person who is very temperamental and quirky. In Act II, when Buonafede inquires whether his daughters and servant may join him on the moon, Ecclitico answers that, yes, these women, due to their constant changes in appearance and mood, belong on the moon, since they are most definitely lunatics (*Sono lunatiche, oh signor, sì!*). Later in Act II, Cecco dresses as the emperor of the moon. He tells Buonafede that his earthly world is crazy and lists the follies of various kinds of people, concluding that everything on earth is backwards (*al rovescio tutto va*).

In recognition of the fact that Cecco's world is the world of the moon, one soon realizes that the most enlightened remarks about man and society come not from the upper classes but from the two *buffo* servants, Cecco and Lisetta. In Act I, sc. vi, Cecco's recitative reprimands Ernesto, his master, for following the 'stupid world' (*il mondo stolido*) and for changing the labels given to certain types of people—for example, by calling a hypocrite 'very pious', a miser 'economical' and a prodigal 'generous'. The following aria continues to expound upon human naivety in a world that is highly fraudulent (Example 4). Reality is only appearance and should be recognized as such.

CECCO

Mi fanno ridere quelli che credono che quel che vedono sia verità. Non sanno i semplici che tutti fingono: che il vero tongono di falsità. Mi fanno ridere, ecc.	Those people make me laugh, who believe that what they see is true. These simpletons do not know, that everyone pretends: that falsehoods colour the truth. Those people make me laugh, etc.

Example 4

Haydn characterizes Cecco's roots in the servant class by maintaining the typical musical syntax of the *buffo* style. At the same time he is sensitive to Cecco's acute understanding of human nature, and he illustrates this understanding through the larger, formal dimensions of the music. In setting the aria, Haydn repeats the text three times. In the initial presentation of the text, the final line ends in the dominant key and leads back to what one thinks is merely a recapitulation. However, after the first eight bars, new material is presented, creating a false recapitulation. While Haydn frequently employed the technique of false recapitulation in his instrumental music, he used this technique only this once in *Il mondo della luna*, thereby consciously restating '*falsità*' (falsehoods). The true recapitulation then begins with the third presentation of the text and remains in the tonic key throughout.

The sentiments of the text are translated musically in the context of the overall form of the aria and in the harmonic language of the orchestral accompaniment. At the moment when the false recapitulation is concluding on the text '*di falsità*', the initial cadence (Example 5, mm. 64-65) is a diminished seventh chord resolving to the notes D and F sharp (in this context the tonic triad of D major, the dominant key). This is considered to be a standard concluding phrase in terms of eighteenth-century harmonic practice. But Haydn does not end the section here. The following bar, which begins a semitone higher on E flat, maintains the previous chord tones of the diminished seventh chord (C sharp, G and B flat), thereby creating a German sixth chord in the tonic key of G major. Once again this cadence resolves to the note, D; but this time it must be reinterpreted as the dominant chord of the tonic key, reinforcing the compulsion to return to the home key area in the third and final repetition of the text. In this five-bar section, in reference to the text, one can perceive that the two resolutions to the harmony of D produce two different results: the first time one is 'falsely' led to hear a final ending in the dominant key, while in the second cadence the note, D, functions as an important linkage back to the tonic key.

The duet in Act II of *Il mondo della luna* again focuses on the relationship between the sexes. Here one finds the most intense confrontation between Buonafede and his servant girl, Lisetta. Earlier in the libretto Buonafede states that lunar relationships between men and women are entirely without sexual ulterior motives; yet while he extolls the purity of lunar society and the innocence of his own intentions, he also makes a pass at Lisetta (Example 6). Their dialogue is highly imbued with sarcastic and witty remarks that playfully underscore the forceful manipulative techniques used by both sexes to attain their goal.

In setting the duet, Haydn employs musical irony. The vocal line first sung by Buonafede is calm and free-flowing, perhaps even coy, barely hinting at the underlying tension and anxiety (Example 7). Lisetta's sardonic text repeats this graceful music verbatim, blatantly mocking Buonafede's flirtation. Her retort is ironical, because she uses Buonafede's melody but expresses exactly the opposite sentiment. However, the

Example 5: *Il mondo della luna*, Act I, no. 14 (1777, 1979-81 vii/117, mm. 63-68)

emotionalism of the flirtation releases itself and is exhibited by an increase in the accompaniment's rhythmic tempo from quarter notes to triplet eighths. The music at Buonafede's line, 'As I would my little dog', changes to *presto*. Although, initially, Lisetta continues to respond by singing Buonafede's vocal line, the tempers begin to rise, and we hear a three-note

Il mondo della luna, Act II, no. 41

BUONAFEDE
Non aver di me sospetto,
malizioso io non ho il core.

BUONAFEDE
Do not be suspicious of me,
I have no malice in my heart.

LISETTA
Vi conosco, bel furbetto,
malizioso è il vostro amore.

LISETTA
I know you, cunning sir,
the malice is in your love.

BUONAFEDE
Non è ver.

BUONAFEDE
It's not true.

LISETTA
Non me ne fido.

LISETTA
I don't trust you.

BUONAFEDE
Son pupilo.

BUONAFEDE
I am innocent.

LISETTA
Io me ne rido.

LISETTA
This makes me laugh.

BUONAFEDE
Via, carina,
una manina.

BUONAFEDE
Come, pretty girl,
a little hand.

LISETTA
No, non voglio.

LISETTA
No, I don't want to.

BUONAFEDE
Oh crudelità!

BUONAFEDE
Oh, how cruel!

LISETTA
Vi conosco.

LISETTA
I know you.

BUONAFEDE
Come fò alla mia cagnina,
le carezze io ti farò.

BUONAFEDE
I'll give you caresses, like
I do for my little dog.

LISETTA
Ed io qual da una gattina
le carezze accetterò.

LISETTA
And I'll accept your caresses
like a little cat.

BUONAFEDE
Vieni, o cara barboncina.

BUONAFEDE
Come, oh dear little poodle.

LISETTA
Vieni, o cara piccinina.

LISETTA
Come, oh dear little one.

BUONAFEDE

BUONAFEDE

Vien da me, non abbaiar.

Come to me, don't bark.

LISETTA
Frusta via, mi vuoi
graffiar.

LISETTA
Get away, you want to scratch
me.

BUONAFEDE
Come fò alla mia cagnina,
ecc.

BUONAFEDE
I'll give you caresses,
etc.

Example 6

Example 7: *Il mondo della luna*, Act II, no. 41 (1777, 1979-81 vii/306, mm. 1-6)

dissonant figure in the strings. This dissonance is created by the violins ascending scalewise, while the lower strings have the same pattern descending (Example 8). The second half of the text is repeated with the voices singing together. Customarily, these vocal parts were set in parallel thirds so that each singer had the same melodic line a third higher or lower than the other. But Haydn does not follow this formula here; instead, he has set the two parts in contrary motion in order to suggest the two opposing positions of Buonafede and Lisetta. The contrary motion figure in the strings continues to be heard at various times, thereby reinforcing the unresolved discord of both text and music.

In the context of the complete opera, the key of this duet is significant, because it is one of only two numbers in Act II that adds tension. In comparison to the two earlier works, the tonal areas of each act of this opera create a pattern that directly relates the dramatic function to the choice of keys. The entire opera is considered to be in the key of D major, the tonality of the second and third acts, while the first act is in the key of

Example 8: *Il mondo della luna*, Act II, no. 41 (1777, 1979-81 vii/312, mm. 56-57)

E-flat major, the flatted second or Neapolitan relationship to D. Each act is a self-contained tonal structure.

The first act opens in E-flat major with a chorus, has three intermediary numbers in E flat and concludes in this key. The second act begins in D major, has two numbers that are in D and a finale that commences in D but, because of Buonafede's anger, changes to d minor. The third act also concludes in D major.

Figure 2 represents the tonal areas for all the numbers in the three acts. This Figure is based on Rosen, who summarizes the eighteenth-century's use of keys in relation to their degree of tension as follows:

. . . the keys of III and VI (mediant and submediant) are sharp keys close to the dominant and imply an increase in tension (or dissonance on the level of structure) and to some extent they can substitute for a dominant; the flat mediant and submediant are largely subdominant keys, and are used like the subdominant to weaken the tonic, and lower tension; . . . the tonalities at a distance of the tritone (diminished fifth) and the minor seventh are most remote or, in other words, most dissonant in their large-scale effects (1972: 27).

Rosen also explains that the supertonic is one of the tonal areas most remote from, and contradictory to, the tonic. In Figure 2 each tonality has

Musical Number	Key	Character(s)	Tension
		ACT I	
Sinfonia	C		
Chorus	Eb	Ecclitico, Scholars	tonic
Chorus	F	Scholars	increases
Sc. iii	G	Buonafede, Ecclitico, Scholars	increases
Entr'acte	D		increases
Cavatina	D	Buonafede	increases
Entr'acte	D		increases
Cavatina	D	Buonafede	increases
Entr'acte	Eb		tonic
Cavatina	Eb	Buonafede	tonic
Aria	F	Buonafede	increases
Aria	Eb	Ecclitico	tonic
Aria	D	Ernesto	increases
Aria	G	Cecco	increases
Aria	C	Flaminia	increases
Aria	A	Clarice	increases
Aria	F	Lisetta	increases
Finale	Eb-Bb-Eb	Ecclitico, Lisetta, Buonafede, Clarice	tonic
		ACT II	
Sinfonia	D		tonic
Concertino	F		lowers
Ballet	Bb		lowers
Chorus	D	Ecclitico, Buonafede, Knights	lowers
Aria	F	Ecclitico	lowers
March	C		increases
Aria	G	Cecco	lowers
Aria	g minor	Ernesto	lowers
Aria	D	Buonafede	tonic
Duet	A	Lisetta, Buonafede	increases
Aria	G	Lisetta	lowers
Ballet	F		lowers
Aria	F	Flaminia	lowers
Aria	Bb	Clarice	lowers
Finale	D-G-d minor	Everyone	tonic minor
		ACT III	
Sinfonia	g minor		lowers
Duet	Bb	Clarice, Ecclitico	lowers
Finale	D	Everyone	tonic

Figure 2: Musical Structure for *Il mondo della luna*

been assigned as either an increase or decrease in tension in relation to the tonality of the entire act. An obvious pattern arises: all the keys used in Act I intensify the harmonic tension, paralleling the dramatic excitement; the keys in Act II release the harmonic tension, paralleling the decrease in suspense, with the exceptions of the march to which Cecco enters dressed as emperor and the aforementioned duet of Buonafede and Lisetta in which Buonafede flirts with Lisetta while she mocks him. Act III continues the pattern of dramatic *dénouement* and its accompanying harmonic equalization.

According to the schematization in Figure 2, it is clear that Haydn's tonal plan represents musically the dramatic action. Act I introduces all of the characters' personalities as well as Ecclitico's intentions to secure the marriage of Buonafede's two daughters and maidservant for himself, Ernesto and Cecco. Buonafede's gullibility and greed are exposed by Ecclitico's cunning. Flamina's and Clarice's philosophy of love, involving rebellion against their father if need be, and Lisetta's coyness to her master are heard in their dialogue. Tension is slowly built up in the act until the climax is reached in the finale, a high point not only for the first act but for the whole opera.

At this point Buonafede has drunk what he assumes is a potion to enable him to fly, while Clarice and Lisetta think that he is dying and may even already be dead. The dramatic highpoint rests on the question of whether Ecclitico will succeed in his plan, or what the consequences will be if he fails. From this point on the tension is slowly released. Buonafede absolutely believes in the moon's viability for human life. Ecclitico's plan unfolds smoothly: Buonafede asks for the three girls to be transported to the moon, and it is now only a matter of time before each girl is escorted away by her future husband. Thus, by the end of Act II the only element of conflict left is Buonafede's anger at being deceived. But this is soon appeased by Buonafede's forgiveness at the beginning of Act III, sc. i, so the conflict is over, and the rest of this act is devoted to a love duet and jubilation over the triple marriage.

Conclusion: Haydn as Musical Dramatist

From these three operas one may observe a pattern of change in the librettos Haydn chose to set to music. In lieu of the fact that all these librettos were written and first performed in Italy between 1750 and 1752, Haydn would probably have had access to any one of them. Therefore, the choice in terms of the Eszterháza chronology was probably based on the Prince's taste and the capabilities of the opera troupe. The earliest opera, *Lo speziale*, in its original version easily facilitated a change in the number of characters from seven to four. The libretto, especially in comparison to other works of Goldoni, does not contain deep psychological significance or penetrating social analysis. The texts of the arias and types of characters are similar to Haydn's other comic operas written around this time period (1768). *Le pescatrici*, since it was performed initially as part of a marriage celebration, was probably chosen because it contained aristocratic characters who could be represented musically in *opera seria* style. The rural setting would have appealed to the royal audience, since it was in keeping with the eighteenth-century fashion of a 'return to nature'. Haydn, having had the experience of writing an *opera seria* in his very first opera for Eszterháza, *Acide*, composed the needed 'aria types' for the serious characters but maintained the *buffo* style where appropriate.

It is the last opera, *Il mondo della luna*, that unites Goldoni's acute social commentary with music that enhances its didactic yet entertaining message. The musical characterization, word painting and atmospheric effects for the lunar world, combined with Haydn's witty, yet subtle, musical humour, leads one to consider this composer's works in the same light as Mozart's operas. Haydn's ability to interpret and musically translate the libretto proves that he justly deserves an honoured place in operatic history.

Acknowledgment

All musical examples have been used with the kind permission of G. Henle Verlag, Munich, from their publication, *Joseph Haydn Werke*, series xxv, vol. 3 (© 1959) and series xxv, vol. 7, Parts 1 and 2 (© 1979 and 1981). The translations of the libretto given in Examples 3, 4 and 6 are my own.

References

EMERY, Ted A.
    1985 'Carlo Goldoni as Librettist: Theatrical Reform and the *drammi giocosi per musica*', Ph.D. dissertation, Brown University (UM No. DA8519831)
GOLDONI, Carlo
1787/1926 *Mémoires*, tr. John Black, New York: Alfred A. Knopf
1751/1969 *The Comic Theatre*, tr. J.W. Miller, Lincoln: University of Nebraska Press
HAYDN, Joseph
    1768 *Lo speziale*. Dramma giocoso, ed. Helmut Wirth, *Joseph Haydn Werke*, series xxv, vol. 3, Munich: G. Henle, 1979 and 1981
    1777 *Il mondo della luna*. Dramma giocoso, ed. Günter Thomas, *Joseph Haydn Werke*, series xxv, vol. 7 (3 parts), Munich: G. Henle, 1979 and 1981
LANDON, H. C. Robbins
    1976-80 *Haydn: Chronicle and Works*, 5 vols. , London: Thames and Hudson

ROSEN, Charles
    1972   *The Classical Style: Haydn, Mozart, Beethoven*, New York:
            W.W. Norton
STEELE, Eugene
    1981   *Carlo Goldoni: Life, Work and Times*, Ravenna: Longo
            Editore
ZEMAN, Herbert
    1976   *Joseph Haydn und die Literatur seiner Zeit*, Eisenstadt:
            Institut für Österreichische Kulturgeschichte

Music as a Sight in the Production of Music's Meaning

Richard Leppert

Abstract

In this paper the author investigates the relation of the sight of music's production to the semiotics and affects of music's sound. Vision focuses attention upon the physicality of music making, just as hearing focuses on the abstract sonorities produced by the body's actions when making music. Because musical sound is ethereal, its meanings and affects are, in part, dependent upon the sense of sight to help the auditor render the experience concrete and meaningful. The sight of music's performance associates the abstract sonoric phenomenon with the social; it locates sound in relation to the larger community of shared experiences from which people both produce and draw their perceptions of reality. The history of musical semiotics' connection to sight can be analyzed via images on musical subjects, that is, by considering the single form of expression that most closely replicates the act of seeing: visual art. The author demonstrates this through a detailed examination of a single seventeenth-century Dutch portrait, an allegory of marriage, wherein music serves as the primary organizing principle, the governing metaphor for marital fidelity and, in a larger sense, for male-female relations, gender hierarchy, class distinction and social order itself. It was possible (and appropriate) for the painter to represent musical activity in this manner—that is, possible for his intended audience to comprehend his intention—precisely because, within the culture, in actual practice, music embedded these myriad associations.

Introduction

The practice of music, for performers, calls on the sensory perceptions of hearing, touch and sight; for listeners, on hearing and sight alone. Historiographers, however, have concentrated their attention on music as sonoric phenomenon and have ignored the role played in the production of musical semiotics by its visual component.[1] In this paper I hope to demonstrate some of the ways by which the sight of music's production functions in close linkage with sonority to produce music's affects. My more specific aim will be to suggest how the sight of music in production constitutes a visual-sonoric simulacrum for social organization and cultural value.

My concern with vision focuses upon the physicality of music making itself (the sight of the body's labors to produce sound), and on the (ironic) fact that the 'product' of this activity—musical sonority—lacks all concreteness and disappears without a trace almost instantly once the musician's 'physical labors' cease (acoustic decay). Precisely because musical sound is abstract, intangible and etherial—lost as soon as it is gained—the visual experience of its production is crucial to both musicians and audience alike for locating and communicating the place of music and musical sound within society and culture. I am suggesting, in other words, that the slippage between the physical activity to produce musical sound and the abstract nature of that which is produced creates a semiotic contradiction that is ultimately 'resolved' through the agency of human sight. Music, despite its phenomenological sonoric ethereality, is an embodied practice, like dance and theater. As such, its visual-performative aspect is no less central to its meanings than are the visual components of these other performing arts. This is profoundly obvious as regards musical theater—opera, masque, etc. (though in fact this linkage is little discussed in musicological literature); but with respect to other sorts of art music, the connection between sight and sound remains untheorized. The single case study I will discuss here is of that variety.

My general interest in the sight of music focuses on music's representation in visual art rather than on eye-witness written accounts of musical performances. My reasons for subordinating written accounts are several. In the first, and less important, instance, *detailed* written accounts of non-theatrical musical events, especially prior to the public concerts of the nineteenth century, are surprisingly rare, though this presents only a practical, not a theoretical problem. Moreover, very few eye-witness accounts have as their particular concern the sorting out of sonority's relation to the sight of its production (my topic), though these accounts naturally depend for their existence on both eyes and ears. Second, written eye-witness accounts of musical activity filter the retinal action of the eyes through the transliterating process of language: the 'image' of the activity is reproduced in the 'mind's eye' of the reader of that account, and the reader's eyes confront the sight of words which in turn produce *linguistic* images. The representation of musical activity in art, by contrast, remains specifically visual in its 'translation' of the three-dimensional and sonoric world into a two-dimensional and silent 'argument' for and about the world.

The affects (meanings) of music, which in performance are produced both aurally *and* visually, in painting must be rendered visually only. Thus, the way of seeing incorporates the way of hearing: the artist must produce images in such a way that their meanings will be congruent with those produced by sight and sound together in the lived experience of the original and intended viewer. To render visually meaningful the *acoustic* phenomenon of music, the artist (discursively) calls upon semiotic codes that operate as a *sight* when music is actually made in real life. The artist does not invent a new visual code, one different from life-practice, for the simple reason that there is no point in doing so. (If artists failed in the endeavor, if their envisioning confused viewers, it is inconceivable that musical subjects could have been painted in the West for many centuries with such abundance as survives.) These codes function through the human body in its efforts to produce and receive music.

When people hear a musical performance, they see it as an *embodied* activity. While they hear, they also witness: how the performers look and gesture, how they are costumed, how they interact with their instruments and with one another, how they regard the audience, etc. Listeners also see themselves in relation to other listeners as well as to the performers. Thus, the musical event is perceived (received) by listeners as a socialized activity. Visual representation in effect summarizes by encapsulation more or less all of this, not as a 'disinterested' record of events but as a 'coherent' and *discursive vision* of the varied relations within the context of which sound occurs and, hence (as I shall argue), sound means. Visual art cannot replicate musical acoustics, but it can provide an invaluable hortatory account of what, how and why a given society heard and, therefore, what the sounds meant. (I should add that visual representations, except perhaps those which include decipherable musical inscriptions, tell us nothing specific about particular pieces of music; instead, they suggest the range of semiotic possibilities for specific compositions performed under conditions similar to those represented.)

I want to draw attention briefly to the account by Lowe (1982: 2-83) of the changing 'histories' of seeing and hearing during the time and place of my larger concern, post-medieval Western Europe, since this may further help explain the significance of sight to the hearing of music. Lowe outlines a history of human sensing around the organization of human communications. He points out that in oral cultures (*e.g.*, during the Middle Ages), where information is passed on by word of mouth and knowing cannot be separated from the knower's own memory, hearing enjoys a privileged position in the hierarchy of sensing. By contrast, in chirographic cultures (*e.g.*, predominant in and after the Renaissance), the separation of knowledge from the memory of the embodied human subject is possible since it exists in writing—though prior to the development of typography such knowledge is nevertheless highly restricted. With the printing press knowledge can be separated from the person who knows (e.g., the author) and relocated in the (mass-produced) book. Whereas in oral culture hearing (and touching) predominates over seeing in the transmission of knowledge,[2] in typographic culture (the culture of reading not listening) sight gains predominance over other senses. My concern is with this latter historical period, when sight became the prime means by which Western European culture came to terms with reality. Presuming the accuracy of Lowe's thesis, change in the hierarchy of sensing strengthens my argument for the importance of sight to the production of acoustic meaning in life practice and so also for the importance of visual art as a means by which to fathom these meanings.

What follows concerns a painting by the seventeenth-century Dutch artist, Jan Miense Molenaer, which I will employ as a case study to demonstrate the relation of sight to sound in the production of musical semiotics [Plate 1].

Plate 1: Jan Miense Molenaer (1606/10-1668), *Music Party (Allegory of Fidelity in Marriage)* (1633). Richmond, Virginia Museum of Fine Arts.

1. *Music Party* (1633): A Case Study

Molenaer's painting, entitled *Music Party*, was the subject of an important essay by the art historian, van Thiel (1967/68)[3], whose ideas I shall summarize before adding to them my own reading. Van Thiel convincingly demonstrated that the painting constitutes a marriage portrait, allegorizing, and highly valorizing, marital fidelity.[4] Music provides the interpretative key to the picture, musical *mesure* standing in visually as a referent for order, regulation, temperance and fidelity—stressed most notably by the woman sitting in the middle holding a partbook at once singing and marking time with her right hand (a gesture of self-restraint that serves to keep together an ensemble that includes a lutenist and cellist). Van Thiel draws particular attention to the male figure standing directly behind the woman who holds the partbook. In a spectacular, indeed, preposterous gesture borrowed from a contemporaneous emblem representing the virtue of Temperance, he waters down wine held in a glass at his side by pouring from a jug held high above his head.[5] The semiotic importance of this detail is evident not only from the singularity of the man's action but also from the fact that the pitcher is compositionally located at the upper center of the picture frame. It casts its significance over everything and everyone beneath it.

Van Thiel argues that the painting is formally organized around the proposal of a thesis (marital temperance) set against a subsidiary antithesis (intemperance). The latter (antithesis) is shown in two vignettes: a background vignette at the extreme left and in small scale showing two men in the act of stabbing each other with knives, hence representing anger (*ira*); and a foreground vignette, lower left, showing a chained monkey ridiculously embracing a cat, hence representing enslavement to the senses and to pleasure—in a word, lust (the cat being a common symbol of libidinous temperament). The cat and monkey are offset by the dog (fidelity, *fides*)—not coincidentally male—standing guard by the newlyweds. Van Thiel comments that the picture is a 'Mirror of virtue' for the husband and wife alike and a 'key to an harmonious married life' (1967/68: 99).[6]

I wish to pursue the semiotics of this painting a bit farther so as to suggest two additional points closer to my own concerns. First, moderation or temperance is articulated as a class issue. Moderation is a possibility for, and the obligation of, the upper classes. It is the peasants who are violent and who behave with anarchical excess; hence, they are threats to themselves and to the social order whose calm they disturb. The painting's sights engender sounds in opposition, namely, the sounds of art music versus the sounds of brutality (for fights are punctuated by animal-like grunts and groans and often by cries of pain). The painting invites (compels?) its viewers to *envision* and *hear* the difference between chaos and order, the antisocial and the social.

But the issue is not quite so simply articulated. In the main part of the image, wherein the musical performance takes place, sonority as such is accorded privilege, despite the fact that we cannot actually hear any sound.

This is so on account of the visually commanding presence of the instruments, the lute and violoncello. They are striking objects in a painting where every object included has been carefully chosen; and they occupy considerable, and compositionally 'prestigious', pictorial space. By contrast, the fighting peasants, whose in-life sounds would doubtless greatly overpower and upset the musical tranquility of the main scene, command attention only by the visual incongruity of their inclusion which, even in so small a detail, is still striking—and purposely worrisome. They possess what the well-to-do burghers had to surrender in exchange for their status and their art: physicality. The peasants' movements are spontaneous and unpredictable, whereas those of their betters are planned and constrained. Indeed, the paved terrace upon which the central characters stand outlines a spatial logic enshrining the opposite of spontaneity.

My second point, one I must describe in greater detail before returning to questions about music, is that the moderation valorized in this image is visually gendered. It is made the responsibility of the woman more than the man (and here my view diverges from Van Thiel's argument about equal responsibility), a fact that relates to the larger issue of gender hierarchy in marriage. Marriage portraits were characteristically ordered by husbands; thus, the marriage portrait might be a gift to one's wife. But it was a gift with strings attached, for it informed her of his expectations of her in all the permanence of its visibility. Not for nothing does the husband wear garb for the outdoors (always the hat, cape and boots): he is not always, or even commonly, going to be around. The burgher's domain is extra-domestic. Thus, the famous Dutch emblematist, Jacob Cats: 'The husband must be on the street to practice his trade/The wife must stay at home to be in the kitchen' (quoted in Schama 1988: 400). The painting, on the other hand, will be prominently displayed in the dwelling as a surveillance (ideally, a surveillance of herself) intended to address the husband's prime anxiety produced by his absences: his wife's sexual fidelity,[7] which in Dutch culture was the cornerstone of domestic *and* social order.[8] In this regard, then, it is not going too far to suggest that the painting's musical metaphor stands in for the very possibility of Dutch culture itself. It incidentally helps clarify the importance in musical life of access to, and sanctioned understanding of, the 'right' kind of music.

The newlyweds (at the extreme right[9]) are posed quite differently from each other and for a purpose. The lady is statuesque, virtually immobilized in drapery; from the waist down she is almost leaden. Her costume and pose may suggest a pregnancy, though this would present some difficulties in classifying the image simply as a 'marriage' portrait.[10] Her husband, lithe by contrast, is not only ready to move but actually taking a step that would lead him into the space occupied by the viewer outside the picture. (And he will move with a gracefulness disallowed the fighting peasants posed in spread-legged brutishness.) That the wife is the lesser of the pair, physically and metaphorically, is emphasized by Molenaer's placing the husband closer to the front picture plane and, hence, further increasing his apparent stature at her expense. (His body also cuts off part of hers.) He gestures to move; she stands stock still. Moreover, she demands even less visual attention than the woman in the center with the partbook—an invidious comparison that cannot be made of the husband and the male musicians (the husband, while off to the side, is painted so as to look physically larger than either of these other men). Indeed, his importance as a person is visually affirmed by the striking way that Molenaer has painted the husband's doffed hat; its darkness takes up a lot of space and powerfully draws the viewer's eyes toward him and away from the woman with the partbook, the painting's putative central figure. More accurately, the viewer's eyes are denied stability of locus: they shift back and forth between the woman musician and the husband. By producing this visual instability, Molenaer brilliantly encodes into the act of the viewer's looking a reminder that the painting's ideological function is like a surveillance; and, as I have suggested, the ideal viewer for the image is the wife herself, who as a viewer must hence watch herself being watched.[11]

There is something about her look—or *where* she looks—that interests me. It is compositionally obvious that music provides the painting's central event. Yet, Molenaer focuses the newlyweds' eyes elsewhere. The man appears to look outside the picture plane, as if towards where he is heading (into the world); the woman by contrast looks inward. She stares slightly downwards, though not, I think, specifically at anything (such as the cat-monkey vignette). Hence, as regards the musical ensemble around which the image is constructed, what the viewer *sees*—ideally, the wife looking from outside the picture in at herself—within the picture she (only) *hears*. She does not look; she listens. In other words, *for the characters inside the painting music accrues meaning as a sonoric phenomenon, whereas from outside the painting for the viewer (who can see but cannot hear the events represented) music signifies as a sight.* For the one intended and ideal viewer, the wife, the two elements of the semiotic equation—sight and sound—converge.

2. Music as Visual Metaphor

Why is music such an apparently important visual metaphor for driving home such extra-musical ideas? What does Molenaer's image feed upon? Despite its very musical 'look', what has all this to do with music?

The vignettes of the watering-down of wine, of the monkey and the cat and of the dog are demonstrably located in the history and use of emblems. Their function, in the specific context of *this* image, is hence quite clear; and on precisely that account it is easier for us to 'read out' the semiotic function of the musical details. Yet, the meaning of music is not related to emblem books specifically but to a praxis fully congruent with emblematic symbols. The emblems present themselves to the viewer as symbolic, because something about each of them registers a visual slippage from lived experience. No one watering their wine would risk the mess that does *not* occur in the painting but which would occur in reality were not the laws of physics temporarily suspended. Monkeys and cats do not embrace. Dogs, of course, do stand guard, like Molenaer's, but his painted dog takes on symbolic quality in its exaggerated degree of stiffness. The same cannot be said for any of the central human subjects, though, again, there is a rupture between the upper-class figures and the profiled, icon-like servants behind the musicians at the left. The three musicians have semiotic functions to carry out, just like the emblematic vignettes, though the consumate naturalism of their representation and the activities they engage in would seemingly deflect such a reading—except for one crucially important detail, their compositional placement, which looks 'wrong'. The difficulty hinges on the identification of the musicians, in particular their social class status and, in relation to class status, the gender of the dominant figure in the musical ensemble, the woman seated in the painting's center who holds the partbook.

Who are these musicians? Molenaer renders them ambiguous. They could be family members or hired professionals (in family portraits of the time it was conventional for all adult men present to wear hats, though to our eyes this might signal the presence of outsiders). The lutenist and cellist are dressed expensively; in fact, they are overdressed, for they are more elegantly attired than the husband and, hence, overshadow him, as is best seen by looking at the lutenist, since none of his body is blocked off. Most noteworthy are his shoes, which, by comparison with the husband's boots, are at once conspicuous and impractical—common enough qualities in Dutch life of the time but ones consistently condemned by Calvinism and rather out of place, it would seem, given the apparent seriousness of the picture. The same may be said of the lutenist's rakish pose, taken directly from the conventions of the often bawdy Merry Company paintings of the period. Similarly, the dress of the woman seated with partbook overshadows the comparatively understated costume worn by the wife (compare the collar and cuffs in particular). The somber facial expressions of all three suggests a family connection; but sartorial inconsistencies— ones with negative moral associations in a patently moralistic image—may indicate outsiders. The real point, of course, is that the musicians are functionally non-persons, despite the naturalism of their representation: their purpose is metaphoric.

Given the normal circumstance of a wedding celebration, the musicians would be hired professionals, except that a female professional would be extraordinarily unusual and certainly unacceptable as a character—a central character—in a marriage portrait: female professional musicians at the time were socially *déclassé*. Yet, in Molenaer's painting it is the lady who, by marking time with her hand, keeps the two young male musicians in tow. Both are dashing in youth and costume alike, hence invested with erotic energy; they register the extra-domestic sexual danger against which the wife must guard.[12] Perhaps this is the point. Molenaer makes an otherwise curious choice in posing the woman, one that can be explained, I think, only if she functions with the ambiguity implicit in the foregoing remarks. I refer to the fact that her right foot is visible protruding from under her voluminous drapery, made so by being placed atop a footstool. With one foot raised, her pose formally echoes that of the lutenist beside her; the formal relationship in turn links her visually to him. And the pose itself endows her with a sensual potential akin to his own much more obvious sexuality, because it emphasizes the outline of both her legs and the separation between them. Her lifted leg, in art of the period suggestive in itself, allows her dress fabric to fall between her legs, showing them to be apart.[13] Nevertheless, as the man standing behind the lady and watering down his wine most clearly indicates, it is her responsibility to maintain *mesure*. The lady concentrates dutifully on her partbook—literally a text, the *word*, so to speak, by which her metaphorical (musical, temperate) duties are *pre*scribed, namely, the control of her sexual drives visually acknowledged and foregrounded. Word and image, in other words, conspire to define her duties, just as the terrace beneath her feet delineates a black and white regularity, a predictability.

Molenaer could only have employed this musical motive for the larger purposes of the painting if actual musical practices of the same sort (potentially) carried complementary meaning—meaning that would affect the sound as well as the sight of the music. Were that not the case, the painting could not make sense to its original and ideal viewer. But this is not to say that only 'one' meaning was possible; indeed, contrary meanings attended musical imagery of this sort, as Molenaer was well aware. Musical imagery could not be used unproblematically, simplistically; its semantic 'surface' encompassed potential ruptures and ambiguities—some of which, like the relation of musical sound to social class, to theological belief and to gender hierarchy, must of social necessity be handled gingerly.

In the Low Countries in the seventeenth century, as elsewhere, art music was a suspect practice among the upper classes on two grounds. First, there was growing uncertainty that acquiring musical skills or music-making itself, whether social or solitary, were appropriate to the upper classes and, especially, upper-class men. Indeed, art music was well on its way to being classified as a female activity, though this ideology would not gain full precedence for another century. Second, and closely related, art music (indeed, all secular music) was viewed suspiciously in Calvinist theology, though to what degree has often been considerably overstated. While in one sense, then, the practices of art music registered themselves as exercises of sonoric order mirroring social order, in another sense they signalled precisely the opposite, a threat to that order. The reasons that this is so depend upon two competing sets of criteria. *As order*, a desideratum whose terms were defined by the hegemonic classes, the sonorities of art music could only mean in opposition to their opposite, the music of the lower classes, the Dutch peasantry. Lower-class music, directly or indirectly, was theorized as disorder, a sonic and social threat *from outside* (I will return to this later). But art music *as disorder*, by contrast, located the enemy as a threat *from inside*; its terms were no longer those surrounding class difference but gender distinction within the upper social strata. Music was potentially effeminizing; it was a specific threat to masculine identity. And worse, when confined to women's practice, its specific relation to physicality and to sexual arousal was perceived as a challenge to husbands' authority (Leppert 1977, 1979 and 1988).

All this being so, why employ a musical motive at all in the painting? Why not try for a less conflicted practice to drive home the same point about fidelity? I think there are two reasons. In the first instance, music's association with love *and* sexuality was entirely enshrined in the culture and had been for many centuries. Marriage was the approved of locus for sexuality and the sexual availability of the woman. Music as an expression of desire, and as a well-practiced device for the production of desire, was fully valorized and theorized. Ribald song texts, not to mention the literary feast of Dutch proverbs, preserve such references endlessly, just as numerous published Calvinist diatribes condemned them and the practices they described.[14] Molenaer's painting, in other words, walks a fine line. To satisfy his male patron/husband, Molenaer instructs the wife to be sexually temperate and sexually active. The art music is *the* metaphor by which to delineate this desideratum, since in life-practice art music simultaneously played conflicting roles as the sonoric simulacrum for order and disorder, arousal and calm, mind and body, etc. Sound, in its abstraction, is by itself semiotically very difficult to control, though control over its semiotics is as socially and culturally essential as for any other form of human expression and communication. By resort to the sight of musical practices, music's inherent sonoric semiotic ambiguity, though it can never be totally overcome, can often be channelled to a degree sufficient to connote acceptable meanings. In this respect, specific visual reference to music's semiotic ambiguity is ideologically useful (more so than pretending to deny the existence of dichotomy), for its acknowlegment both identifies the problem and presents the solution—and the musical problem is inevitably important in this regard, because it stands in for much larger questions about social institutions and organization.

The second reason, I think, has to do with class difference. The practices of art music in the Dutch seventeenth century were increasingly emerging as an important component of class distinction in a world rapidly changing from a feudal order to a mercantilist, pre-capitalist order. Medieval economic stasis was being replaced by economic dynamism, by the building of new fortunes. But a good deal of the cultural implications of these changes were being invented as the socio-economic changes occurred, following the successful separation from the rigidly feudal political hegemony of conservative Spain during the religious wars of the late sixteenth and early seventeenth century (Blok 1900, Geyl 1936, 1958 and Parker 1977). Dutch culture was middle class in the ways that historically later determined what that meant for the West generally. Dutch culture created for itself the challenge of class self-definition. The rules it adopted included those of conspicuous consumption that effectively aped the acquisitional habits of the European aristocracy, even though the price paid was enormous guilt (Schama 1988).

Music was a prime component of this practice—*visually* so in the form of expensive musical instruments, *sonorically* in the sorts of music they played: increasingly sophisticated and complex, inevitably composed and notated and *collected* in printed form. Musical instruments, expensive to purchase if they were made with precious or rare materials (exotic woods, ivory, silver, etc.), were clear signs of excess wealth: they did not 'do' anything except produce sound. As such, they were perfect symbols of social arrival, the very ethereality of what they 'produced'—sound—assuring the correct reading. Indeed, sermons condemning music during the seventeenth and eighteenth centuries in Holland and elsewhere commonly point to just this fact.[15] To make music well takes much time, yet music made well *is* nothing—simply air. Thus, the ubiquitous '*vanitas*' still-life paintings of the period commonly include musical instruments—usually only those associated with art music—and while, as vanities, instruments are 'literally' condemned (for example, by visual reference to life's brevity via an hour glass, a burned-down candle, etc.), they are visually celebrated [Plate 2], along with other consumer objects, to an extent that seriously undercuts such paintings' didactic function *(see* Bergström 1956: especially 153-6, de Mirimonde 1964: 107-43 and Fischer 1975: 45-72). Thus, *vanitas* paintings do not sort out the conflicts I am delineating but only affirm their existence and, indeed, add to the impossibility of their resolution.

The musical sonorities that can be assumed in Molenaer's painting stand in silent opposition to the noise judged characteristic to the music-making of peasants.[16] David Teniers the Younger, a contemporaneous Flemish painter—but whose work ideologically complements Dutch images from the same period[17]— specialized in arch representations of peasants in paintings obviously produced for the upper, especially urban, social strata (peasants did not buy paintings). A particular musical scene he produced in several versions shows peasant listeners who themselves belittle peasant players behind their backs, as if to assure the viewer that even they know the stuff stinks (Leppert 1978: 95-8 and figs. 24-25). By noise I do not mean simply that peasant musicians played poorly or that their instruments were incapable of sounding well. Indeed, quite the opposite was undoubtedly true, though extremely few instruments of this sort have survived on which to base a judgment. The issue is not circumscribed by the skills of players or

Plate 2: Dutch School (17th Century), The Yarmouth
Collection (*Vanitas*), Norwich, U. K., Castle Museum

makers. It develops instead from the ideological necessity to differentiate
the sounds of classes according to principles that delineate the *socio-
politically* superior qualities of the one over those of the other, as
established by the particular group enjoying power. The sounds of the
lower classes are associated with anarchy, registered *visually* as extreme,
vulgar, caricatured physicality and drunkenness [Plate 3]; and as leering,
virtually uncontrolled sexuality [Plate 4]. By contrast, the sounds of the
upper classes are associated with the high degree of order, registered
visually as extreme physical *self*-control, as in the case of Molenaer's
painting, one among many.

I need to comment further on this last image [Plate 4], for like
Molenaer's painting it (ironically) concerns a new marriage. Being a
peasant affair, it provides Teniers with the opportunity for caricature
(Leppert 1978: 141-2). The terms of the visual argument, and of the sonoric
one upon which it depends, reverses the discourse employed by Molenaer.
Teniers places a bagpiper together with the newlyweds and, like Molenaer,
he moves them to the edge of the image. The bagpipe is the location of

Plate 3: David Teniers the Younger (1610-1690) and Lucas van Uden (1595-1672/73), *Peasants Dancing*. Dublin, National Gallery of Ireland. Copyright A.C.L., Brussels.

sexual energy (Leppert 1978: 141 n.140), since its chanter pipe and windsack together replicate the male genitalia, a fact not lost to contemporaneous proverbs.[18] Further, the bagpipe is decorated with the head of Pan, whose lechery and fertility go hand in hand. The husband's coarse arousal is captured in his face, and the bovine stupidity and incomprehension registered by his bride's profile is made more ludicrous on account of the crown she wears.

The visual differentiations between Molenaer's and Teniers' images could hardly be more extreme. And the same holds for sonoric distinctions. The sounds of Molenaer's ensemble are soothing, easy on the ear. Those of Teniers' bagpipe are raucous, especially in that the instrument is blaring virtually into the ears of the whispering lovers who, in truth, under the circumstances would not have a chance of hearing one another. But, of course, that does not matter, for in this image marriage is not temperate—the union does not depend on the prescribed 'word' of Molenaer's lady's partbook. It merely follows the guidance of biological rhythm, whereby the peasantry are reified as animals whose responsibility it is the *noblesse oblige* of the upper classes to control and their right to belittle. And it is the *noise* of peasants' music that defines them, as much as

Plate 4: David Teniers the Younger (1610-1690), *Village Wedding* (1648). Vienna, Kunsthistorisches Museum, Gemäldegalerie. Copyright A.C.L., Brussels.

the non-noise of Teniers' and Molenaer's patrons that by contrast defines them. The political difficulty here, of course, is that only one side is empowered to represent their judgments in historical memory by preserving the image of the social order of sound long after the sounds themselves have decayed.

Conclusion

From the tenor of this discussion it should be clear that the pleasure of music is not at issue in Molenaer's painting. (Indeed, nothing in the picture seems to produce the slightest joy; all of the participants are uncannily serious for a wedding celebration.) This conflicts with what we know to have been the historical reality in Dutch culture, as with virtually any other culture. But for Molenaer's presumed patron, the present-absence of pleasure is useful for driving home an underlying fact of social organization: that the personal, including the personally pleasurable, is political (and politics is inevitably a serious business), that 'entertainment' and politics do not exist in separate spheres.[19] The arts, music notably included, discursively 'transliterate' the political process into an aesthetic chronicle (Durant 1984, Small 1980: 60-96 and Norton 1984: 138-230), even—perhaps especially—when, as with later Romanticism, the arts are theorized under the guise of the philosophical rejection of the political (Adorno 1976 and Marcuse 1968: 88-133). Music's pleasure or pain can only be experienced as a sonoric account of the world. The confusion about this only enters as the result of the enormous efforts, throughout our history, to mystify the social relations of music, most notably via philosophical aestheticization, so as to deny that musical expression engages our lives in this way. Ironically, but hardly surprising, the most vocal theorization of music's connection to politics has mostly come from those who condemn music—or certain music—on precisely this account: for example, Plato (*Republic* 398e1-2, 9-10, 399a3-c4) and Bloom (1987: 68-81).

The concatenation of pleasure and politics is evident in the history of musical notation, which contains within it an anxiety about meaning as well as about preservation. The only purpose in preserving—making replicatable—sounds is that they mean something and that their meaning will help stabilize the social and cultural order from which they are born. It is no accident that the early history of notation coincides with the codification (regularization for ideological purposes) of the liturgy in the medieval church. It is no accident that musical manuscripts were often elaborate productions, visually stunning as well as musically so, or that much of the printed art music of the nineteenth century carried dedications to rich patrons. The latter goes beyond the mere economic gain hoped for by impoverished composers. It begs the question why such commissions of manuscripts and dedications in printed music might matter to patrons. The value implied exceeds the physical possession of notated music which, by its very nature, is the possession of far less than, say, a painting that can be hung up and looked at, fully and permanently realized. The value instead comes with the faith (sometimes *not* justified) that the experiential phenomena promised by the score has transliterated a particular world order into the properly aestheticized and aural form. Molenaer emphasizes the stakes of the issue, that order must be defined and specified if *mesure* is to result. In his picture the partbook occupies the exact center of the composition because, already by the seventeenth century, the life that art music ideally replicated was itself a 'scored' experience, not an 'improvisatory' one. The woman (madonna and whore) holding the partbook encompasses in her bifurcated body—torn between 'reason' and desire— both the reward promised for the accepted observance of this order and the cost she must endure to gain the specified rewards: society constructed according to one set of rules by no means wholly, or even particularly, in her interest.[20]

Notes

[1] The sense of touch gains musicological attention in studies of performance practice.

² In this regard musical memory, and music as an aid to memory, plays a special part, as in the 'recitation' of epics, etc.

³ I have previously commented on this painting; *see* Leppert 1979: 13-4.

⁴ *See further* Smith (1982), most of whose study concerns the pair portrait (separate pictures for husband and wife pendants), by far the more common type of marriage picture produced by Dutch artists.

⁵ Emblem collections provided both an image and a verbal gloss which together gave the opportunity to nail down meaning to a considerably greater degree than might be the case with images alone. The success and power of emblems to do precisely this is evident in the degree to which emblem illustrations found their way into the cultural vocabulary of other discursive practices like painting and, indeed, music. *See further* Landwehr (1962), de Jongh (1967) and Praz (1964).

⁶ The visual antithesis to the temperance emblem is the servant at the left peering into the jug (he is a *kannekijker*, that is, a tippler). In emblematic literature such a figure commonly defines gluttony, according to van Thiel (1967/68: 93). On the uniqueness of the monkey-cat representation, *see ibid.*: 95-6. The 'domestic' enclosure at the right, conceivably but not likely the representation of a real dwelling, is a symbolic fortress of the marriage vows; it is metaphorically mirrored on the painting's left by the ivy-covered wall topped off by two pots of carnations. Van Thiel (1967/68: 98-9) describes the emblematic associations: the wall alluding to the husband, the ivy to the wife and the flowers to fidelity. For additional information on the broad range of symbols conventionally employed in Dutch marriage portraiture, *see* Smith (1982: 57-89).

⁷ According to Schama (1980: 7): 'Woman, as the incarnation of caprice, vulnerable to the enticements of the world, had to be confined within a system of moral regulation. . . . [W]omen in Dutch art were immediately encumbered with a massive baggage of secondary associations concerning their duties in the home and towards their husband. . . . These took the form of a comprehensive inventory of symbols and visual allusions. . . . Planted conspicuously in the middle of genre paintings, or portraits, they turned ostensibly anecdotal subject matter into visual disquisitions on human frailty.' For information on misogynist literature, *see ibid.*; and for a fuller treatment of this topic, *see* Schama (1988: 445-54).

⁸ 'The home was of supreme importance in determining the moral fate, both of individuals and of Dutch society as a whole. . . . In other words, the home was irreducible primary cell on which, ultimately, the whole fabric of the commonwealth was grounded' (Schama 1988: 384, 386).

⁹ This is not a conventional arrangement, though it is not unique. *See*, for example, Rubens' famous *Garden of Love* in the Prado (reproduced in Janson 1962: 395), representing Rubens himself with his second wife

standing together at the left edge of a strikingly rectilinear painting as witnesses to the allegorical celebration of their marriage which occupies the rest of the canvas. In Molenaer's portrait, the man's coat sleeve is actually slightly cropped by the frame; the painting may have been trimmed, judging from a similar slight cropping of the fighting peasant's feet at the far left.

10 Van Thiel (1967/68: 95) points to the wife's hand gesture as itself symbolic of marital fidelity.

11 It is not to be automatically assumed, however, that a Dutch wife felt compelled to define herself precisely in the terms set out by her husband. Though prevailing ideologies of gender and domestic relations in Holland were not different from those of the rest of Western Europe, during the seventeenth century foreign visitors commonly remarked, usually critically, on the freedoms enjoyed by Dutch women (*see* Schama 1980: *passim*, 1988: 402-4, 420-7).

12 The vast majority of Dutch marriage portraits (*i.e.*, pendants) are devoid of such overt sensual charge (*see* Smith 1982: 28-30).

13 Sexual referents were common in Dutch art of the period and ran the gamut from the symbolically obscure to the bawdily obvious. *See*, for example, the discussion of several paintings by Jan Steen in Schama (1988: 204-11), who elsewhere pointed out that: 'Money, as well as sex, was something of a Dutch fixation . . . (and it) is represented by the visual equivalent of a wink, a leer or a nudge: the proffering of a single coin, or a glass of wine held at the stem, or a *strategically placed foot*. The point of this symbolism was not to expose sexual behavior but to shroud it behind a gauze of allusions and metaphors' (Schama 1980: 12, italics added).

14 *See* Schama (1988: 388-480 on 'Housewives and Hussies: Homeliness and Worldliness'). Dutch prostitutes even carried lutes with them into taverns as a sonoric-visual device advertizing their profession. This meets in head-on conflict with emblematic references to the lute in conjunction with the virtue of temperance (on which *see* van Thiel 1967/68: 91) and with numerous Dutch paintings that visually connect the lute to prostitution in particular via the visual topos of the procuress (*see* Leppert 1977: i/185).

15 *See* Leppert (1988) for the situation in England and *ibid.* (1979) for the Low Countries. Though the concern was continent-wide, the severity of the complaint varied over time and place, across religious divides, etc. Concerning the ideological significance of expensively-made musical instruments, *see* Leppert (1989).

16 Among all instruments employed by Dutch burghers as part of art music practices, only the violin and, occasionally, the lute crossed class boundaries, as the latter's use by prostitutes (note 14 above) indicates. In the Spanish Netherlands, if not in Holland, the lute's use (potential or real) by the lower orders was itself a subject for the mocking enjoyment

of the upper classes (*see* Leppert 1978: 77-82, 96-7). On the musical opposition between noise and order, *see* Attali (1985).

[17] For example, despite notable stylistic differences, there is little ideological divergence between Teniers' representations of the lower classes and those of many other Dutch and Flemish painters (*e.g.*, Cornelis Bega, Pieter de Bloot, Andries Both, Joos van Craesbeek, Egbert van Heemskerck, Frans van Mieris the Elder, Bartholomeus Molenaer, Adriaen van Ostade, Isaac van Ostade, David Ryckaert the Younger, Pieter Verelst and even Jan Miense Molenaer). Examples of relevant work by these painters are reproduced in Bernt (1970).

[18] '*Met een goed gevulde buik wil het zingen beter lukken*': it's better to sing with a well-filled belly (here, the bagpipe's swelled windsack). The meaning of 'sing' here is preserved in another proverb: '*Voor het zingen de kerk uit*': Before singing leave the church (in reference to *coitus interruptus*).

[19] The seriousness of portraiture as a genre is of course conventional, for precisely the reasons I am suggesting, without regard to whether musical activities are included. Such seriousness, however, is antithetical to Dutch Merry Company scenes, including those with musicians like Molenaer's lutenist. Regarding the (musically inappropriate) decorum of sitters in another group picture by Molenaer, *see* Smith (1982: 29-30).

[20] Schama (1980: 13) writes: 'This uncompartmentalised world, fraught with confusion, disguise, ambiguities and stratagems was, by definition, riddled with anxiety (even if Calvin had not added his own brand). In keeping with its undifferentiated components, women were rarely seen as exclusively given to either vice or virtue, to the purified world of the conjugal home, or the soiling world of vanity and lust. It was precisely the daunting suspicion that the two identities—paragon and hussy— might cohabit within the same frame that, literally, *bedeviled* Dutch men. . . . Culture and nature; morality and instinct, were locked in perpetual and unresolvable combat in the Dutch mentality.'

References

ADORNO, Theodor W.
>   1976 *Introduction to the Sociology of Music*, tr. E.B. Ashton, New York

ATTALI, Jacques
>   1985 *Noise: The Political Economy of Music*, tr. Brian Massumi, Minneapolis, Minnesota

BERNT, Walter
>   1970 *The Netherlandish Painters of the Seventeenth Century*, tr. P.S. Falla, 3d edn., 3 vols., New York

BERGSTRÖM, Ingvar
>   1956 *Dutch Still-Life Painting in the Seventeenth Century*, London

BLOK, Petrus Johannes
　　1900　*History of the People of the Netherlands*, (Part 3: The War with Spain) tr. Ruth Putnam, New York
BLOOM, Allan
　　1987　*The Closing of the American Mind*, New York
DE JONGH, E.
　　1967　*Zinne-en minnebeelden in de schilderkunst van de zeventiende eeuw*, Amsterdam
DE MIRIMONDE, Albert Pomme
　　1964　'Les natures mortes à instruments de musique de Peter Boel', *Jaarboek, Koninklijk Museum voor Schone Kunsten* (Antwerpen): 107-43
DURANT, Alan
　　1984　*Conditions of Music*, Albany, New York
FISCHER, Peter
　　1975　*Music in Paintings of the Low Countries in the 16th and 17th Centuries*, Amsterdam
GEYL, Pieter
　　1936　*The Netherlands Divided (1609-1648)*, tr. S.T. Bindoff, in collaboration with Pieter Beyl, London
　　1958　*The Revolt of the Netherlands* (1555-1609), 2d edn., London
JANSON, H. W.
　　1962　*History of Art: A Survey of the Major Visual Arts from the Dawn of History to the Present Day*, Englewood Cliffs, New Jersey
LANDWEHR, John
　　1962　*Dutch Emblem Books: A Bibliography*, Utrecht
LEPPERT, Richard
　　1977　*The Theme of Music in Flemish Paintings of the Seventeenth Century*, 2 vols, Munich and Salzburg
　　1978　'David Teniers the Younger and the Image of Music', *Jaarboek, Koninklijk Museum voor Schone Kunsten* (Antwerpen): 63-155
　　1979　'*Concert in a House*: Musical Iconography and Musical Thought', *Early Music* 7/1: 3-17
　　1988　*Music and Image: Domesticity, Ideology and Socio-Cultural Formation in Eighteenth-Century England*, Cambridge
　　1989　'Music, Representation, and Social Order in Early-Modern Europe', *Cultural Critique* 12: 25-55
LOWE, Donald M.
　　1982　*The History of Bourgeois Perception*, Chicago
MARCUSE, Herbert
　　1968　'The Affirmative Character of Culture', *Negations: Essays in Critical Theory*, Boston

NORTON, Richard
    1984   *The History of Western Tonality: A Critical and Historical Perspective*, University Park, Pennsylvania

PARKER, Geoffrey
    1977   *The Dutch Revolt*, Ithaca, New York

PRAZ, Mario
    1964   *Studies in Seventeenth-Century Imagery*, Rome

SCHAMA, Simon
    1980   'Wives and Wantons: Versions of Womanhood in 17th Century Dutch Art', *The Oxford Journal* 3/1: 5-13
    1988   *The Embarrassment of Riches: An Interpretation of Dutch Culture in the Golden Age*, Berkeley

SMALL, Christopher
    1980   *Music – Society – Education*, London

SMITH, David R.
    1982   *Masks of Wedlock: Seventeenth-Century Dutch Marriage Portraiture*, Ann Arbor, Michigan

VAN THIEL, P. J. J.
  1967/68 'Marriage Symbolism in a Musical Party by Jan Miense Molenaar', *Simiolus*, 2/2: 90-9

Music and Shamanic Power in the Gesar Epic

Geoffrey Samuel

Abstract

A connection between epic bards and shamans has been regularly observed in the ethnographic literature for Central and North Asian societies, but the meaning of this connection is far from clear. A general model of shamanic processes derived from Victor Turner's work on African ritual and Roy Wagner's studies of Melanesian society suggests that the key element is the shaman's ability to manipulate the community's perceived reality. This is an ability which the epic bard also shares. Performances of the Gesar epic of Tibet only occasionally involve the bard entering a quasi-shamanic visionary state, but they can generally be interpreted as narratives about contests between shamanic heroes. The victor, Gesar, is himself less a king than a shaman invoking and manipulating the powers of the Buddhist Tantric deities of whom he is the earthly representative.

Introduction

The term 'shamanism' has been variously defined and used by anthropologists and other scholars. It is nevertheless quite common to read that the Gesar epic and other Asian epic traditions (Stein 1959, Chadwick and Zhirmunsky 1969: 234-67) have 'shamanic' connections. In a recent work on anthropological theory (in press), I have argued that shamanism can be understood in terms of a framework for analysing cultural processes. My analysis may be regarded as an extension of Victor Turner's work of the transformative effects of ritual (*e.g.*, 1968) and Roy Wagner's work on what he terms the 'tropic' use of metaphor (1978). I regard shamanic processes, in other words, as bringing about changes through analogical or metaphorical argument. The key feature of these processes, which range from small-scale healing rituals carried out for a single sick person to visions leading to a radical transformation of a community, is that they involve a change in people's analogical perception of a situation.

Processes bringing about changes in how the world is experienced are not confined to shamanic societies, but in such societies they are characteristically grounded in and justified by communications from some sphere of existence conceived as 'deeper' and more fundamental than the appearances of everyday life. The shaman is a mediator between this world, which is in effect a storehouse of alternate possibilities for social life, and the world of ordinary appearances. In shamanic societies the other world is often conceived of as inhabited by spirits or gods whom the shaman invokes.

Communications from the other world take a variety of forms in different societies. A shaman may journey in a dream or other visionary state to the world of the spirits to find healing or revelation. A local deity may state his or her requirements through a medium. A Tibetan lama may enter a visionary state (*daknang*) as a result of Tantric yoga and return from the profound realm of the Tantric deities with new rituals, with instructions for the discovery of a 'hidden valley' or of concealed books or Buddhist sacred objects. All these are forms of shamanic vision; and if the communication is accepted by its audience, it creates a transformation (an analogical shift) in the relationship between individual human beings and their biological, social or physical environment (*cf.* Samuel in press). Such procedures amount to the exercise of a kind of power over individuals and social group which is no less real for its apparently magical or supernatural origin. Shamanic cultures are typically very much concerned with power of this kind, with its use for the good of the community, and with its possible abuse for anti-social ends (sorcery or witchcraft).

1. The Gesar Epic of Tibet

Here I shall examine a specific epic tradition, the Tibetan epic of King Gesar of Ling, as a narrative about such shamanic processes. Gesar is the central figure of a cycle of epic stories widely known among both Tibetans (David-Neel 1933, Roerich 1942, Hermanns 1965, Stein 1956, 1959, 1969, 1979) and Mongols (*e.g.*, Heissig 1983). The stories resemble in general outline those of other epic cycles among the Mongols and among the Turkic peoples of Central Asia (Chadwick and Zhirmunsky 1969, Heissig 1979, 1982, 1985), as well as European epic traditions such as the Arthurian cycle. King Gesar has a miraculous birth, a despised and neglected childhood and then becomes ruler and wins his (first) wife, Drukmo, through a series of marvellous feats. In subsequent episodes he defends his people against various external aggressors, human and superhuman.

Instead of dying a normal death he departs into a hidden realm from which he may return at some time in the future to save his people from their enemies (*see* David-Neel 1933). Gesar also became the central figure of a Mongolian and Manchu cult in which he was regarded as a god of war and assimilated to the Chinese war-god Kuan-ti (*see* Heissig 1980: 97-101).

In Tibet the Gesar stories form the principal repertoire of the so-called bards (*drungpa*). There is a central core of episodes concerning the sending of Gesar from the realm of the gods, his birth, his youth and the horse-race through which he becomes King of Ling, and his wars against the demon king of the North, the kings of the Hor (a Turkic people in Northeast Tibet), Jang (the Naxi people to the Southeast of Tibet) and Mon (to the South of Tibet). There is an indefinite series of further episodes, some of them created in recent years by known authors and generally taking the form of Gesar's war against one or another neighbouring kingdom. My examples in this paper will be drawn mainly from the Horse-Racing or *Tagyuk* episode, one of the core episodes, in the version edited and translated by Stein (1956: 275-350 and 87-140) and further studied by Helffer (1977), and from the Turquoise Fortress of Kashmir or *K'ach'e Yudzong* episode, which is one of the additional episodes, though from internal evidence probably fairly old (Kaschewsky and Tsering 1972).

Traditionally, Mongol and Turkic epic cycles were performed in a variety of ways, the most common being a continuous narrative in song or heightened speech with or without instrumental accompaniment. The Tibetan Epic of Gesar is, however, traditionally performed without instrumental accompaniment in *chantefable* style. The singer, usually male, alternates between prose narrative, recited in a kind of heightened speech with exaggerated tonal inflections, and songs for the various characters in the story. The songs are sung to a small repertoire of melodies which correspond to different characters and character-types. Manuscript and printed (blockprint) versions of the epic also strictly follow this *chantefable* form and frequently name a specific melody to be employed for each song (Helffer 1977, 1979, 1982).

A significant point about this *chantefable* form in Tibetan society is that it is by no means confined to the Gesar epic. It is also employed in biographies (*namt'ar*) of religious heroes such as Jetsün Milarepa, Yeshe Tsogyel or Drukpa Kunlek, in the dance-dramas (*ach'e lhamo*) performed to religious stories, and in various Buddhist liturgical and ritual performances. That a similar alternation between speech and song occurs in a variety of performance genres suggests that for Tibetan listeners these genres may be less diverse than they seem to a non-Tibetan and that the speech-song alternation may serve similar purposes in all of these genres. As we shall see, the songs of Milarepa provide an illuminating comparison with the Gesar epic. A second feature which the Gesar epic has in common both with some of these other genres and with other contexts of Tibetan life is the presence of what I refer to here as song-contests. These are sequences of two or more songs in which competing persons or groups carry on an argument or contest through successive songs. Such contests are a significant theme in Tibetan culture and their frequent occurrence in the epic in combination with the *chantefable* form is a clue to the meaning of the epic and its songs.

The stories of the Gesar epic exist both as extemporized performances and in the form of books. Contemporary singers often read from a written or printed text, which follows the prose-verse structure indicated above. The prose carries the major part of the narrative, while the songs represent statements by the various characters. These 'statements' are of various kinds which will be considered in detail below. The musical example (Figure 1) is from near the beginning of the *K'ach'e Yudzong* episode. This

Figure 1: Gesar Recounts Guru Rimpoch'e's Prophecy*

*Filler syllables (without lexical meaning) are underlined

episode concerns the war between Gesar's kingdom of Ling, along with its allies, and the King of K'ach'e (Kashmir), a war which culminates in the conquest of the Turquoise Castle of Kashmir by Gesar and his followers (Kaschewsky and Tsering 1972). In the opening scene, set at the Kashmiri court, the Kashmiri king, unable to bear the suggestion that Gesar is more powerful than he, has determined to attack Ling. The action moves to Ling, where the divine guru, Guru Rimpoch'e (Padmasambhava), visits the meditating Gesar. Guru Rimpoch'e, who brought Tantric Buddhism to eighth-century Tibet, is regarded as a second Buddha, and Gesar is often described as his emanation. Guru Rimpoch'e tells Gesar of the forth-coming attack and predicts the means by which the Kashmiri king may be defeated. Gesar then summons the leading men of Ling to a council where he addresses them in this song. The translation begins with the last sentence of the prose narrative and includes slightly over half of the song itself:

Gesar then sang in this Endless Vajra Melody that the time had come for the attack on the Turquoise Castle of Kashmir and that Guru Padmasambhava had made a prophecy:

OM MANI PADME HŪM HRĪH
Refuge Lama, Yidam and Three Jewels,
Lotus-Born Lord, Pema T'ötr'engtsel,
The Ruler of Ling invokes you with devotion.
Remain for ever as an ornament on my head.
As for this place, if you don't know where it is,
It is the Ratak Plain of Tr'amo,
As for me, if you don't know who I am,
I am King Gesar of Ling.
Listen, chiefs and ministers of Ling:
Last night when dawn was breaking,
At the time when appearances become clear,
The Knowledge-Holder, the Lotus-Born Guru
In person made this prophecy.
He who was once born as the Bön minister Lupel,
Has been born in our time as the Kashmiri king,
By name called Tr'iten Lupel.
Through the power of his perverted desire
This lord has brought under his control
The three kingdoms of Nepal, Gurkha and Nyugk'a.
Now his goal is our Tr'amo Ling.
With him is first the hero Luyak Ruring,
Second the matchless Dogö Mebar.
Third the fierce T'oktr'i Putsen,
Along with ten other great warriors
And 30,000 excellent horsemen.
[Guru Rimpoch'e] says that before a month has passed
They will attack Tr'amo Ling.
He says that unless our vanguard is in place in time
White Ling will certainly be destroyed.
He says that unless we wear white silk armour
We won't be able to resist the sharp swords of Li.
He says that unless we summon troops from all directions
Our forces will be insufficient.
He says that unless we overthrow the Kashmiri king
The heretical Bön religion will spread

And do harm to the Buddha's teachings.
He says that eventually we must attack the Turquoise
     Castle.
He says that unless I, Masang Kyebu Dondrup [= Gesar],
perform various magical exploits
We will not be able to obtain victory.
His words are the teaching of the primal guru.
If we do not follow these teachings
The consequences will be evil in this life and the next (Text 1: 24-5; Text
2: 13-4; cf. Kaschewsky and Tsering 1972: 297-8, 366).

In the remainder of the song, Gesar orders preparations for the coming
war. The text of this song is in the standard seven-syllable line of Tibetan
verse, frequently extended, as is normal, to eight syllables (Helffer 1977:
428):

chab lama yidam könch'o sum
je ts'otr'ung Pema T'ötr'engtsel
Ling kyebü küpey solwa dep
ku mindrey kyewö gyen la shu
sa di sango masheyna
Dura Tat'ang Tr'amo ser
ngadra ngango masheyna
Ling-je Kesar gyelpo yin

This song has a number of formal characteristics typical of songs in the
Gesar epic. First, there is the preceding mantra—usually, as here, OM
MAṆI PADME HŪM HRĪH, the mantra of Avalokiteshvara, *bodhi-
sattva* of compassion, who is closely associated with Padmasambhava and
through him with Gesar. Second, the initial invocation of deities occurs in
almost all songs. Here the invocation (the first four lines of the song) is to
Guru Rimpoch'e, addressed by his 'secret name' Pema T'ötr'engtsel. This is
appropriate since it is Guru Rimpoch'e whose revelation is being
recounted. In practice the deity or deities who are invoked vary from song
to song. The heroes of Ling usually invoke Buddhist deities or the
protective local deities of Ling; the warriors of other regions invoke their
own protective deities, Hindu gods, etc. Third, the stereotyped formulae—
'If you don't know this place, it is called. . .'; 'If you don't know who I am, I
am . . .'—occur in most (not all) songs, although frequently, as here, the
audience within the story would hardly fail to know where they were or
who was addressing them. There is also a frequent ending formula (with
variations and not included here): 'If you understand this song, it's an
ornament to your ears; if you don't understand it, there's no commentary'.
'There's no commentary' evokes the frequent practice in Tibetan Buddhist
literature, going back to Indian sources, of giving a condensed verse text,
suitable for memorization, along with an extensive prose commentary.

Musically, this performance is typical of Gesar singing (Helffer 1977,
1979). A clearly defined melody covers two or three—here three—lines of

the text at a time, with some use of filler syllables, and it is simply repeated over and over again until the end of the song is reached, with no particular attention to the syntactical units of the text (*see* Figure 1). There are minor variants in the melodic outline which incorporate the varying numbers of syllables and to some degree also reflect syllable-tone, which has phonemic value in most Tibetan dialects. I have transcribed four repetitions (numbered in Figure 1).

A skilled singer will use a dozen or more different melodies in performing an episode from the epic, the choice depending on the character and the situation. As an example, in Mireille Helffer's study of a performance of the *Tagyuk* episode, the singer, Lobsang Tenzin, used thirteen different tunes for a total of fifty-six songs (Helffer 1977). This singer employed one tune for the thirteen songs of Drukmo, Gesar's future wife and the main female character in the episode; another for the five songs of Tr'ot'ung, Gesar's wicked and treacherous uncle; another for the two songs by Gesar's half-brother Gyats'a, and another for the two songs by Gesar's horse. Some melodies are associated with particular kinds of characters, such as older protective females, or with particular kinds of song, such as premonitory dreams. Others are general-purpose tunes. Gesar himself has four different tunes in Lobsang Tenzin's performance of the *Tagyuk* episode.

2. *Namt'ar, Gur* Songs and Song Contests

As I mentioned above, the *chantefable* form is also employed in many *namt'ar* or biographies of religious heroes such as the well-known Tibetan poet and yogic practitioner, Jetsün Milarepa. These *namt'ar* narratives consist of an alternation between prose narrative and songs (*gur*), which are mostly but not always attributed to the central figure. The songs cover a variety of themes, but they are all in one sense or another expressions of the yogi's Buddhist insight. Some are condensed expositions of the teachings, whereas others, more like the songs of the Indian siddhas to which the whole *gur* tradition goes back (Templeman 1987), are direct statements of the yogi's realization, often in highly allusive or condensed language.

In the late fifteenth and early sixteenth centuries, the Kagüypa yogi and guru, Tsangnyön Heruka, and his followers gathered together many of these songs into biographies and collections of stories of Milarepa and other teachers in the Kagüypa lineage (Smith 1969). The major texts of this corpus have now been translated into English (Evans-Wentz 1969, Lhalungpa 1979, Chang 1977, Trungpa 1982, Kunga and Cutillo 1978, 1986, Guenther 1963). These texts were not the first texts to be known as *namt'ar*, but they provided an important model for future texts and established the *chantefable* type of *namt'ar* within Tibetan literature. The *namt'ar* form as used by Tsangnyön and his followers was widely adopted by subsequent writers, as with the *namt'ar* of Drukpa Kunlek (Stein 1972, Dowman 1980) or that of Yeshe Ts'ogyel (Tarthang 1983, Dowman 1984).

Such texts may be read silently, but they may also be performed as a sequence of prose narration alternating with singing for the *gur* sections. The style of the prose narration is identical to that used for the epic. The songs are sung in a variety of styles varying from simple chants using three or four notes to more complex and melismatic forms. They are generally unaccompanied. Many of Milarepa's songs are in the same seven-syllable metre as the epic songs, although later *gur* are more varied in formal structure. Like the Gesar songs, the *gur* of the Milarepa corpus almost all begin with an invocation, which in Milarepa's case is usually of his lama Marpa seen as a Tantric deity, and they often include formulaic elements similar to those of the epic songs:

If you don't know my name
I'm Milarepa of Gungthang Plain—
A beggar wandering by myself (Kunga and Cutillo 1978: 55-7; Text 3: 117a ff.).

The literal meaning of the Tibetan term, *namt'ar*, is 'complete liberation', implying that the narrative is intended to be an exemplary and inspiring account of the central figure's progress to enlightenment. The term is applied generally to life-histories of lamas or other holy personages. It is also sometimes applied to the Gesar stories, which may be seen as episodes in the *namt'ar*, the exemplary progress to enlightenment, of Gesar himself.

Episodes from the Milarepa corpus frequently involve a degree of dramatic structure and occasionally include elements of contest of a kind common in the epic. An example is the account of Milarepa's first meeting with his female disciple, Rechungma, in the Gurbum, a text which was edited by Tsangnyön himself in around 1488. Before accepting Milarepa as her guru, Rechungma and four girlfriends test him by challenging him in a song contest at Mount Kailash. In the girls' first song they describe Mount Kailash and the local places of power as being famous from afar but mere ordinary rocks and lakes now they have actually visited them. Milarepa and his disciple are also famous from afar, but all the girls can see is a couple of poorly-clothed beggars in cotton robes. Their journey to Kailash has been wasted. The song ends with a formula reminiscent of that mentioned earlier for the epic songs:

If you understand our song, answer it;
If you can't understand, let the yogis move on elsewhere (Text 4: 267, *cf.* Chang 1977: I, 261)!

Milarepa takes up the challenge, pointing out both the virtues of Mount Kailash and the level of yogic attainment underlying his humble appearance. His song ends as follows:

Here is the answer from the old man's mouth;
If you can understand it, these are the real teachings.

If you don't understand it, it's just a little song.

We, the yogis, are happy doing whatever we choose.

You visitors should go back home (Text 4: 271; *cf.* Chang 1977: I, 265). After this exchange Rechungma is convinced of Milarepa's attainment. She offers him the jewelry she is wearing and asks for teachings in a third song. Milarepa refuses the jewels; but after testing Rechungma and her companions' resolve in two further songs, he agrees to give them the teachings (*see* Chang 1977: I, 259-74).

Several further examples of such song-exchanges may be found in the Milarepa corpus. Among them are the contest between Milarepa and a Bön magician (Chang 1977: I, 215ff.) and the exchanges with the goddess Ts'eringma and her entourage (*ibid.*: I, 296 to II, 361), which Charles van Tuyl has suggested may predate the Gurbum as a whole (1975).

The similarities are striking between *gur* songs, particularly the older songs in the Milarepa corpus, and Gesar songs. While the *gur* of Milarepa may have undergone substantial change in oral transmission before being written down, their written forms are several centuries prior to the oldest written episodes of the Gesar epic known to us. Since the songs were clearly not influenced by the epic in its modern form, we can assume that the *gur* songs and the epic as we now know it are more or less independent indications of a Tibetan tradition of narrative which goes back at least to the fifteenth century and is characterized by prose-verse alternation, the epic metre, the formulaic features noted above and the presence of sequences of song-exchanges with elements of contest.

Song contests, in the form of partly-improvised competitive exchanges of verses, are a frequent form of entertainment among young Tibetans (Snyder 1972, *see also* Norbu 1967, Samuel 1978). These improvised song-exchanges use a standard verse-form with four lines of eight syllables each, sung to one of a small number of standard tunes. Most of the verses are already known to the participants, but inventing a witty variation is particularly appreciated. The verses are highly allusive and metaphorical in nature. A boy may sing

On the Eastern mountain of India

Peacocks open their feathers brilliantly

But there is only one peacock

Whose feathers could be used for the prince's parasol

to indicate to a girl that there are many girls he likes, but she is the only one he trusts (Norbu 1967). Her reply, predictably, might take the affair a stage further or alternatively suggest that the peacock (deer, apricot-tree, or whatever) has other plans in mind. Incidentally, such exchanges appear to be widespread in East and Southeast Asia (Bidyalankarana 1926, Miller 1985: 27-31, Yang 1988). Song-contests also occur as formalized exchanges of questions and answers between the bride's and bridegroom's party in traditional Tibetan weddings (for examples, *see* Francke 1901, Tucci 1966: 33-8, 52-8, Ribbach 1986: 63-90; *see also* Aziz 1985) and as similar formalized exchanges between opposed parties at annual festivals such as the songs of the local protective deities from Western Tibet edited by Tucci (1966: 61-112).

3. The Gesar Epic and Shamanic Vision

We can now return to the question of the shamanic nature of the Gesar epic. I shall argue that, as in the *namt'ar* or biographies of saints such as Milarepa, the formal features we have been considering are related to the epic's functioning as a narrative about shamanic power. First, however, it is worth noting that there are several features of the epic which are directly indicative of shamanic visionary processes. For example, the performance of the epic may involve some kind of direct 'shamanic' vision of the events being described. Thus, David-Neel describes a bard who would gaze at a sheet of white paper while performing, claiming to see the text of the story on it (1933: 19). She comments that the bards she encountered in Eastern Tibet in the 1920s did not 'learn' the epic but claimed to sing through inspiration by Gesar 'or some other divine personage' (David-Neel 1933: 18). In a recent survey Yang Enhong (1989) mentions twenty-six contemporary bards of this so-called *babdrung* type, and a further singer who gazed at a mirror while performing, seeing in it the events of the story (*cf. also* Chödpa Dondrub 1989).

According to Chagdüd Rimpoch'e (personal communication, November 1987), performers are also thought of as 'remembering' the events of the epic from previous lives in which they had been actors in the events they narrate. The paper-gazing bard mentioned by David-Neel claimed to be a rebirth of Dikchen Shenpa, a leading character in the epic (David-Neel 1933: 18). The concept of remembering the narrative from a previous life is reminiscent of the idea that *tertön* or discoverers of 'hidden texts' were reborn disciples of Guru Rimpoch'e. Guru Rimpoch'e is held to have concealed either the texts themselves, or knowledge of where to find the texts in written form, within the consciousness of the *tertön* in their previous lives (Gyatso 1986, Thondup 1986). The effect of these ideas is to 'ground' a particular text in a revelation from another sphere of existence (the mythical time of Gesar or of Guru Rimpoch'e).

Most performances today are from memorized, written or printed texts. The creation of new written episodes can nevertheless still involve shamanic vision. The eighth K'amtrul Rimpoch'e Döngyüd Nyima (1929-1980), a well-known Kagyüpa lama and a prominent figure among the refugee community in India, was responsible for several new episodes which were revealed to him when in a visionary state (informants at Palampur, 1978). In a short English biography of the eighth K'amtrul, the circumstances are described as follows:

> In the succeeding year [when Khamtrul Rimpoch'e was twenty-six, in around 1955], having been requested by the King of Nangchen to give

spiritual instructions according to the desires of his audience, Khamtrul experienced a vision of himself as King Gesar surrounded by Gesar's eighty protectors and ministers—this vision seemed to last a vivid two hours although in reality only two minutes had passed, but it was sufficient for the young Rinpoche to realize a strong connection [*i.e.*, with Gesar] and as a result of this, he spontaneously composed three faultless volumes, needing no further correction, of a total of fourteen hundred pages on the life and adventures of King Gesar. . . . (Anon. n.d. : 6).

Several of K'amtrul Rimpoch'e's Gesar episodes, including the *Jar Ling* and the *Uyen Ling*, have since been published in India and Bhutan. It is also worth noting that, according to Chagdüd Rimpoch'e, some episodes from the epic have particular 'magical' properties: the War against Hor (*Hor Ling*) suppresses demons, the War against Persia (*Tak Ling*) creates wealth. A household may commission a recitation for these reasons. Here a shamanic transformation of reality is seen as created through the performance of the episode.

These points do not add up to a consistent theory or doctrine of the Gesar epic as shamanic revelation. This is not surprising, as shamanic processes rarely do have a consistent doctrinal basis. In the Tibetan context, intellectual consistency of this kind is found in the highly systematized and philosophically sophisticated 'clerical' Buddhism of the monasteries. The Gesar epic has certainly been influenced by such formulations, but its basis is precisely in the less formalized, more variable and creative, shamanic side of Tibetan religion (Samuel 1989). This does not imply that the Gesar epic today is in any real sense non-Buddhist. The shamanic aspects of Tibetan religion are as characteristically Buddhist in their vocabulary, their concepts and their assumptions as the clerical aspects; and the epic in particular is deeply infused with Buddhist ideas and concepts.

4. Shamanic Power in the Gesar Epic.

In fact, the epic gives us a revealing glimpse into the shamanic aspects of Tibetan Buddhism, within which the search for this-worldly power and the quest for Buddhist enlightenment are inextricably linked (*see* Samuel 1989). This is particularly so when we move on from the shamanic processes involved in the creation and performance of the epic to consider the epic itself as a narrative about the nature of shamanic power and its relationship to Buddhism. The question of shamanic power, its nature and its proper usage, is at the centre of the Gesar epic. Power here is not a question of brute force or even of a better set of magical techniques. The ultimate source of power in the epic, as in the shamanic side of Tibetan society more generally, is the Buddhist enlightenment. Gesar cannot be defeated because he is, in Buddhist terms, the most evolved and spiritually realized character in the epic—with the exception, that is, of Guru Rimpoch'e and other Tantric deities who appear to give him aid. Significantly, Gesar can be held in subjection by the wife of the Demon King of the North only because she gives him a potion which leads him to forget his mission and his true identity (*e.g.*, David-Neel 1933: 140-2).

In order to substantiate this suggestion, I now turn to examine the dramatic function of songs within the epic. First, though, the frequency of competitive exchanges of songs within the epic may be noted. In the *K'ach'e Yudzong*, the episode from which my musical example was taken (Figure 1), the first twenty-eight songs include six sequences of two songs in which the second answers or counters the first (1-2, 9-10, 11-12, 14-15, 16-17, 19-20) and one series of three songs (3-4-5, *see* Kaschewsky and Tsering 1972). In the *Tagyuk* episode, which contains fifty-six songs, there are seven sequences of two songs (11-12, 13-14, 22-23, 33-34, 37-38, 50-51, 52-53) and two sequences of three songs (3-4-5 and 41-42-43, *see* Stein 1956, Helffer 1977). These exchanges are of two kinds. In the first, two characters are engaged in a contest as to what course of action should be taken. Gesar's uncle, Tr'ot'ung, announces his intention of holding the horse race; his wife counsels him against it; Tr'ot'ung rejects her advice (*Tagyuk* 3-4-5). Gesar's mother sings to Gesar's horse to capture him; the horse sings his refusal (*ibid.* 21-22). The second kind of exchange is very common in the battle sequences which take up large parts of episodes such as the *K'ach'e Yudzong*. It consists of two warriors each boasting of their might, the power of their generals and the invincibility of their armies (*e.g., K'ach'e Yudzong* 16-17, 25- 26). Such exchanges frequently lead to a fight in which one or the other is victorious. What both kinds of exchange have in common is that they are about the exercise of what may, in a general sense, be referred to as 'power'. What is at issue in either case is whose will is going to predominate. One might also say that it is a question of whose analogical definition of reality will prove the stronger.

Here we may recall the song-contests of the Milarepa epic, which are resolved by the 'defeated' partner being tamed or subdued by Milarepa's Buddhist shamanic power and becoming his disciple. We may also consider the more light-hearted competitive exchanges of verses between young Tibetan men and women which I mentioned earlier. These exchanges are also about competing definitions of reality, even if what is here at issue concerns the roles of the boy and girl in a potential amorous encounter. (I would interpret the formalized song-contests associated with marriages, by contrast, as establishing the equality rather than the inequality of the contesting parties.) Such kinds of analogical 'play' are typical of what may be called 'shamanic' cultures and represent, among other things, a kind of socialization into their mode of operation (Samuel in press).

If we now turn back to the epic, we can see that a very high proportion of the songs is in some sense enunciating an analogical definition of reality, announcing what is going to happen, making a statement of power which may stand or be contested, and which may or may not be borne out by the subsequent course of events. This process, which I regard as a key element within shamanic cultures, is realized in a variety of ways within the epic. There are songs which are direct prophecies, generally combined with advice as to how the recipient of the prophecy should behave. There are songs in which a particular course of action is ordained or refused and songs which act as omens (*tendré*) helping to bring about the events which they foretell. Prophecies may be retold by the recipient, as in the song in the musical example (Figure 1). Songs of false prophecy and deliberate deception are also common. Gesar is frequently responsible for such prophecies as a way of tricking his opponents into doing what he desires. In the table below (Figure 2) the fifty-six songs of the *Tagyuk* episode and the twenty-eight songs of the first part of the *K'ach'e Yudzong* episode are categorized. Such a categorization is rough, since songs may fit into more than one category, but it indicates the extent to which the songs of the epic do in fact fall into the types suggested. All the categories in Figure 2 can be interpreted in terms of the 'contest of power' model suggested above, and several of the eleven songs listed as 'Other' can also be interpreted in these terms.

TYPE OF SONG	*Tagyuk*	*K'ach'e Yudzong*
Prophecies, omen-songs, recounting dreams	16	4
Announcement of course of action; decision	8	3
Refusal of course of action	5	3
Disguise, deception, false prophecy	11	5
Warning against false prophecy	1	2
Songs of transformation and magical action	3	0
Appeal to gods for help	2	0
Boasting of one's power	0	11
Other	10	1

Figure 2: Categories of Songs in the *Tagyuk* and *K'ach'e Yudzong* Episodes

At this point we can begin to perceive how the songs in the epic might be experienced by a Tibetan listener and also to see the appropriateness here as in other Tibetan genres of *chantefable* form. If each song articulates a particular definition of reality and derives from a particular vision of the world, then each song represents an instance of the non-ordinary ('shamanic') consciousness from which such world-visions ultimately derive. In this sense the movement from speech to song corresponds to the movement from ordinary consciousness to the shamanic consciousness within which a particular vision of the world is enunciated. States of consciousness and analogical definitions of reality are in a sense simply different sides of the same coin (Samuel in press).

The presentation of what I have called 'analogical definitions of reality' is most obvious in the case of the many songs of prophecy and foretelling. These are particularly common in the *Tagyuk* which is concerned with the initial establishment of Gesar's kingdom. In fact, the *Tagyuk* begins with a song of this kind, and ends with three in succession (54, 55, 56). Other types of songs such as those of announcement of a course of action or decision, of transformation and magical action, and of disguise, deception and false prophecy, can easily be assimilated to the same model. The many songs in the *K'ach'e Yudzong* in which a character boasts of his strength and valour can be seen in similar terms. If 'magical' processes in a society such as our own tend to be assimilated as techniques to a technological model, the reverse is true in a shamanic society. The hero succeeds not because he is physically the stronger, because he can deliver a greater force in pounds per square inch, or even because he is a technically more skilled fighter, but because he rates higher in terms of spiritual power or magical protection or possesses supernaturally powerful weapons.

Thus, we could say that the characters who boast of their strength and ability are also fulfilling through their songs the quasi-prophetic function of staking a claim to the outcome of the next episode. That claim is frequently tested directly in the next round of combat. In the case of major characters, however, a fight to the finish is likely to be averted until near the end of the episode and suspense is maintained by devices which avoid and postpone conflict and confuse the listener's expectations, such as the treachery of Gesar's uncle, Tr'ot'ung, and the false prophecies and deceptive appearances of Gesar and other characters.

Given this view of the epic as a competition between states of consciousness and their associated definitions of reality, the invocations at the start of each song may be more significant than they might at first appear. As mentioned earlier, deities in Tantric Buddhism are essentially symbols for states of consciousness. In invoking one or another deity or sets of deities, the characters are telling us where their allegiance lies in the interplay of possible realities and to what kind of consciousness they commit themselves, on a scale which leads up to the central Tibetan Buddhist deities, Avalokiteshvara and Padmasambhava, who are closely associated with Gesar himself. The music of the songs signals and evokes the various kinds of consciousness associated with the different characters as well as marking the movement back and forth from the ordinary consciousness of the background narrative. In any given performance particular characters or character-types are systematically associated with a specific melody. Gesar himself, as the central character and supreme master of shamanic transformations, has a number of melodies which correspond to his different modes of activity in the epic.

5. Conclusion

All these suggestions could be further substantiated by a detailed examination of more of the songs, and I hope to do this on another occasion. Here I shall conclude with a comment on the status of Buddhism in the epic.

In the last analysis, the interplay of realities in the epic generally comes down to that between Buddhism, with all its associated powers, and the opposition, who are somewhat indiscriminately labelled *mutik* ('heretical', usually referring to the non-Buddhist traditions of India) and bön (which refers to non- and pre-Buddhist traditions in Tibet). To quote from Padmasambhava's prophecy to Gesar in the *K'ach'e Yudzong*, 'unless we overthrow the Kashmiri king the heretical [*mutik*] Bön religion will spread and do harm to the Buddha's teachings'. Thus, the King of Kashmir's view of himself and of the world, based as it is on a denial of Gesar and the power of Buddhism, has ultimately to be shown to be wrong. Put otherwise, the kind of consciousness which he represents has to be shown to be perverse and self-destructive. At the end of the day, Gesar and the people of Ling will triumph. However, the fight needs to be a close one, and the result has to at least appear to hang in the balance or the victory of the Buddhist forces would seem empty.

All this may be some way from the Buddhism of, say, the London Buddhist Society or the Mahabodhi Society; but it does, I suggest, tap into some fundamental Tibetan orientations towards Buddhism, as well as helping to explain the significance of the epic's formal structure. Certainly, this perspective on Gesar takes us beyond seeing the epic simply as a pre-Buddhist story onto which Buddhist meanings have been arbitrarily superimposed. Such an approach may make sense in purely historical terms, but if we want to understand what Gesar means today it is quite inadequate. Gesar for the Tibetans has to be perceived as a whole (*see* Samuel 1989). I have suggested above some of the lines along which we can see Gesar as a genuine hero of the 'shamanic Buddhism' of Tibet. I have also suggested some of the concerns which may lie more generally behind epic traditions such as those of East and North Asia. What I have called 'shamanic power' is a matter of real importance in such societies, and it is not surprising that its proper usage is a major theme of their literature. It is perhaps more intriguing that in our own society, where related forms of analogical manipulation of reality have developed into a highly sophisticated and pervasive art dedicated to selling us everything from cars, perfumes or tobacco to political leaders (*see* Samuel in press), there is less evidence of such concern.

Glossary

ACH'E LHAMO (*A che lha mo*): Dance-drama performed to religious stories

BÖN (*bon*): General term for pre-Buddhist and non-Buddhist Tibetan religious traditions

DAKNANG (*dag snang*): Visionary state

DRUNG (*sgrung*): Epic narrative

DRUNGPA (*sgrung pa*): Bard

GUR (*mgur*): A class of songs or poems on religious themes

K'ACH'E YUDZONG (*Kha che g.yu rdzong*): Episode of the Gesar epic dealing with the defeat of the King of K'ach'e (Kashmir)

MUTIK (*mu stegs*): 'Heretical'; usually refers to non-Buddhist religions of India

NAMT'AR (*rnam thar*): Biographical account of lama or religious hero

TAGYUK (*rTa rgyugs*): Episode of the Gesar epic dealing with the horse-race by which Gesar becomes King of Ling

TENDRÉ (*rten 'brel*): Omens, karmic connections

TERTÖN (*gter ston*): Lama who discovers concealed scriptures and other religious objects

Acknowledgments

I should like to acknowledge the assistance of Mr N.T. Maja of Darjeeling, who sang the musical example for me in 1979, Lama Chagdüd Rimpoch'e, Yang Enhong and Lissa Stutchbury.

References

ANON.
    n.d.   *Brief Account of the Life History of Venerable Kalzang Dhong-yud Nyima, the Eighth Incarnation of Khamtrul Rinpoche (1931-1980)*, Tashi Jong Community, Palampur, H.P., India

AZIZ, Barbara
    1985 'On Translating Oral Traditions: Ceremonial Wedding Poetry from Dingri', B.N. Aziz and M. Kapstein (eds.), *Soundings in Tibetan Civilization*, New Delhi: Manohar, pp. 115-32

BIDYALANKARANA, H. H. Prince
    1926 'The Pastime of Rhyme-Making and Singing in Rural Siam,' *Journal of the Siam Society*, 20: 101-27

CHADWICK, Nora K. and ZHIRMUNSKY, Victor
    1969 *Oral Epics of Central Asia*, Cambridge: Cambridge University Press

CHANG, Garma C.C.
    1977 *The Hundred Thousand Songs of Milarepa*, 2 vols., Boulder and London: Shambhala

CHÖDPA DONDRUP (*gcod pa don grub*)
   1989   'Dmangs khrod kyi ge sar rgyal po'i sgrung pa'i rigs la rags
          tsam dpyad pa', *Krung go'i bod kyi shes rig (China
          Tibetology)*, Tibetan edition, 2: 101-14
DAVID-NEEL, Alexandra and Lama YONGDEN
   1933   *The Superhuman Life of Gesar of Ling, the Legendary Tibe-
          tan Hero, as Sung by the Bards of his Country*, London: Rider
DOWMAN, Keith
   1980   *The Divine Madman: The Sublime Life and Songs of Drukpa
          Kunley*, London: Rider
   1984   *Sky Dancer: The Secret Life and Songs of the Lady Yeshe
          Tsogyel*, London: Routledge and Kegan Paul
EVANS-WENTZ, W. Y.
   1969   *Tibet's Great Yogi Milarepa: A Biography from the Tibetan
          [. . .] according to the late Lama Kazi Dawa-Samdup's
          English rendering*, Oxford: Oxford University Press
FRANCKE, A. H.
   1901   'The Ladakhi Pre-Buddhist Marriage Ritual', *Indian
          Antiquary*, 30: 131-49
GUENTHER, Herbert V.
   1963   *The Life and Teaching of Naropa*, Oxford: Clarendon Press
GYATSO, Janet
   1986   'Signs, Memory and History: A Tantric Buddhist Theory of
          Scriptural Transmission', *Journal of the International
          Association of Buddhist Studies*, 9, 2: 7-35
HEISSIG, Walther
   1979   (ed.) *Die Mongolischen Epen: Bezüge, Sinndeutung und
          Überlieferung (Ein Symposium)*, Asiatische Forschungen 68,
          Wiesbaden: Otto Harrassowitz
   1980   *The Religions of Mongolia*, tr. from the German edition by
          Geoffrey Samuel, London: Routledge and Kegan Paul
   1982   (ed.) *Fragen der mongolischen Heldendichtung: Teil II*,
          Asiatische Forschungen 73, Wiesbaden: Otto Harrassowitz
   1983   *Geser-Studien: Untersuchungen zu den Erzählstoffen in den
          'neuen' Kapiteln des mongolischen Geser-Zyklus*,
          Abhandlungen der Rheinisch-Westfälischen Akademie der
          Wissenschaften 69, Opladen: Westdeutscher Verlag
   1985   (ed.) *Fragen der mongolischen Heldendichtung: Teil III*,
          Asiatische Forschungen 91, Wiesbaden: Otto Harrassowitz
HELFFER, Mireille
   1977   *Les chants dans l'épopée tibétaine de Ge-sar d'après le livre de
          la Course de Cheval: Version chantée de Blo-bzaṅ bstan-'jin*,
          Paris and Geneva: Librairie Droz
   1979   'Réflexions concernant le chant épique tibétain', *Asian Music*,
          10, 2: 92-111

1982   'Les Airs dans l'épopée de Ge-sar: Tradition orale et tradition écrite', in Heissig 1982: 231-44

HERMANNS, Matthias
1965   *Das National-Epos der Tibeter Gling König Ge sar*, Regensburg: Verlag Josef Habbel

KASCHEWSKY, Rudolf and TSERING, Pema
1972   'Gesars Anwehrkampf gegen Kaschmir', *Zentralasiatische Studien*, 6: 273-400

Lama KUNGA Rimpoche and CUTILLO, Brian
1978   *Drinking the Mountain Stream: Further Stories and Songs of Milarepa, Yogin, Poet, and Teacher of Tibet*, New York: Lotsawa
1986   *Miraculous Journey: New Stories and Songs by Milarepa*, New York: Lotsawa

LHALUNGPA, Lobsang P.
1979   *The Life of Milarepa: A New Translation from the Tibetan*, Frogmore: Granada

MILLER, Terry E.
1985   *Traditional Music of the Lao*, Westport, Connecticut: Greenwood Press

NORBU, Namkhai [= N.N. Dewang]
1967   'Musical Tradition of the Tibetan People. Songs in Dance Measure', *Orientalia Romana: Essays and Lectures*, 2, Serie Orientale Roma 36, Rome: IsMEO

RIBBACH, S. H.
1986   *Culture and Society in Ladakh*, tr. from the German by John Bray, New Delhi: Ess Ess

ROERICH, George N.
1942   'The Epic of King Kesar of Ling', *Journal of the Royal Asiatic Society of Bengal*, 8: 277-311

SAMUEL, Geoffrey
1978   'Songs of Lhasa', *Ethnomusicology*, 20, 3: 407-49
1989   'Clerical and Shamanic Buddhism in Tibet', unpublished paper
in press *Mind, Body and Culture: Anthropology and the Biological Interface*, Cambridge: Cambridge University Press

SMITH, E. Gene
1969   'Preface', Lokesh Chandra (ed.), *The Life of the Saint of Gtsang by Rgod-tshaṅ-ras-pa Sna-tshogs-raṅ-grol*, Sata-Pitaka series 79, New Delhi: International Academy of Indian Culture

SNYDER, Jeanette
1972   'Some Popular Songs of Tibet', *Malahat Review*, 21: 20-39

STEIN, R. A.
1956   *L'épopée tibétaine de Gesar dans sa version lamaïque de Ling*, Paris: Presses Universitaires de France

1959   *Recherches sur l'épopée et le barde au Tibet*, Bibl. de l'Institut des Hautes Études Chinoises 13, Paris: Presses Universitaires de France

1969   'Les Conteurs au Tibet', *France-Asie*, 197: 135-46

1972   *Vie et Chants de 'Brug-pa Kun-legs le Yogin*, Paris: G.-P. Maisonneuve et Larose

1979   'Introduction to the Gesar Epic', in Tobgyel and Dorji 1979, 1: 1-20; reprinted in *Tibet Journal* (1981), 6,1: 3-13

TARTHANG Tulku

1983   *Mother of Knowledge: The Enlightenment of Ye-shes mTshorgyal*, Berkeley: Dharma

TEMPLEMAN, David

1987   'Buddhist Tantric Song—Doha, Vajragiti and Carya Songs', paper for the Australian Anthropological Society conference, Newcastle, New South Wales, August 1988

THONDUP Rinpoche, Tulku

1986   *Hidden Teachings of Tibet: An Explanation of the Terma Tradition of the Nyingma School of Buddhism*, London: Wisdom

TOBGYEL, Kunzang and DORJI, Mani
        see Stein 1979

TRUNGPA, Chögyam

1982   *The Life of Marpa the Translator, by Tsang Nyön Heruka*, tr. from the Tibetan by the Nalanda Translation Committee under the direction of Chögyam Trungpa, Boulder: Prajna

TUCCI, Giuseppe

1966   *Tibetan Folk Songs*, 2d edn., Ascona: Artibus Asiae

TURNER, Victor

1968   *The Drums of Affliction: A Study of Religious Processes among the Ndembu of Zambia*, Oxford: Clarendon Press

VAN TUYL, Charles D.

1975   'The Tshe rin ma Account—an Old Document Incorporated into the Mi la ras pa'i mgur 'bum?', *Zentralasiatische Studien*, 9: 23-36

WAGNER, Roy

1978   *Lethal Speech: Daribi Myth as Symbolic Obviation*, Ithaca: Cornell University Press

YANG Enhong

1989   'On the artists who perform the epic "King Gesar" ', paper for the First International Symposium on Gesar Epic Studies, Chengdu, November 1989

YANG Mu

1988   'Erotic Musical Activity in China's Multi-Racial Society: Examples of Cultural Interaction Through Music', paper for the Symposium of the International Musicological Society, Melbourne, August 1988

Tibetan Texts

1. *Ma sang skyes bu'i rnam thar las kha che'i g.yu rdzong phab pa'i rtog brjod mtshar gtam gyi phreng ba.* [Modern Indian edition in microfiche reprint by IASWR, Suny Stonybrook = LMpj 011, 060.]

2. *Gling ge sar rgyal po'i sgrung (gling rjes kha che'i g. yu rdzong phab pa'i rtogs brjod).* Bod ljongs mi dmangs dpe skrun khang, Lhasa 1979.

3. *Rje btsun mi la ras pa'i rdo rje mgur drug sogs gsung rgyun thor bu pa 'ga'.* [Blockprint; microfilm of copy in India Office Library, London, Tib MS Lhasa I 87 (Lhasa J 18 d).]

4. *Rje btsun mi la ras pa'i rnam thar rgyas par phye pa mgur 'bum.* (Complete Biography of Milarepa by the Yogi Rupa'i Gyan Chen). Published by Lobsang Tsultim, Sarnath, Varanasi 1971.

The Javanese Court Bedhaya Dance as a Tantric Analogy

Judith Becker

Abstract

The central Javanese court dance, bedhaya, *is performed by nine women, who are usually relatives of the ruler, on the anniversary of his accession to the throne. The long, slow performance is accompanied by a* gamelan *(gong and drum ensemble) and is considered to be the most sacred and spiritually potent of court performances. Two different interpretations— one exoteric, widely known and public, the other esoteric, restricted to the inner circle of the court—are invoked to explain the meaning of the dance. Although Java is an Islamic country and, since the earliest conversions in the fourteenth and fifteenth centuries, has become increasingly orthodox, echoes of the Tantric Śaivism (Śiva worship) and Tantric Buddhism of Java's medieval period remain. Centuries-old cultural memories resurface not only in the exoteric stories told to explain the* bedhaya *performance but also in the esoteric interpretation of the choreography itself. Both types of interpretation are rooted in Tantric beliefs, and both are based on the similarities of the dance to some other aspect of the world. But the dance also is sacramental, since through the transformative power of the ritual it becomes that which it represents.*

Introduction

In most parts of the world music and dance are understood as referring to meanings other than those deriving from acoustical or musical attributes such as timbre, pitch, duration and intensity or melodic line, harmonic progression and rhythmic organization. Although musicians and dancers appreciate acoustical and musical elements, those who listen to the music or watch the dance usually do not regard those elements as significant.

Instead, they invest the performance with extra- musical meaning, and this meaning differs both within and across cultures. The process by which meaning is expressed in language always involves analogy—the understanding of music or dance as being in some way similar to, and therefore representing something other than, itself.

No performance can have exactly the same meaning for everyone, since each person brings different experience to an event and understands the event within the framework of an individual history. Complete consensus on the meaning of a performance, or complete overlapping of individualized meanings, never happens. Meaning inheres in a complex system of implied or explicit relationships which pertain between a person and a performance. As Ricoeur (1981) has pointed out, extracting meaning from a performance is like reading a poem: if a reader brings a wealth of experience to the poem, he or she will apply more imaginative associations in reading the poem and will therefore become more enriched by the experience of reading.

Different levels of meaning are found in the Central Javanese court dance, *bedhaya*. At the esoteric level, it is regarded as a symbol of transformation. At appointed times of the year, particularly the anniversary of the accession to the throne, nine chosen females, generally relatives of the ruler (his wives, daughters or concubines), are rehearsed for several weeks before they perform *bedhaya* before a select private audience.[1] Some kind of female dance called '*bedhaya*' has been known in Java at least as far back as the fourteenth century, the time of the Majapahit empire of East Java (*see* Hill 1960: 102-3). Since the founding of the Central Javanese Mataram dynasty in the seventeenth century, the *bedhaya* has been claimed as a creation and a special sacred heirloom (*pusaka*) of the Mataram court.

The dance takes several hours to perform and is accompanied by singing, as well as by a small *gamelan* ensemble in Surakarta and a full *gamelan* in Yogyakarta [Plate 1]. Until very recent times, it was considered an honor for anyone outside the immediate court circle to attend a court *bedhaya* performance. A religious aura pervades both the preparations for, and the performance of, *bedhaya*. Preceding the event dancers must fast and undergo purification. During the event an atmosphere of subdued fear fills the audience hall, since all participants expect to encounter spiritual forces from another realm.

In the following pages I treat two different interpretations of *bedhaya*, the one esoteric—known only to those close to, or a part of, court circles, the other exoteric—known to the general public. The two different interpretations derive from two different 'texts', using text here to mean 'the inscription' of meaning by writing, telling or action (Ricoeur 1981: 197-221; Becker 1979: 211-6; Geertz 1983: 30-1). My two 'texts' are the dance formations of *bedhaya* and the story about its origins. It is my purpose to show that the dance formations encode a particular religious teaching, whereas the story encodes a re-enactment of the origin myth of the dance.

Plate 1: A palace *gamelan* ensemble, Surakarata, Central Java; from Th. B. van Lelyveld, *La Danse dans le Theatre Javanais*, Paris: 13B Boulevard Saint-Germain, 1931, plate 38

In my treatment of the first 'text', the choreography, I am indebted to the work of Hostetler (1978, 1982) who pointed out that

> Association with meditation is . . . found in the mystical interpretations given to the formal designs of the dance, particularly as espoused by dance experts in Yogyakarta. In these interpretations, the dance is regarded as a symbolic portrayal of a person's spiritual life culminating in the experience of mystical oneness (Hostetler 1982: 128).

In the diagrams of the dance formations, I have standardized the number designation and followed the system of Hostetler (1978, 1981) and Vetter (1984). All diagrams are based upon those found in Tirtaamidjaja (1967: 48-56), Hostetler (1978: Appendix III: 22), Hadiwidjojo (1981: 46-7) and Vetter (1984: 47-9). 'Based upon' means that I have made minor changes, either by standardizing the numbers or by adding the names of the dancers to the diagram.

1. The Dance Formations: Inscribing Esoteric Meaning

The first 'text' which interprets *bedhaya* is the dance formations, in which there are nine dancers, all of whom are female. Each has a name (with variants) translated as follows:

1. Desire, constant/fixed desire (*èndhèl/èndhèl ajeg*)
2. head, mind (*pembatak/batak*)
3. neck (*gulu/jangga*)
4. chest (*dhadha*)
5. tail, genitals, lower end of spinal column (*buncit/bunthil*)
6. right arm, also right flank, front flank (*apit ngajeng/apit ngarep*)
7. left arm, also rear flank (*apit wingking/apit mburi*)
8. right leg, also emergent desire, front emergent desire, outside desire (*èndèl weton/èndhèl wedalan ngajeng/èndhèl jawi*)
9. left leg, also quiet flank, rear emergent desire (*apit meneng/èndhèl wedalan wingking*).

These names designate a particular position in the changing dance formations, although in the written sources there is a slight variation in the assignment of names and numbers to each dancer. Nevertheless, all the writers on *bedhaya* agree as to the basic formations of the dance and the positions of each dancer in the basic formations.

Dancer No. 1, desire, represents various kinds of attachment: for example, the attachment of the individual to other individuals; the attachment to the ego-bolstering comfort of friends; the attachment to the security of one's home, family or job; and the attachment to one's own understanding and interpretation of the world. In Tantric teachings attachment is the primary obstacle to proper meditation and enlightenment. The next four dancers, head, neck, chest and genitals, correspond to the four standard centers of psychic energy (*cakras*) [Figure 1]. According to the Buddhist *anuttara yoga tantras*, these centers are located along the spinal column and are activated in meditation (Snellgrove 1987: i/248). The remaining dancers—right arm, left arm, right leg, left leg—complete the representation of the human body.

The choreography of *bedhaya* may be divided into three large sections, preceded and concluded by a stately processional to and from the dance area. Each section of the dance consists of a lengthy series of dance formations which change slowly in an ordered sequence.[2] After the processional from a room behind the audience hall, the dancers assume the opening position, all of them facing the Susuhunan who sits on his throne [Plate 2]. In order to show how the dance presents detailed and specific Tantric teachings, I have reduced the long and complex sequences to a diagramatic schema, which serves as an outline of the dance's 'plot' or 'narrative structure' [Figures 2-5]. In the first diagram the dance formation represents desire and the Tantric psychic body; in the second, the conflicting forces within the Tantric body; in the third, the integration or absorption of desire; and in the fourth, the dissolving of conflicts and the body formation into the universe.

The audience and performers together participate in the processes of

Figure 1: A representation of the seven psychic centers (*cakras*); from Joseph Campbell, *The Mythic Image*, Bollingen Series 100, © 1974 Princeton University Press, plate 306 (drawn by Mark Hasselriis) reprinted by permission of Princeton University Press

incorporating desire into the psychic body, thus breaking the impetus to action precipitated by various kinds of attachments. In addition to the symbolic nature of the dance, the performance has a didactic purpose, for it serves as training in the technique of meditation and, hence, is part of religious practice.

2. The Story: Inscribing Exoteric Meaning

The second 'text' which interprets *bedhaya* is the story of its origin in the encounter between the first king of the Mataram dynasty, Sultan Agung (seventeenth century) and the goddess of the south sea, Kangjeng Ratu Kidul.[3] Many versions of the story of Sultan Agung and Kangjeng Ratu Kidul are current in oral tradition. Among textual sources the most notable are the nineteenth-century versions told in the *Babad Tanah Jawi* and the *Serat Babad Nitik*.[4] In this set of myths the king and the goddess

Plate 2: The opening position of *bedhaya*; from B. van Helsdingen-Schoevers, *Tari Serimpi dalam Istana Soerakarta*, Weltevreden: Balai Poestaka, 1925, photo 10

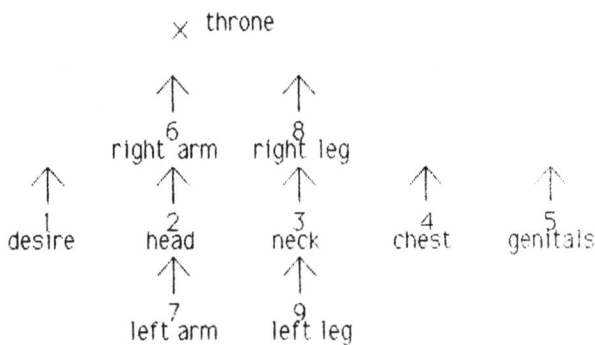

Figure 2: Position 1
The Tantric body and desire

group 1   group 2
6 →   ←8
right arm   right leg
        1 →   ←2   ←3   ←4   ←5
    desire   head neck chest genitals
7→   ←9
left arm   left leg

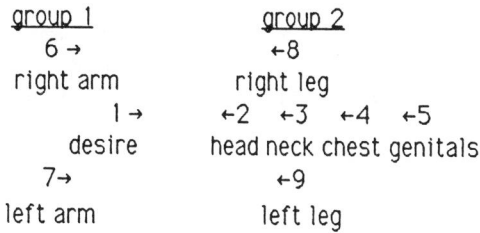

Figure 3: Position 2
Conflicting forces: The Tantric body in opposition to desire

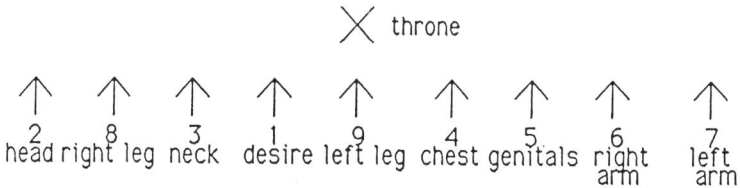

✕ throne

↑   ↑   ↑   ↑   ↑   ↑   ↑   ↑   ↑
2   8   3   1   9   4   5   6   7
head right leg neck desire left leg chest genitals right   left
                                                    arm   arm

Figure 4: Position 3
Integration: Desire absorbed and the body dissolved

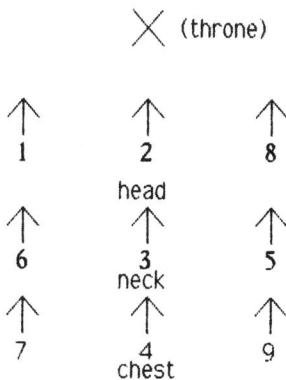

✕ (throne)

↑   ↑   ↑
1   2   8
              head

↑   ↑   ↑
6   3   5
              neck

↑   ↑   ↑
7   4   9
              chest

Figure 5: Final position
Perfection: Body and desire dissolved, the three main *cakras* become the universe

fall in love, consummate their love, suffer the pain of separation and the joy of reunion. They have strong, clearly delineated personalities and are equals in terms of power and creativity; and their union is necessary for the prosperity of the kingdom. Intimate feelings and strong emotions are involved.

Briefly told, the story is as follows. Sultan Agung, through his meditation on Mount Girilaya, caused the volcanic Mount Merapi to erupt and the southern sea to roll and boil. Many spirit followers of the south sea goddess, Kangjeng Ratu Kidul, were destroyed by the tumultuous sea. The goddess herself went to confront Sultan Agung; but when she saw him, she fell passionately in love with him. She persuaded him to come to her resplendent underwater palace, where their love was consummated and where she danced for him the first *bedhaya*. She tried to prevail on him to remain forever with her, but he was drawn back to his palace by his sense of his destiny as a ruler.

There is a rich mythology surrounding Kangjeng Ratu Kidul, some of which indicates an overlap with the fertility goddess, Dewi Sri (Jordaan 1984). But in the myth of the origin of *bedhaya*, Kangjeng Ratu Kidul is not a life-giving force or an agricultural deity. Rather, she is magnificent, beautiful and destructive. Her realm, the southern ocean, is the source of demons, pestilence and disasters. If a *bedhaya* performance and the preceding rehearsals do not follow the prescribed procedures, such as proper offerings and purifications of participants, it is believed that some misfortune will befall the palace and its inhabitants. Yet, the goddess's involvement with the ruler of the Mataram dynasty is essential for sustaining the monarchy and the prosperity of the realm. When the destructive, regenerative power of Kangjeng Ratu Kidul is brought within the sphere of the king, it serves to support both king and kingdom.

When the story of *bedhaya* is applied to the dance itself, it is clear that the nine dancers represent Kangjeng Ratu Kidul: she is the female energy (*śakti*) which must be drawn to the king and incorporated into him for his success as a ruler and as a man. Moreover, the goddess is his ultimate 'other' or opposite. In Tantric terms she is his *śakti*. In the texts of the singers who accompany a *bedhaya* performance, the erotic attraction of Kangjeng Ratu Kidul to Sultan Agung is underlined as in the following:

> . . . sleeping with pillows on the floor, oh, my great lord,/ who has pity on this passionate longing, oh, my great lord,/ light of the world, beautiful *danurwenda* flower, oh, my great lord,/ with you in the bedchamber, oh, my great lord,/ heaven is forgotten, oh, my great lord/ (Tirtaamidjaja 1967: 58-9 tr. Becker; Brakel-Papenhuyzen 1988: 106-17 tr. Becker).

In all the versions of the story, it is the goddess who longs for the Sultan, for she is irresistibly drawn to him and comes to his palace each year. A *bedhaya* performance, in its exoteric interpretation, represents the story of the sexual union of opposites, the union of the king with *śakti*, the female energy of the universe.

Conclusion

In the dance formations and the story of the origin of *bedhaya*, the sacredness and sexuality of the event are joined. Indeed, the two aspects are inseparable in the dance and in the religious systems that fostered the dance. With the decline of the court traditions, the court *bedhaya* has become almost extinct. But other forms of *bedhaya* continue as artistic performances. These may be performed either in a palace, but without the presence of a prince, or on a stage, where the audience pays an admission fee. One no longer need be a member of the nobility or connected to the court to perform this dance. The choreography is now changing to focus on narratives, in which the dancers enact episodes from popular *wayang* stories (Vetter 1984). In this form contemporary *bedhaya* has largely severed its Tantric roots.

By contrast, the ancestor of the new generation of *bedhaya* dances, the Surakarta *bedhaya Ketawang*, still retains its Tantric doctrines. In the commemoration of the first union of the goddess, Kangjeng Ratu, and Sultan Agung, and in continuation of this union into the present, the *bedhaya Ketawang* dance is performed on the anniversary of the consecration of the Susuhunan of Surakarta. Kangjeng Ratu Kidul, the *śakti* of the king, is believed to be present at the performance and to be united sexually with the Susuhunan (Hadiwidjojo 1972: 121). Although the *bedhaya Semang* of Yogyakarta is no longer performed, the late Sultan also felt that he had contacted the goddess (Jordaan 1984: 100).[5]

Notes

1 During some periods of the nineteenth century, the *bedhaya* dancers were youthful males dressed as women (Pigeaud 1938: 299). The transvestite role in Indonesia has often been a ritual one and is considered to have a special power. For a survey of the literature on transvestism and ritual in Indonesia, see Wolbers (1989: 8-10).
2 For a description of the formations and lengthy transitions between them, see Vetter (1984: 45-63) and Brakel-Papenhuyzen (1988: 172-80).
3 Kangjeng Ratu Kidul is known by many names, each of which relates etymologically to one or several of the stories regarding her origin. Combined, they present a rich overlay of meanings and associations with the south sea goddess (see Jordaan 1984: 99-116).
4 The *Babad Tanah Jawi* and *Serat Babad Nitik* are collections of manuscripts, the former of which is from Surakarta and the latter, from Yogyakarta (see Ricklefs 1972: 285-315 and Hostetler 1982: 129-35).
5 The late Sultan of Yogyakarta, Hamengku Buwana IX, died 3 October 1988. According to a story reported in the Indonesian weekly magazine, *Tempo* (15 October 1988: 43), Kangjeng Ratu Kidul visited the Sultan one last time after his death. The night before the funeral, several palace servants were keeping watch over the small building in a corner of the

central courtyard in which the body had been placed. They saw a darkly-dressed figure enter the gate of the courtyard, and they immediately gave chase. The figure mysteriously disappeared into the small building. Only after a struggle were the palace servants able to open the door to the building. When they finally succeeded, they were startled by a whirlwind rushing past them out the door, followed by a sweet fragrance. No one doubted that Kangjeng Ratu Kidul had come to say the last goodbye to her former lover.

Glossary

anuttara yoga tantras: the 'supreme' category of Tantric Buddhist scriptures
apit ngajeng: right arm/right flank
apit ngarep: right flank/right arm
apit meneng: left leg/rear emergent desire
apit mburi: rear flank/left arm
apit wingking: left arm/rear flank
batak: mind/head
buncit: tail, genitals/lower end of spinal column
bunthil: lower end of spinal column/tail, genitals
cakras: center of psychic energy
danurwenda: a kind of flower
dhadha: chest
èndhèl: desire
èndhèl ajeg: constant/fixed desire
èndhèl jawi: outside desire
èndhèl wedalan ngajeng: emergent desire, front emergent desire
èndhèl wedalan wingking: quiet flank, rear emergent desire
èndhèl weton: right leg/emergent desire
gamelan: gong and drum ensemble
gulu: neck
jangga: neck
pembatak: head
pusaka: sacred heirloom
śakti: female energy of the universe
wayang: Javanese shadow-puppet theater

References

BECKER, A. L.
    1979 'Text-building, Epistemology, and Aesthetics in Javanese Shadow Theatre', *The Imagination of Reality: Essays in Southeast Asian Coherence Systems* ed. A. Becker and A. Yengoyan, Norwood, New Jersey: Ablex Publishing Corporation: 211-43

BECKER, A. L. and Judith
1981 'A Musical Icon: Power and Meaning in Javanese Gamelan Music', *The Sign in Music and Literature* ed. W. Steiner, Austin, Texas: University of Texas Press: 203-15

BRAKEL-PAPENHUYZEN, Clara
1988 *The Sacred Bedhaya Dances of the Kratons of Surakarta and Yogyakarta*, Leiden: State University of Leiden

GEERTZ, Clifford
1983 *Local Knowledge*, New York: Basic Books, Inc.

HADIWIDJOJO, K.G.P.H.
1972 'Danse Sacrée à Surakarta: La Signification du *Bedojo Ketawang*', Archipel 3: 117-32
1981 *Bedhaya Ketawang: Tarian Sakral di Candi-candi*, Jakarta: Balai Pustaka

HILL, A. C.
1960 'Hikayat Raja-Raja Pasai', *Journal of the Malayan Branch of the Royal Asiatic Society*, 33, pt.2 (no. 190): 3-215

HOSTETLER, Jan
1978 'Bedojo Semang: Reconstruction of a Masterwork', Unpublished manuscript
1982 'Bedojo Semang: The Sacred Dance of Yogyakarta', *Archipel* 24: 127-42

JORDAAN, Roy E.
1984 'The Mystery of Nyai Lara Kidul', *Archipel* 28: 99-116

PIGEAUD, T.G.Th.
1938 *Javaanse Volksvertoningen: Bijdrage tot de Beschrijving van Land en Volk*, Batavia: Volkslectuur

RICKLEFS, M. C.
1972 'A Consideration of Three Versions of the Babad Tanah Djawi, with Excerpts on the Fall of Madjapahit', *Bulletin of the School of Oriental and African Studies* 35, pt.2: 285-315

RICOEUR, Paul
1981 'The Model of the Text: Meaningful Action considered as a Text', *Hermeneutics and the Human Sciences*, Cambridge: Cambridge University Press

TIRTAAMIDJAJA, N.
1967 'A Bedaja Ketawang Performance at the Court of Surakarta', *Indonesia* 1: 31-60

VETTER, Valerie Mau
1984 'Behaya Durma: Change and Continuity in a Javanese Court Dance', M.A. thesis, University of Wisconsin, Madison

WOLBERS, Paul
1989 'Transvestism, Eroticism, and Religion: In Search of a Contextual Background for the Gandrung and Seblang

Traditions of Banyuwangi, East Java', *Progress Reports in Ethnomusicology 2*, nos. 4-7: 1-17

Belian as a Symbol of Cosmic Reunification

Ashley Turner

Abstract

The drum associated with the Petalangan shamanic healing ritual, belian *is attributed with extraordinary powers which are believed to be capable of creating a nexus between the human world and the spirit world. While the overt function of shamanic drum music is to socialize the occasion and to accompany the shaman's dancing, drum rhythms also provide the motivic force by which the shaman enters into trance and journeys in the spirit world to obtain healing on behalf of his community. The key to this aesthetic power is a system of esoteric analogies which charge the drum with cosmological and social meaning. The cosmological significance of these analogies suggests a reason why music is an integral part of shamanic healing ritual. According to Petalangan philosophical thought, the divided cosmos is temporarily re-joined through ritual and music.*

Introduction

This paper presents an analysis of a musical shamanic ritual called *belian*, which is practised by the Petalangan Malay people of Riau province on the east coast of Sumatra (*see* Figure 1). A shaman is defined as someone 'who can enter at will into a non-ordinary psychic state (in which either his spirit undertakes a journey into the spirit world or he himself becomes possessed by a spirit) for the purpose of making contact with the spirit world on behalf of members of his community' (Reinhard 1976: 16). The Petalangan shaman, the *kemantan*, makes use of his inherited esoteric knowledge (*ilmu gaib or kaji*) about the essential interconnectedness of the cosmos, to create within and of himself a symbolic and literal nexus between the reality of everyday life and the extraordinary reality of spirits, dreams and

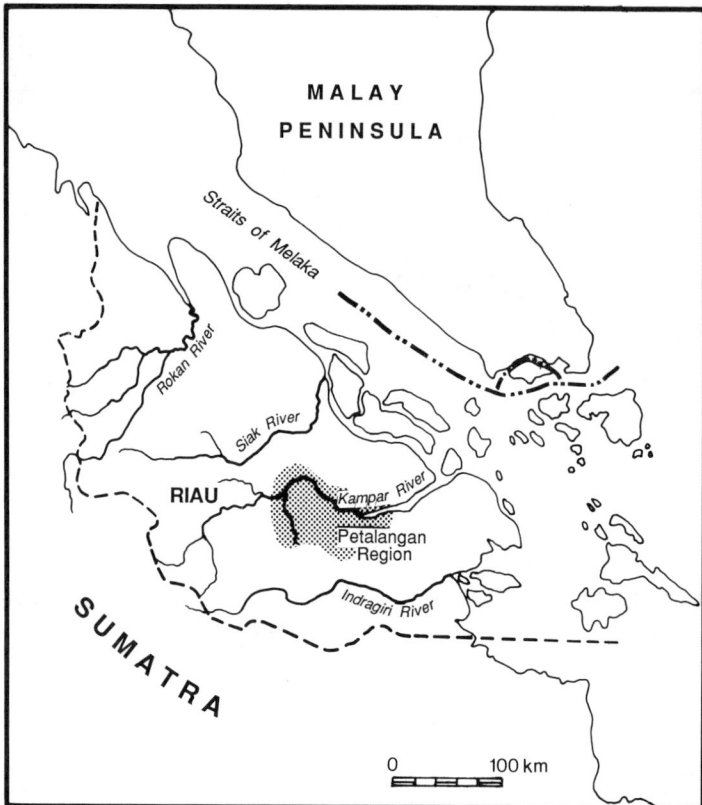

Figure 1: The Petalangan region

the mythical past. He accomplishes this transformation through a self-controlled trance, assisted by ritual action, sensory deprivation, the driving rhythms of the *ketobung* drum, prayers and charms and the power of public expectation. Having attained this state, he makes a journey in the cosmos to obtain from the spirits protection and healing (*obat*) for members of his community.

The concepts and secrets which form the *kemantan's* knowledge are usually embodied in origin stories, metaphors and symbols which the *kemantan* consciously manipulates to achieve magical transferences. A significant part of these concepts also relate, either directly or indirectly, to the *ketobung* drum (Plate 1), its players and its rhythms, and the role they play in helping to re-unify the divided cosmos and propel the *kemantan* on his journey. The analysis presented in this paper aims to interpret the roles and meanings of the shamanic drum in the context of observable shamanic performance and in the symbolic and cosmologic context evoked through

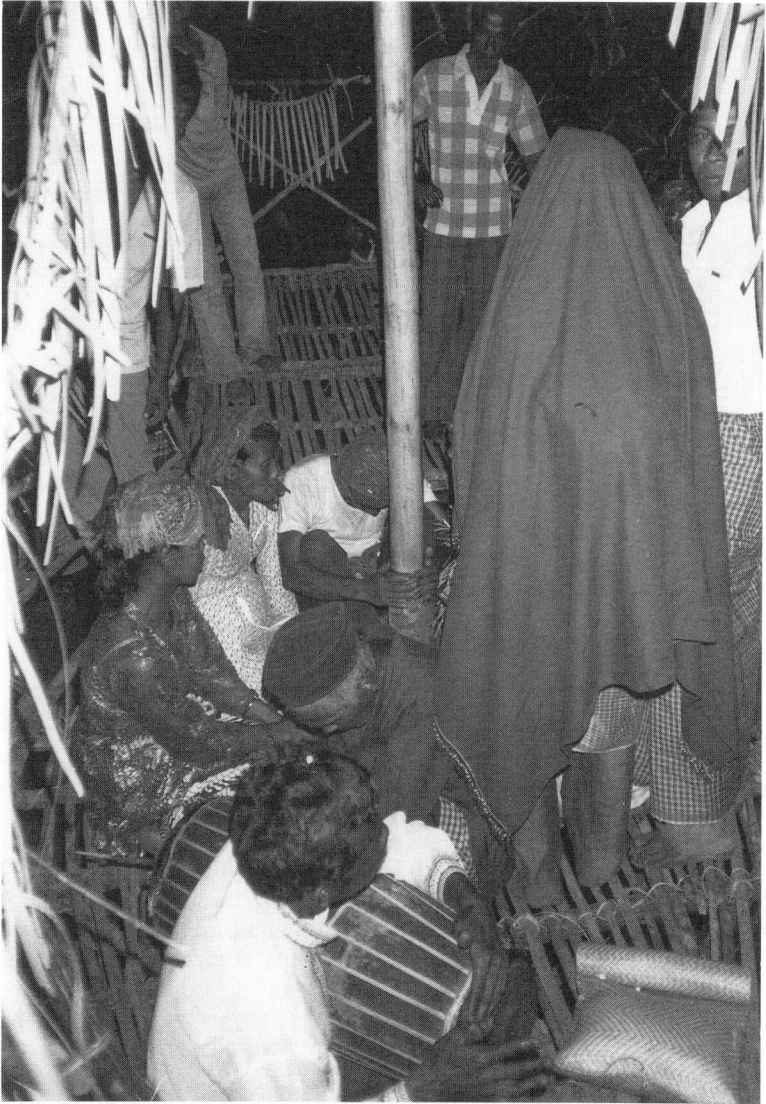

Plate 1: The *ketobung* drum, an indispensable part of the *belian* ritual.

ritual (*see* Figure 2). My approach, which is informed most notably by Effendi's analysis of Petalangan shamanic ritual (n.d.), Feld's paper on the social symbolism of the Kaluli drum (1983), Kartomi's work on Mandailing musical aesthetics (1983) and Laird's analysis of Temoq shamanism (1978 and 1983), is to identify structural commonalities between musical and non-musical systems inherent in *belian*, as well as in Petalangan society and in Petalangan philosophical thought. The main sources for the data are *belian* performance practice, Petalangan social organization and musical culture generally, and the *kemantan's* body of esoteric knowledge.

Ketobung in the Microcosm	Ketobung in the Macrocosm
Informs everyone in the district that a performance of belian is imminent or in progress.	Informs all sentient nature of community's need and intention to hold a shamanic ritual.
Calls the community together.	Invokes the spirits.
Provides a continuous background for program of ritual activities.	Provides continuity for the shaman's journey in the cosmos.
Creates a continuity between the inside and outside of the ritual house.	Creates a continuity between the visible and the hidden realm.
Assists the shaman to internalize symbols and to trigger his trance.	Resident spirit in drum helps to empower and transform the shaman.
Accompanies the shaman's dance.	Conducts the shaman in the cosmos.

Figure 2: Macrocosmic and microcosmic functions of the shaman's drum

Religious trance rituals throughout the world are often associated with music (Rouget 1985: xvii). Explanations for this association range from the suggestion that certain types of music have an intrinsic ability to induce trance states by stimulating the human nervous system (Neher 1962: 152) to the claim that music does nothing more than socialize trance (Rouget 1985: 326). However, most scholars agree that music can be highly effective in producing an atmosphere conducive to the production, control and maintenance of trance. The case study presented in this paper demonstrates that the trance of the Petalangan shaman—his transition from the mundane, everyday state to the condition of a traveller in the cosmos and his safe return—depends not only upon the accurate performance of specific drum rhythms but also upon the wilful application by the shaman of a series of symbolic systems which give meaning and power to the music.

However, these rhythms are only effective when they are played upon the spiritually powerful *ketobung* drum and only in the context of shamanic ritual. Under these conditions the shaman perceives the drum rhythms as *suao duwato* (the voice of the deity) which guides him on a journey in the macrocosm. To the audience in the ritual house, the various stages of the shaman's journey manifest themselves as a dance in which the shaman perambulates back and forth, sings, speaks and makes gestures as though to an invisible third party. The relations between the overt performance features of *belian* and the shaman's reported experience of the performance are shown in Figure 3 and its Key.

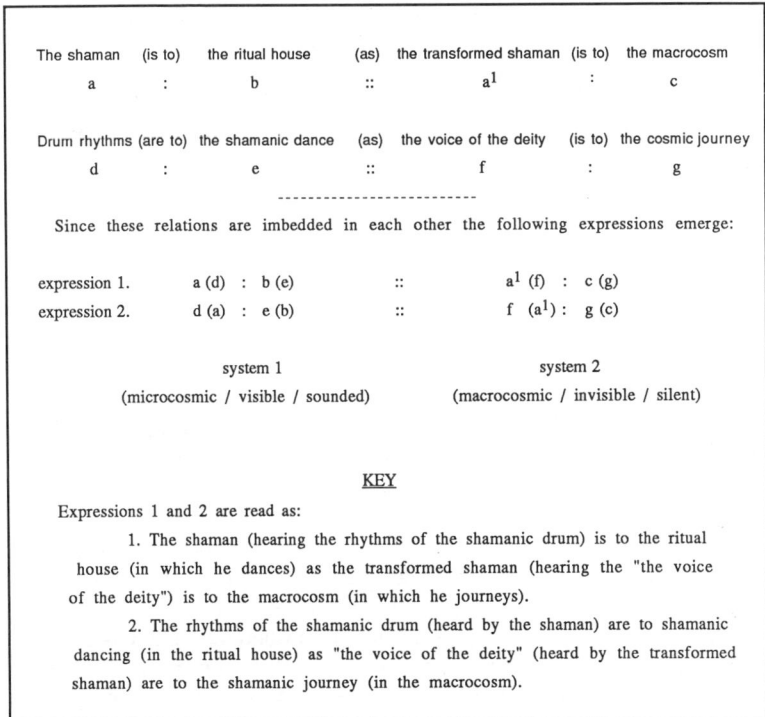

The shaman   (is to)   the ritual house   (as)   the transformed shaman (is to)   the macrocosm

   a   :   b   :: a^1 :   c

Drum rhythms (are to) the shamanic dance   (as)   the voice of the deity   (is to)   the cosmic journey

   d   :   e   ::   f   :   g

- -

Since these relations are imbedded in each other the following expressions emerge:

expression 1.   a (d) : b (e)   :: a^1 (f) : c (g)
expression 2.   d (a) : e (b)   ::   f (a^1) : g (c)

system 1   system 2
(microcosmic / visible / sounded)   (macrocosmic / invisible / silent)

KEY

Expressions 1 and 2 are read as:

    1. The shaman (hearing the rhythms of the shamanic drum) is to the ritual house (in which he dances) as the transformed shaman (hearing the "the voice of the deity") is to the macrocosm (in which he journeys).

    2. The rhythms of the shamanic drum (heard by the shaman) are to shamanic dancing (in the ritual house) as "the voice of the deity" (heard by the transformed shaman) are to the shamanic journey (in the macrocosm).

Figure 3: Relations between the performative aspects of *belian* and the shaman's reported experience [after Laird (1983)]

1. The Petalangan World

The Petalangan are a homogeneous group of rural Malays who live in local communities along the thickly forested middle and lower reaches of the Kampar river where they engage in hunting, fishing, dry-rice cultivation, vegetable gardening and collecting forest-products. The basis for their economic, social and cultural survival is cooperation and reciprocity in the use of their traditional lands. The ethos of cooperation which extends throughout Petalangan society is especially strong within and between families, within the eight matrilineal kinship groups, and between the numerous villages throughout which the kinship groups are dispersed.

The Petalangan cosmos is divided into two interrelated domains: the visible realm of directly observable reality in which everyday life proceeds (*alam nyato*), and the hidden or invisible realm of the spirits (*alam gaib*). Petalangan people often attribute events in the world around them to the actions of spirit beings, especially when sickness and misfortune are involved. Spirits fall into three categories according to their relationships with humans: evil and antagonistic spirits who are believed to cause affliction and misfortune; spirits who are sympathetically inclined towards humanity and which can be counted upon to assist the shaman in his fight against sickness and misfortune; and neutral spirits who may be swayed to perform either good or evil acts. In many ways the realm of the spirits is thought to be homologous with the visible human realm. Just as Petalangan society is organized around hierarchical structures, so the spirit world consists of vertically ranked classes of beings. The supreme authority of both realms is Allah. Petalangan shamans always begin their rituals by praying to Allah for assistance in securing the services of His invisible subjects.

The inhabitants of the invisible realm, which are referred to corporately as 'invisible beings' (*makluk gaib*), include Islamic saints (*ko'amat*), ancestral spirits (*ninik moyang*), elemental spirits (*jembelang*), forest sprites (*mambang*), ghosts (*jin* or *antu*), celestial spirits (*dewo*), and a host of animal spirits, the most powerful of which is the tiger-spirit (*antu a'imau*). Petalangan shamans usually control at least one tiger-spirit which they call upon for assistance and protection during healing rituals. Another type of spirit-being with whom Petalangan shamans have frequent dealings is the *o'ang bunyian* (sound-people). These are forest-dwelling, human-like beings who have the ability to become invisible at will. It is believed that *o'ang bunyian* live in villages and have gregarious social and cultural lives just like their human counterparts. Though usually invisible, it is said that they can sometimes be detected by the sounds (*bunyian*) which they make as they socialize and play music. Some musicians claim that their ancestors originally learned particular musical traditions by copying *o'ang bunyian* musicians whom they happened to overhear.

2. The Relations between Petalangan Music and the Spirits

The Petalangan regard music in general to be a powerful medium for communication between humans and spirits. Music, like all other cultural practices, descends from the ancestors, and the Petalangan always invite the spirits of ancestors to attend on formal musical occasions. The sign of a formal invitation is the presence of a box containing betel nuts and leaves which is provided by the host of the occasion and which is usually placed before the performing musician. Betel nut and leaves are chewed on social occasions, and their presence signifies good will and sociability. The invitation to the ancestors may also be reinforced by the astringent aroma of incense, invocations and, in some cases, the sacrificing of a chicken. Certain types of music, such as narrative epic songs (*nyanyi panjang*), are thought to be of particular interest to the spirits because of their subject material. As epic songs are specifically concerned with the exploits and travels of the ancestors, their performance is thought to have an invocatory effect upon the ancestral spirits.

While musical communication between the visible realm and the spirit realm is often a by-product of the close associations between music and the ancestors, certain types of ritual music also have the explicit aim of creating channels of communication between the human world and the spirit world. These include certain drum rhythms, melodies played on the spike-fiddle (*obab*) and invocatory songs associated with possession ceremonies, such as *main dewo* (playing the deity), *main Adin* (playing the spirit Adin) and *anggung* (ascending), in which a dancer enters into a trance identified with the possessing spirits. Possession trance dances are performed mainly for the community's entertainment, though occasionally they may be performed to obtain minor healing from the spirits or to divine the whereabouts of lost objects. However, the most powerful music for communicating with the spirits is the drum music played for the shamanic healing ritual, *belian*.

The Petalangan believe that direct contact between humans and spirits occurs mainly during dreams and rituals. However, dreams constitute an uncontrolled conduit between realms, whereas ritual occasions provide various strategies for creating a spatial, temporal and social framework within which a safe and controlled passage may take place. Music-making is one of the principal strategies employed for this purpose. Indeed, it is characteristic of *belian* to be immersed in an ambience of continuous musical and social sounds. This musical environment results from the combination of drumming, singing, the sounds of thumping as the shaman dances and perambulates back and forth, the jangling of his bell-chime bracelet (*gonto*) and shouts of excitement and encouragement which come from the audience (*see* Figure 4). For the duration of the performance, which usually lasts about four or five hours, the players of the *ketobung* drum provide an almost unceasing rhythmic flow and pulse to accompany the shaman's dancing (*see below* Section 7: Figure 9). This flow and pulse is the main source of continuity for the shaman's trance and the program of ritual events. The shaman and his assistants (*bujang pebayu*) also sing

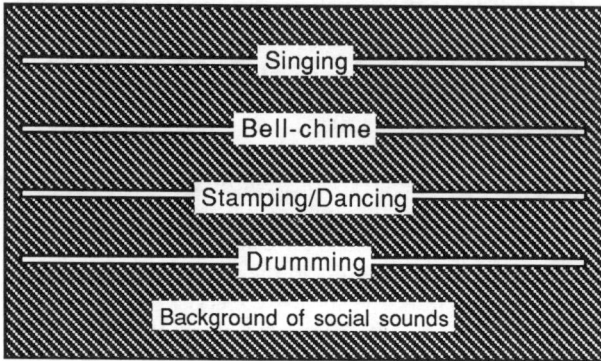

Figure 4: The musical environment of *belian*

charms and invocations which cajole and command the spirits and which inform everyone present of the shaman's progress on his journey among the spirits.

3. Forms and Functions of *Belian*

According to Petalangan shamans and their assistants with whom I have spoken, *belian* literally means 'a purchase'. The paramount aim of the *belian* ritual is to create a connection between the visible realm and the spirit realm. The shaman's transition from one realm to the other—his travels among the spirits and his meetings with benevolent spirits— manifest themselves to the audience as a sacred drama involving trance, drumming, singing, dancing, miming and esoteric symbolic and ritual action. Petalangan shamans are usually male, though it is possible for a woman to become a *kemantan*. A female *kemantan* enters into trance, sings and performs ritual actions just like her male counterpart. However, in accordance with Islamic prohibitions, Petalangan women never dance in public. Instead, the female *kemantan* remains sitting while a male assistant performs the shamanic dance.

For Petalangan communities, even mild sickness (*sakit biaso*) is regarded as a serious matter which, if left unattended, can lead to untimely death or to the afflicted individual becoming a burden upon the rest of the community. Since the occupations of dry-rice farming and collection of forest-products rarely produce a surplus, the Petalangan community cannot afford to support a sick person for long. Individual sickness is regarded as a threat to the viability of the community and is therefore always a matter of public concern. *Belian* is called for whenever it appears that individual or communal sickness or misfortune may threaten the community's social viability. The Petalangan people believe that the *kemantan* is capable of compelling or supplicating the ancestral spirits to assist him in his efforts to reverse sickness by endowing him with their healing powers, by providing information about the nature of sickness and the preparation of a remedy, or by intervening directly to remove the invisible sources of affliction.

There are five different types of *belian*, distinguished according to the nature of the affliction (*see* Figure 5). The most common type is called

BELIAN TYPE	PURPOSE
1. Belian obat biaso	To heal individual and communal sickness and misfortune.
2. Belian gegawe	To protect a village against a marauding tiger.
3. Belian bainang	To protect a pregnant woman and her unborn child against future misfortune.
4. Belian membaye utang	To "repay a debt" to spirits understood to have intervened on a past occasion to restore health and good fortune.
5. Belian pole	To initiate or heal a shaman.

Figure 5: Five types of shamanic ritual distinguished according to their function

belian obat biaso (belian for ordinary sickness). The performance takes place in a conveniently located home which has been prepared with ritual objects made from woven palm leaves. Less frequently performed is *belian gegawe* (*belian* for obtaining a protective talisman), in which the *kemantan's* own tiger-spirit guardian is enlisted to protect the community against a tiger known to be marauding the village. Another rarely performed type is *belian bainang* (*belian* for pregnancy). This prophylactic ritual protects a woman in her first pregnancy, and the child whom she carries, by securing a guardian spirit for them.

If the *kemantan* succeeds in obtaining protection or a remedy, it may be necessary for the beneficiary family or community to repay their debt to the spirits. Their debt-repayment takes the form of a performance of *belian membaye utang* (*belian* for paying a debt), during which twenty-one plates of food are presented to the spirits. After the spirits have consumed the invisible essence of the food, the remaining physical substance is shared evenly among everyone present. Failure to tend to this obligation, it is believed, may cause the return of the undesirable conditions for which shamanic intervention was initially sought.

The relationship between the *kemantan* and the community is essentially one of interdependence and reciprocity. Not only does the community perceive a need for the services of the *kemantan*, but the *kemantan* needs to be nurtured continually by the community. When a person first becomes a *kemantan*, he usually endures a prolonged period of sickness and crisis which is brought on by the arrival of tutelary familiar spirits (*akuan*) who later guard and guide him in his encounters in the spirit world. During the crisis he is completely dependent upon the community to look after him. To facilitate his recovery and to conduct him into his full powers, the community hosts a performance of the initiatory form of shamanic ritual called *belian pole*. Unlike all other forms of *belian*, which take only one night to perform, *belian pole* is conducted over three nights. A major part of the performance on the second night takes place in the open air on a ritual scaffolding (*balai*), the design of which may vary according to particular needs of the ritual. Whereas other forms of *belian* are rites of transformation in which the *kemantan* undergoes a temporary change of state and status, *belian pole* is a rite of passage through which the novice *kemantan* becomes initiated into his full status, a status which he retains for the rest of his life. As long as he remains ritually active, the community which he serves keeps a close check on him for any signs that the crisis may be returning. At the first sign of a relapse, he must undergo another *belian pole*.

4. Social Structure and Origins of *Belian*

Belian performances are always public occasions, and participation in the preparations and performance are held to be public responsibilities. Everyone in the village contributes to the successful mounting of *belian*, by helping to collect building materials from the forest, by assisting in the preparation of the needed ritual artifacts and by attending the night-time performance. Their contributions, however, are not made on an ad hoc basis. Rather they follow the directions of a matriarch, the *tuo longkap* (the complete old-one), whose knowledge and skills have been acquired through apprenticeship to a previous *tuo longkap*. She is symbolically, and often literally, the wife of the *kemantan*.

Petalangan society is governed by an hierarchically organized body of men consisting of heads of villages and leaders of the eight kinship groups. However, they are also subservient to the authority of the *tuo longkap* as the community focuses upon the tasks of preparing for and performing *belian*. The main roles of the *tuo longkap* are to mediate between the community and the *kemantan* and to consult with him about the type of ritual preparations needed. It is she who decides upon the date and place for the performance, delegates the responsibilities for overseeing the collection of materials and preparation of ritual artifacts and secures the services of several ritual assistants (*bujang belian*), including two male musicians to play the *ketobung* drum. The social and ritual success of the occasion depends largely upon her knowledge of ritual matters and her social skill in organizing the community.

It is helpful to refer to the origin story of *belian* in order to understand, more fully, the role of the *tuo longkap* and her relationship with the *kemantan*, the community, the two realms of the cosmos and the *ketobung* drum. The story is as follows:

A healer called Datuk Alam (Lord of Nature) and his wife, Puti Bunyian (Princess of the Invisible Folk), lived in peace and happiness by carefully observing the articles of faith. Several years after they had been married, Puti Bunyian became pregnant and began to crave for the taste of a *seminai* fruit. She implored her husband to go into the forest to obtain the fruit for her. However, as a healer it was utterly forbidden for Datuk Alam to pick the *seminai* fruit. To explain his refusal, he told her: "If I bring you a *seminai* fruit we will certainly be punished. For one of the conditions binding my magical healing power is that I am forbidden to pick the *seminai* fruit." Still, Puti Bunyian would not contain her longing, and she continued to press Datuk Alam. Finally, moved by her tears, he went into the forest to get a piece of *seminai* fruit for her. However, the instant that he presented it to her, he started to fade from her sight. When Puti Bunyian realized that Datuk Alam was completely hidden from her, she cried with remorse.

Several months later, when Puti Bunyian felt that the birth of her child was imminent, she prayed to Duwato that she might be with her husband once again. Her prayers were answered one night when an image of Datuk Alam appeared before her. He gave her some medication to ensure her safety and to ease her childbirth, and then he disappeared again. Saddened but hopeful, Puti Bunyian then prayed that her husband would always be with her, albeit in spirit only. Eventually, Duwato spoke from the sky to Puti Bunyian, telling her that whenever she or her grandchildren wished to meet Datuk Alam, or wished to request his help, they should perform a *belian* ritual. To prepare for the ritual, she would need incense (*gau*) and an incense burner, an arrangement of flowers, a candle and a firebrand. In addition, she should construct a miniature house, boat and raft and a drum known as a *ketobung*. Then, if she would light the candle and firebrand, burn some incense, beat the *ketobung* drum and cry out to Datuk Alam, he would appear once again on earth before her (Effendi n.d.: 22-24; edited translation by A. Turner).

The story of Datuk Alam and Puti Bunyian shows a close conceptual link between *belian* and the events which originally led to the division of the once-unified cosmos (*see* Figure 6). The attachment of the shamanic drum to such ancient and powerful thoughts invests the *ketobung* drum with a degree of symbolic and emotional meaning shared by no other musical instrument. Whenever it is struck, it invokes a set of musical, social and cosmologic relations which link everyday reality to the mythical past.

```
┌─────────────────────────────────────────────────────┐
│                                                       │
│                  ACTOR RELATIONS                      │
│                                                       │
│         Kemantan        :      Tuo  longkap          │
│                                                       │
│         Datuk Alam      :      Puti  Bunyian         │
│                                                       │
│         Father          :      Mother               │
│                                                       │
│         Healer          :      Patient              │
│                                                       │
│                                                       │
│                SPATIAL RELATIONS                      │
│                                                       │
│      Invisible  realm   :      Visible  realm       │
│                                                       │
│      Macrocosm          :      Ritual  house        │
│                                                       │
│      Sky                :      Earth                │
│                                                       │
│                                                       │
│              TEMPORAL RELATIONS                       │
│                                                       │
│      Period  prior  to  disjunction  of  cosmos     │
│                                                       │
│                        ::                            │
│                                                       │
│   Ritual  time  evoked  through  belian   performance│
│                                                       │
└─────────────────────────────────────────────────────┘
```

Figure 6: Some structural relations contained in the origin story of *belian*

5. The *Ketobung* Drum as Artifact and Symbol

Double-headed drums are by far the most common musical instruments among the Petalangan. Generally speaking, there are two types of drums: ordinary drums (*gondang biaso*) and drums used for shamanic rituals. The primary musical distinction between the *ketobung* drum and other drums is its sound quality and its repertoire. The *ketobung* drum is tuned much higher than other drums, and the timbre is required to be especially rich in overtones (*bunyi alui*). Its repertoire consists entirely of rhythms (*i'amo ketobung*) associated with shamanic ritual, whereas ordinary drums may play a variety of trance and non-trance music.

Non-shamanic drums usually occur in complementary pairs which provide the basis of an ensemble used to accompany dancing based on the art of self-defence (*silat*). However, the *ketobung* drum has no twin and is always played alone. A parallel condition exists for the *kemantan* who is regarded symbolically as the unmated ninety-ninth child of *Nobi Adam* (the Prophet Adam). The *kemantan*, who usually lives on the periphery of the village, is often regarded as being slightly estranged from the rest of the community, even from his own wife. This is due in part to the villagers' fear of his esoteric knowledge but also to his intrinsic condition as a man who lives continually between two worlds. Even his wife must be ever-vigilant against the competing affections of an *o'ang bunyian* spirit-wife who continually seeks to lure the *kemantan* to remain permanently with her in the spirit world.

The *ketobung* drum is defined by the Petalangan community primarily by its association with the *kemantan* as well as by its attendant ritual function. Thus, it is also called *gondang kemantan* (the shaman's drum) and *gondang belian* (lit., *belian* drum). It forms a part of the *kemantan's* personal ritual paraphernalia, though he never actually plays it himself. Although the *ketobung* drum is thought of as being different from other drums, its distinction is mainly ideological rather than physical. If the *kemantan's* own drum is broken or otherwise unavailable, it may be replaced by an ordinary double-headed drum. In such an event the substituted drum is thought to become (*menjadi*) a *ketobung* drum and is referred to by that name while being played.

One of the objects symbolized by the *ketobung* drum is the human body. Petalangan society places great emphasis upon correct bodily attire, presentation, carriage and control. Great importance is also placed upon accurate representation of the human body through the *ketobung* drum. The body (*badan*) of the drum consists of a hollow wooden cylinder with a length between 65 cm and 70 cm. It represents the human trunk and torso. It is slightly barrel-shaped, with a waist diameter of about 30 cm; and it tapers from the waist to the ends. One head is always slightly smaller than the other, giving the instrument an asymmetry which allows for unmistakable recognition of its head (*kopalo*) and posterior (*buntut*). This asymmetry, which is usually less pronounced in ordinary drums, prevents the *ketobung* drum from being placed inadvertently upon its head. In the waist of the drum a small hole, which symbolizes the human naval (*pusat*), allows the air pressure within the drum to remain in equilibrium with the pressure outside. Goat or deer skin is stretched over each end. Parallel strips of split-cane, representing tendons and veins (*urat*), fasten each skin to a separate plaited cane collar near the waist of the drum. The two collars are held taut by fourteen wooden pegs (seven for each collar) corresponding to the fourteen human ribs. A lacing of braided bark cord, which zig-zags between the collars, helps to maintain the relative pitch of the two skins. An integral part of the *ketobung* drum is a half-metre-long cane beater which corresponds to the human index finger (*ja'i telunjuk*). In keeping with its status as a symbol of humanity (*tando manusio*), the *ketobung* drum is usually slightly larger and more robustly constructed than other drums. Drawn on the inside is a chalk figure of a man (Plate 2).

Plate 2: *Kemantan Lembang Alam*

This figure represents humanity as a whole, the familiar spirit who occupies the drum during *belian*, and an ancestral spirit called *Kemantan Lembang Alam* (the *kemantan* who symbolizes the cosmos) who is one of the shaman's own spirit-mentors (*gu'u*).

Whereas an ordinary drum can be constructed relatively quickly and with no need for ceremony, a *ketobung* drum must be fashioned with painstaking care and meticulous regard for the appropriate rituals, especially during transformational stages of its construction when the drum is especially vulnerable to ritual pollution. Care is particularly important during the felling of the tree from which the drum is to be carved. The *ketobung* drum is usually fashioned from the bough of a *merbau, meranti, tontang, gau* or *loso* tree. However, *merbau* or *gau* are favoured because of their status as sacred trees (*kayu sati*). A sign of their sacredness is the presence of red gum which symbolizes blood. Whichever type of wood is used to construct a *ketobung* drum, the tree from which it is cut is regarded metaphorically as the world-tree (*kayu alam*) and cosmic axis which connects the earth with the sky. In the symbolic domain of shamanic ritual, the *kemantan* ascends the world-tree in order to visit the spirits.

Both *ketobung* drum makers and shamans need to be well-versed in knowledge about the cosmological significance of the world-tree. This body of esoteric knowledge is called *kaji Nobi Adam* (the Prophet Adam's knowledge). In accordance with Islamic mystical teachings (*tarekat*), Petalangan people believe that as well as the gifts of intellect (*akal*) and soul (*jiwa*), Allah bestowed upon mankind certain esoteric knowledge. As the first man in Allah's creation, the Prophet Adam received mankind's first instalment; and the *kemantan* is regarded as one of its custodians. At the heart of this body of knowledge is knowledge about the origins of the *gau* tree (*kaji induk gau*) which concerns the relationship between the world-tree as the central axis of the macrocosm and the human placental cord as the central axis of the microcosm. Thus, Petalangan midwives are also versed in Nobi Adam's esoteric knowledge about the world-tree.

The *ketobung* drum is one artifact within a class of ritual objects and paraphernalia which the *kemantan* inherited from his predecessor. These artifacts include a bell-chime bracelet (*gonto*), a cloth veil and a woven mat. During *belian*, these objects contribute to the reconstruction of the world-tree metaphor, the bell-chime bracelet being its fruit, the cloth veil being its leaves, the mat being the carpet of fallen leaves at the foot of the world-tree and the drum being its trunk. The *ketobung* drum, then, is an integral part of the composite world-tree which the *kemantan* ascends (*naik*) to gain access to the macrocosm. The *kemantan* also envisages the world-tree to be within his own body. Thus, the *ketobung* drum is implicit in both microcosm and macrocosm through its relation to the human body and the world-tree (*see* Figure 7).

	MICROCOSM	
kemantan	(internalizes)	world-tree
ketobung	(body symbol)	kemantan
	MACROCOSM	
kemantan	(ascends)	world-tree
ketobung	(represents/made from)	world-tree

Figure 7: Triadic relations between the *kemantan*, the *ketobung* drum and the world-tree

6. Musical Structures and Petalangan Social Structures

The *ketobung* drum is always played by two men, both of whom must be versed in the esoteric symbolism of the instrument. Sitting cross-legged on the floor, one player supports the *ketobung* drum under an arm and beats the smaller head with both hands. The other player, perched on his haunches at the back of the drum, strikes the rear skin with a cane beater and damps it with his free hand. The part played by the first drummer, called the *penyelalu* (always), consists of a continuous and cyclic succession of five to ten beats per second. A repeating series of rim-shots interspersed through this continuum creates the characteristic rhythmic figure which identifies each particular rhythmic pattern (*see below* Section 7: Figure 9). There are more than fifty such patterns, each associated with particular spirits, particular stages of the ritual and the shaman's journey, and particular styles of shamanic dancing. As many as twenty-five different rhythmic patterns may be played during a single ritual.

The part played on the rear skin of the drum is called the *peningka* (interjector). The *peningka* rhythm is said to derive from the *penyelalu* rhythm. However, whereas the *penyelalu* part constitutes an unambiguous pattern of high and low pitches, the *peningka* often articulates new patterns of accents, causing the *penyelalu* to be heard from different rhythmic perspectives (*see* Figure 8). The combined effect of the *peningka*

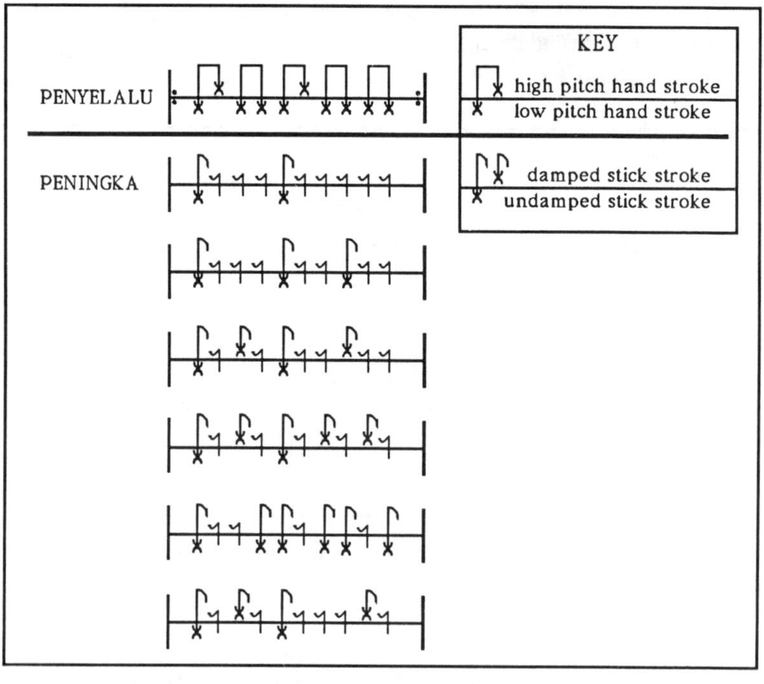

Figure 8: Rhythmic components of shamanic drumming form a figure/ ground relationship [the transcription is to be read from top left to bottom right]

and the *penyelalu* is a shifting figure-and-ground pattern, the high pitched rim- shots and accents forming the figure against a continuous and undifferentiated rhythmic ground. If played properly, the two rhythms are said to fuse together to produce a higher order of rhythmic complexity and unity called *suao duwato* (the voice of the deity). The *kemantan* is particularly sensitive to this rhythmic fusion. Until fusion is achieved, the *kemantan* cannot enter into trance or travel in the cosmos.

To bring about the fusion of *penyelalu* and *peningka* rhythms, players need to practise the highest degree of cooperation. Petalangan drummers say that during a performance, the *ketobung* drum and its two players become a single entity (*jadi satu*). The term used to describe the fusion of the two rhythmic components is *ikut* (join, participate). The *peningka* joins the *penyelalu* in such a manner that their beats compliment each other exactly. The term *ikut* is often applied in a social sense, the idea being that when an individual joins with others in cooperative action, the whole community benefits. Indeed, the welfare of the individual and of the community are regarded as inseparable. Everyone engages in cooperative work to ensure that agricultural projects, ritual occasions and social events are successful. The cooperative efforts made by individuals towards the mounting of a successful healing ritual are seen as benefiting the whole community.

However, even though members of Petalangan society are expected to submit to the general good, the community's most prized resources are generally recognized to be the talents of its individuals. So long as the interests of the individual and the community coincide, individual expression is nurtured through a system of rewards based upon increased social status. Those whom the community judges to be the finest practitioners of the plastic, performing and ritual arts participate in an organization of esteemed elders called *pemuko adat* (the face of customs) who make up the rank-and-file of village government.

7. The Performance Context

The *ketobung* drum is never played outside its proper context for fear of bringing misfortune upon the community. The *kemantan* is particularly vulnerable because of his sensitivity to the power of the drum. The prohibition against sounding the *ketobung* drum finishes at dawn on the day of the performance (*a'i belian*), when the first task for the appointed players is to retrieve the drum from its previous performance venue and to check it for any necessary repairs. Throughout the day the players tune and re-tune the *ketobung* drum so that by the time of the performance it holds a high pitch with ease. This repairing, tuning and re-tuning is believed to be very important, because, if for some reason the skins were to go slack after the *kemantan* had commenced his journey in the cosmos, he could become immobilized (*kebatangan*) and unable to return.

The players use the daytime to familiarize themselves with some of the more difficult rhythms and to teach novices. As well as ensuring that the *kemantan* and the community are provided with many competent and well-practiced drummers for *belian*, the day-time rehearsal serves several other important functions. Firstly, the sound of the *ketobung* drum informs everyone in the district, including people in neighbouring villages, that a shamanic ritual is in preparation. Like other modes of communal activity, an important condition of the *belian* ritual is that it be well attended. If not, the *kemantan's* journey is likely to be fraught with difficulty. The sounding of the *ketobung* drum during daytime ensures that the community is adequately reminded of their social responsibility to attend the forthcoming performance.

Secondly, the *ketobung* drum provides a musical, emotional and symbolic background for the intensive work in which everyone in the village participates as they prepare the ritual houses and ritual objects which will later house the deities. Labour is distributed between several work parties, some of which need to venture deep into the forest to obtain special varieties of cane and wood. It is believed that the sound of the *ketobung* drum is so powerful that it penetrates into the deepest parts of the forest, thus providing an acoustic beacon linking the work parties in the forest with the work parties in the village. Furthermore, the messages inherent in the *ketobung* drum are thought to form a link between the various work parties.

Thirdly, the rehearsal time provides a rare occasion for people to enjoy *ketobung* drum music in its own right. The day preceding a *belian* performance is the only time during which the *ketobung* drum is heard outside the ritual context, though its playing is sanctioned by the imminence of the performance. It is said that *ketobung* drum music in this daytime context is most enjoyable around sunset, when it begins to exert a powerful effect upon listeners.

The *ketobung* drum's communicative power reaches its peak just prior to and during the performance of *belian*, when it is said to inform all sentient beings (*segalo makluk*) in the cosmos that a ritual is in progress. By day the *ketobung* drum is played intermittently, but after nightfall the *ketobung* drum sounds almost continuously and with a vigour which players say is made possible by charms (*monto*) which they use to invoke inner strength (*tenago batin*). Certain charms are also believed to compel the attention of anyone who hears the *ketobung* drum. Anyone not already attending the ritual is believed to be drawn to the performance venue by the sound of the *ketobung* drum.

During *belian*, the *ketobung* drum provides a continuous musical background to the ritual activities surrounding the *kemantan's* entry into trance and his subsequent journey in the spirit realm. The *ketobung* drum's perceived relationship to the performance and to the participants changes continuously throughout the ritual. The drum rhythms are the object of direct audience attention while they accompany the shaman's dancing. This is especially so during the initial danced stages of the ritual, when the shaman bows deeply before the *ketobung* drum as a sign of respect to the occupying spirit. However, the drumming fades rapidly into the background of attention whenever the *kemantan* attends to other ritual activities.

The first stage in the performance proper is a sanctifying and cleansing ritual, during which the *kemantan* invokes the presence and protection of his three familiar spirits, *Akuan Sati, Akuan Sidi* and *Akuan Bu'ung Kopalo Ompat*. Each familiar spirit has a specific region of responsibility in the world-tree and in the body of the *kemantan*, and each has a role to play in protecting the *kemantan* against spirit-attack and ensuring that his journey in the cosmos is fruitful. *Akuan Sati* (sacred akuan) resides in the roots of the world-tree and in the legs and feet of the *kemantan* and assists by sanctifying the re-created cosmos. *Akuan Sidi* (wise akuan), who resides in the trunk of the world-tree and in the hips and waist of the *kemantan*, directs the *kemantan* throughout the journey by means of his knowledge of the layout of the cosmos. *Akuan Bu'ung Kepalo Ompat* (four-headed bird), who resides in the canopy of the world-tree and behind the eyes of the *kemantan*, alerts the *kemantan* to danger and instructs him in the protocol needed to deal with other spirits. During this stage, one of the drum players quietly recites a mantra invoking *Akuan Sidi*, the spirit-familiar responsible for guiding the *kemantan*, to take up residence within the drum (Plate 3). The *ketobung* drum is then said to be alive (*idup*) and mature (*tuo*).

The players then start to play the rhythm, *pejongkuan* (*see* Figure 9), while the *kemantan*, who sits down with a red veil covering his head, conducts himself into trance. His initial entry into trance occurs while he sings a mantra which maps the macrocosm (*alam godang*) onto the microcosm within his own body (*alam dalam di'i*: the cosmos within oneself). A second mantra recasts the microcosm of his body in the form of the world-tree, the trunk of which is represented by the *ketobung* drum. Thus, the *kemantan* creates a multi-referential symbolic domain in which the microcosm of his own body is linked through ritual event and ritual space with the greater cosmos. The multi-referentiality of the *ketobung* drum includes: (1) its concrete existence as a musical instrument and emblem of shamanic power; (2) its representation of the trunk of the symbolically present world-tree which the *kemantan* ascends to the spirit realm; (3) its role as the material 'body' of a spirit-being which guides the *kemantan*; and (4) its symbolic presence in the body of the transformed *kemantan*.

Only after these symbolic internalizations and transformations are complete does the *kemantan* signal to the drum players to stop playing *pejongkuan*. His signal is to give the ever-sounding bell-chime bracelet around his wrist three or four sharp shakes in time with the drumming. At

Plate 3: A musician invokes the *ketobung* drum's resident spirit.

this point he is no longer referred to as *kemantan* but rather *kemantan mudo* (lit., the young *kemantan*), a term indicating his change of status from a healer in society to a prototypical embodiment of the healer in and of the cosmos. He is now ready to begin his journey, starting with a succession of rhythms called *naik tujuh* (sevenfold ascension) which creates a conduit between the visible realm of ritual action and the cosmic realm in which the *kemantan mudo* needs to journey (*see* Figure 9).

Naik tujuh consists of eight rhythms. Each change of rhythm constitutes

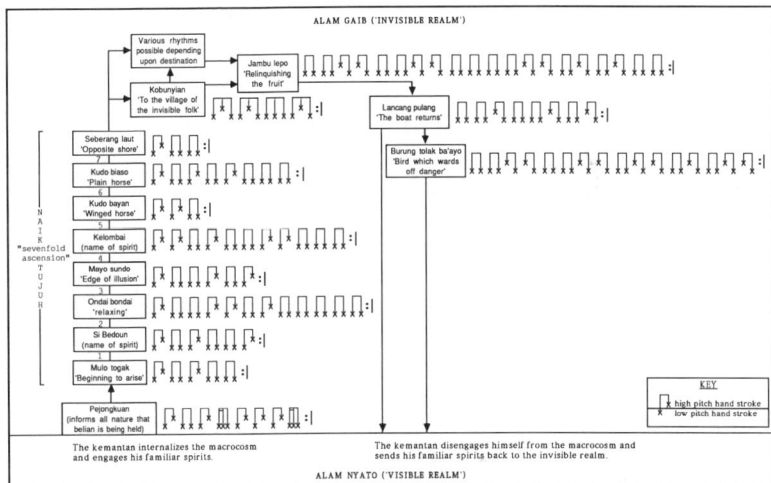

Figure 9: The shaman's cosmic journey is facilitated by a succession of drum rhythms [transcriptions are based on the *penyelalu* parts only]

a single step within the ascension. This is a critical stage in the journey of the *kemantan mudo* because of his vulnerability while existing between worlds. To establish a continuity between the material world and the spirit world, the drum players must perform the eight rhythms as an organic whole, executing each change perfectly without losing rhythmic momentum. The players take their rhythmic cues from the *kemantan mudo*, who indicates each rhythmic change by stamping his foot in time with the new stress pattern. Every shaman with whom I spoke claimed that it was not he himself but rather the familiar spirit residing within the drum, *Akuan Sidi*, who distinguishes between the various drum rhythms. As the *kemantan* ascends, his trance intensifies. Occasionally, he attempts to break free from the prepared ritual space by violently head-butting the sturdy uprights of the house in which the performance is taking place. The fact that he appears unharmed by the apparently massive blows to his head is taken by the excited and noisy audience as a sign of his increasing detachment from the constraints of material existence.

In the symbolic realm of the shaman's journey, the sevenfold ascension has four different levels of meaning. Firstly, it is an ascension of the world-tree which connects the earth and the sky. Secondly, it is a reconstruction of the human body, beginning with a handful of earth (*sakopal tana mulo jadi*, lit., a handful of earth begins to become [human]). Thus, the ascension process provides a systematic means for the *kemantan* to survey the macrocosm while internalizing it within the microcosm of his own body. At a third level of symbolism, the continuity created by the sevenfold ascension represents the human placental cord, which Petalangan midwives traditionally tie with seven pieces of string. Thus, the ascension process also provides a means for the symbolic rejoining of the *kemantan* to his biological origins and, by extension, to the source of his spiritual existence. The fourth level of symbolism is available, however, only to people who have entered into a formal teaching relationship with the *kemantan*. This level is referred to as the *keputusan kaji* (mastery of esoteric knowledge), in which all the layers of symbols condense to form a single supreme truth (*akekat*).

If all goes well, the ascension may take only a few minutes. If the *kemantan mudo* encounters problems (for instance, if he experiences the adverse influence of an antagonistic agent), his ascension may take up to an hour, during which time the drummers must play with unrelenting vigour. Occasionally, a player needs to be replaced after a particularly arduous ascent, because his physical and spiritual energy has been expended. Another problem which drummers may face during prolonged playing is the splitting of the skin on their palms and finger-tips. If this happens it is taken to be a sign that the player lacks the necessary inner strength or that his physical energy has been depleted.

With the continuity between worlds already secured through the ascension process, the drummers await further instructions from the *kemantan mudo*, who may address them formally with the words: *Wasalamallaikum bujang nobat, kami mau ko koto bunyian* (God's peace be with you, servants of the royal drum, we now wish to go to the village of the invisible folk). The drummers then begin to play the rhythm, *kobunyian*, a rhythm based upon triplets, prompting the *kemantan mudo* to perambulate in a particular lop-sided gait associated with the rhythm. His task is to seek access to a powerful spirit-mentor who can advise him about the availability of a cure for the particular sickness or misfortune which first prompted the request for a *belian* performance. The function of the *kobunyian* rhythm is to conduct the *kemantan mudo* to the village of the invisible folk, where several such spirit mentors reside. Depending upon the advice he receives, he might then ask his drummers to play other rhythms conducting him to other mentors, until finally he may locate the particular mentor who specializes in the remedy he is seeking. If a cure is obtained, the *kemantan mudo* dispenses it to the patient and other recipients among the audience by a laying on of hands and other symbolic gestures.

During the penultimate stage of the ritual, the *kemantan mudo* sings his thanks and praise to his spirit-mentors while the drummers beat the rhythm, *jambu lepo* (relinquishing the fruit). When the *kemantan mudo* finally wishes to return to his mundane state, he signals to his drummers to play the rhythm, *lancang pulang* (the boat returns). If he encounters difficulty in returning to mortal reality, it may be necessary to use an alternative rhythm, *bu'ung tolak ba ayo* (the bird which wards off danger), which is believed to invoke a powerful bird to carry the shaman home. When he has finally returned, he signals to the drummers to cease playing by giving his bell-chime bracelet another three or four sharp shakes. His final ritual act is to recite a charm which is intended to send his familiar spirits back to the spirit realm. The *ketobung* drum is then put away into a yellow or white cloth bag, where it remains until the next performance.

Although the principal actor in *belian* is the shaman, the audience also plays an important role in the ritual. Referred to corporately by the *kemantan* as *anak asuan* (children in his care), members of the audience are the main beneficiaries of the healing ritual. The shaman's performance provides an opportunity for the whole community to experience and participate directly in the therapeutic reunification of the cosmos. It is rare for members of the audience to experience directly the transformation undergone by the *kemantan*. If someone falls into trance, it is taken by the community as a sign of latent shamanic power or possession by a spirit, including one of the shaman's own familiar spirits. Such a person will need to receive formal training from the *kemantan* so that his or her powers can be brought under control. Alternatively, the *kemantan* can intervene through therapeutic ritual to remove the latent power of the novice by adding it to that of his own entourage of attendant spirits. For most people in the audience, *belian* represents an opportunity to witness and participate in the re-making of the cosmos. Nevertheless, they are sharply aware of the communal role which they play in the transformation of the mundane to the sacred. The rhythms of the *ketobung* drum provide one of the main triggers for the transformative experience of shaman and audience alike.

Selected Glossary of Petalangan Terms associated with Shamanic Ritual

Akuan Bu'ung Kopalo Ompat: familiar spirit who takes the form of a four-headed bird

Akuan Sati: name of a familiar spirit who sacralizes the cosmos

Akuan Sidi: name of a familiar spirit who knows the layout of the cosmos

anak asuan: lit., nursing-children; the general public who are in the shaman's care.

anggung: lit., ascending; possession trance ritual

belian: lit., a purchase; shamanic ritual

belian bainang: shamanic ritual for pregnancy

belian gegawe: shamanic ritual for obtaining a protective talisman

belian membaye utang: shamanic ritual for repaying a debt to the intervening spirits

belian obat biaso: shamanic ritual for ordinary sickness

belian pole: shamanic ritual for initiating or healing a shaman

bu'ung tolak ba'ayo: lit., a bird which wards off danger; a drum rhythm invoking a powerful bird to carry the shaman home

bujang nobat: player of the shamanic drum

Datuk Alam: Lord of Nature

gau: forest tree; produces an aromatic resin which is used in rituals; its wood may be used to construct a *ketobung* drum

gondang belian: lit., *belian* drum; see also *ketobung*

gondang kemantan: lit., the shaman's drum

ikut: to join, participate

jambu lepo: lit., relinquishing the fruit; drum rhythm

kaji Nobi Adam: lit., the Prophet Adam's knowledge; knowledge about the cosmological significance of the world-tree

kemantan: shaman

Kemantan Lembang Alam: lit., the shaman who symbolizes the cosmos; name of spirit whose figure is drawn inside the *ketobung* drum

kemantan mudo: lit., young shaman; ritually transformed shaman

keputusan kaji: mastery of esoteric religious knowledge

ketobung: shaman's drum

kobunyian: lit., to the village of the invisible folk; drum rhythm

lancang pulang: lit., returning boat; the drum rhythm invoking the boat by which the shaman usually returns from the realm of the spirits

loso: forest tree; may be used to construct a *ketobung* drum

main Adin: lit., playing the spirit Adin; possession trance ritual in which the dancers become possessed by the spirit Adin

main dewo: possession trance ritual in which the dancers become possessed by celestial spirits

meranti: forest tree; may be used to construct a *ketobung* drum

merbau: forest tree; may be used to construct a *ketobung* drum

naik tujuh: lit., sevenfold ascension; succession of eight drum rhythms by which the shaman ascends into the cosmos

Nobi Adam: the Prophet Adam

o'ang bunyian: lit., sound-people; human-like beings who live in the invisible realm

pejongkuan: first drum rhythm played to conduct the shaman into his trance

pemuko adat: lit., face of customs; a body of esteemed social and cultural leaders who form the rank and file of Petalangan village government

peningka: lit., interjector; intermittent rhythm played on the rear skin of the *ketobung* drum

penyelalu: lit., always; continuous rhythm played on the front skin of the
   ketobung drum
Puti Bunyian: Princess of the invisible folk
seminai: forest fruit which Datuk Alam was forbidden to pick
suao duwato: lit., voice of the deity; a higher order rhythmic unity
   produced by the fusion of the two rhythmic components of the
   ketobung drum
tontang: forest tree; may be used to construct a *ketobung* drum
tuo longkap: lit., the complete old-one; female director who organizes the
   community as it prepares for a shamanic ritual

Acknowledgments

The case study presented above is based upon eleven months of continuous
fieldwork in the Petalangan region in 1984 and 1985, during which time I
worked with several shamans. However, the interpretation of shamanic
practice and symbolism presented in this paper is based mainly upon
information provided by Pak Bantu, a ritually active shaman in the village
of Betung in the sub-district of Pengkalan Kuras on mainland Riau. While
the details of shamanic traditions which I encountered in other Petalangan
villages tended to vary, the underlying patterns remained the same.

I am grateful for the assistance rendered by numerous Petalangan
cultural leaders and, in particular, Bapak Tenas Effendi who first
introduced me to the Petalangan people and who acted as my guide,
informant and adopted father for the duration of the fieldwork. I am also
grateful to the Indonesian Institute of Science (LIPI) under whose auspices
my fieldwork was conducted, and the Department of Music at Monash
University for providing field equipment and other assistance. The Centre
for Southeast Asian Studies at Monash University provided partial
funding for the project which has served as the basis of my Ph.D.
dissertation (Monash University, in progress).

Thanks are also due to Prof. Margaret Kartomi, Dr Steven Feld,
Dr Jamie Kassler and Dr Judith Becker for reading drafts of this paper and
for their invaluable comments.

References

EFFENDI, Tenas
   n.d.   'Uraian Singkat tentang Upacara Belian' (A Brief Analysis of
          the *Belian* Ritual), Pekanbaru, Riau: Unpublished paper
ELIADE, M.
   1964   *Shamanism: Archaic Techniques of Ecstasy*, Princeton:
          Princeton University Press
ENDICOTT, K. M.
   1970   *An Analysis of Malay Magic*, Oxford: Clarendon Press

146 METAPHOR — A MUSICAL DIMENSION

FELD, S.
   1983 'Sound as a Symbolic System: The Kaluli Drum', *Bikmaus* 4(3): 78-89
KARTOMI, M. J.
   1983 'Music Aesthetics in Ethnomusicology with Particular Reference to Analogies in Mandailing Artistic and Philosophical Thought', Unpublished paper
LAIRD, P.
   1978 'Temoq Shamanism and Affliction: A Preliminary Investigation', Unpublished Ph.D. dissertation, Monash University
   1983 'Temoq Shamanism', Unpublished paper read at Monash University, Centre for Southeast Asian Studies, 20 July 1983
NEHER, A.
   1962 'A Physiological Explanation of Unusual Behaviour in Ceremonies Involving Drums', *Human Biology* 1: 151-60
REINHARD, J.
   1976 'Shamanism and Spirit Possession: The Definition Problem', in T.J. Hitchcock and R.L. Jones (eds.), *Spirit Possession in the Nepal Himalayas*, Warminster: Aris and Phillips, 12-20
ROUGET, G.
   1985 *Music and Trance: A Theory of the Relations between Music and Possession*, Chicago: University of Chicago Press (1st edn. 1980)
SKEAT, W. W.
   1965 *Malay Magic*, London: Frank Cass and Co. Ltd. (1st edn. 1900)
WINSTEDT, R. O.
   1961 *The Malay Magician being Shaman, Saiva and Sufi*, London: Routledge and Kegan Paul

Musical Modes and the Medical Dimension: The Arabic Sources (c.900-c.1600)

Amnon Shiloah

Abstract

The keen belief in the overwhelming power of music follows the development of ideas connecting music with medical effects and properties. Subsequently, cosmological speculation is linked to the concrete application of modes (both rhythmical and melodical) in healing treatment. The latter practical aspect led naturally to the principal question: should the musician possess medical qualifications, or, inversely, the physician be versed in the science of music? By reference to evidence drawn in the sources, the author assumes that musico-therapy belongs more to the musician who acts in this respect as an auxiliary to the physician, although he concedes that physicians may also be musicians.

Introduction

From the ninth to the sixteenth centuries, many Arabic sources provide details about the doctrine of music therapy. This doctrine incorporated aspects of the theories of medicine and music. Medical theory was indebted chiefly to Aristotle's doctrine of mixture (Hall 1969). According to this doctrine, physicians established four humours of the human body—blood, yellow bile, black bile and phlegm—by analogy to the four cosmic elements (earth, air, fire, water). They also envisaged four qualities of matter—heat, dryness, moisture and cold—consisting of two pairs of opposites. They then ascribed all material existence to the various mixtures of the four elements and qualities. Accordingly, the doctrine of mixture could account for climate or temperature (caused by a mixture of the four basic qualities) as well as for the different temperaments of people—sanguinic, choleric, melancholic and phlegmatic (caused by a mixture of the four humours that make up the body and the four qualities that make up the climate).

Medieval Arabic musical theory is like a convergence of interlocked ideas and trends. Its blossoming coincided with the highest development of Muslim civilization which reached its zenith at the ninth and tenth centuries. The study of music was then part of the sum of encyclopedic knowledge that every learned man had to acquire. This period saw also the advent of a new type of writing on music which came into being as a result of contacts with the Greek treatises which were being translated into Arabic. This new type represents two major orientations: one focussed mainly on mathematical and acoustical speculations dealing with the elements of music, the science of melody and rhythm; the other treated the conception of harmony as order, linking music with cosmology. In this latter orientation, the study of music was considered as a key to understanding the principles presiding over the universe.

The harmony of all celestial and earthly phenomena was expounded chiefly by means of number. Hence, arithmetical speculations (arithmology) were used to explain the governing principles in the universe as well as in the construction of musical instruments and the compositions of melodies and rhythms. Of all old Arabic sources the tenth-century 'Epistle of Music' of the Brethren of Purity brought numerical symbolism to its most developed form. In their speculations on the properties of numbers, the number four—and by extention the quaternities or fourfold structures—received the highest symbolical consideration. In the 'Epistle of Music' the focal point was the classical *'ūd* or short-necked lute, a favourite musical instrument used also for purpose of didactical demonstration in all theoretical writings. The *'ūd* was indeed strung with four strings, stretched in such a way to sound a fourth apart of each other. Since the predominance of the number four was said to be 'comparable to the natural things' and 'in the image of the science of the Creator', it was supposed that the four strings were comparable to such quaternities as the four elements, qualities, humours, temperaments, seasons, weeks of the month and phases of the moon.

In this paper I draw on a select number of Arabic writings that contain information about the relations between medicine and the musical modes.[1] In order to ascertain the roles of the physician and the musician, I describe three different viewpoints—philosophical, medical and musical. First, I summarize the philosophical viewpoint as contained in the writings of the ninth-century philosopher, al-Kindī, and the tenth-century philosophical sect, Brethren of Purity (Ikhwān al-Ṣafā). Second, I survey the physician's viewpoint as found in the writings of ibn Hindū (d. 1019), ibn Sīna (d. 1037) and al-Anṭākī (d. 1599). Third, I use two anonymous sources as representative of the musical point of view. On the basis of these sources, I draw some conclusions about the respective roles of physician and musician in music therapy.

1. Music Therapy as a Component of Universal Harmony: The Philosopher's Point of View

The first manifestation of ideas linking music, or specific melody types, with medical properties and effects goes back to the earliest Arabic sources that have come down to us and which date from the ninth century. At that period the association of the medical dimension with music was integrated into cosmology, in which speculative music was a model of the order of all things, as well as a science of the harmonic relationships of the universe; and practical music was viewed as a power capable of exerting marvelous effects on the human body and soul.

This approach is particularly evident in the musical writings of the ninth-century philosopher, al-Kindī, who wrote several treatises in which he set forth his ideas regarding the marvelous effect of music. In his lesser-known treatise consisting of three discourses, *Book of Sounding Stringed Instruments, of one to ten strings* (Shiloah 1979: 254-5), he attributes the effect of music to musical instruments; and he also advances one or two ideas that may help us in our attempt to understand the various links between musical modes and medicine.

In the first discourse of his treatise, al-Kindī says:

The instruments help in creating harmony between the soul and the universe. Each people has instruments that reflect their nature and each instrument is said to express the specific beliefs and characteristics of the group to which it belongs. Therefore the skilled musician should make acquaintance in advance with all possible cases, so that he is able to adapt his music to any given situation, like the physician who diagnoses his patients before prescribing suitable treatment.

In the third discourse, al-Kindī characterizes the *'ūd* as the instrument of the philosophers par excellence. This instrument, according to al-Kindī, is used for arithmological and cosmological speculations, because it demonstrates the affiliations of its four strings with the elliptic arcs, Zodiac, position of the stars, seasons, days, ages, elements, words, humours, colours, faculties of the soul and temperaments.

From this brief summary it follows that the musician should develop diagnostic skills parallel to those of the physician in order, like him, to prescribe the suitable treatment. Does this imply that the musician should therefore have some knowledge of medicine or, inversely, the physician some knowledge of music? As far as al-Kindī is concerned, this remains a matter of speculation, although a hint as to what the nature of the musical treatment should be is included in the correspondences of the *'ūd's* four strings. In theory, the *'ūd*, represents a symbolic network of cosmic correspondences; in practice, it is a tranquilizing, introverting and elevating (sublimatory) instrument, like the Greek lyre and the Biblical *kinnor* in the story of David and Saul (I. Samuel 16, 23).[2] In contrast to the drums and wind instruments used in ecstatic ceremonies, the *'ud* and the lyre do not require energetic physical participation and are intended to be listened to and their music absorbed during the process of therapy.

We come somewhat closer to a more concrete association of musical modes and healing procedures in the writings of the tenth-century Brethren of Purity, who formed a society for the pursuit of holiness, purity and truth. In the 'Epistle on Music', which forms part of an encyclopedia in fifty-two tracts (Shiloah 1979: 230-1), music is used as a model to explain the wonders of creation, the phenomena of nature and matters lying within the domain of human creation. The ethical and therapeutic influence of music on man is developed as a central theme: music is regarded as a decisive factor in spiritual and philosophical equilibrium, since it acts toward creating inner harmony among the contradictory forces in man's soul. In the same way the correct use of music under appropriate circumstances has a healing influence on the body: it evokes a change in the condition of the humours, thereby producing an ideal balance among them.

Just as the humours were supposed to be common to all people, so, too, the basic principles of music were believed to be common to all people. Yet, the philosophers also recognized differences between races and nations of the earth. According to the theory of racial differences, as treated by al-Kindī and by the Brethren of Purity, the particular characteristics that distinguish nations and races do not result from inheritance but from geographical location and climate. Hence, people differed in their senses of taste and smell, their clothes and their music. As these differences were natural, they were to be accepted and lived with in the same way one lives with varieties of other natural phenomena (*see* Shiloah 1978: 25-6). According to the philosophers, the development of musical art should be seen as the joint contribution of various men of different periods, and the divergences should be regarded with tolerance and understanding. These divergences should be looked upon as branches of one tree, the roots of which are common to all music.

Dealing with the matter on a general and universal level, the Brethren say that typical melodies, that is, melody types or modes (*alḥān*[3]), which were invented by the Greek philosophers, correspond to different feelings and various circumstances: they refine man's desires; they arouse his courage; they may also influence him to generosity, clemency and renunciation. The Brethren state that the Greek philosophers 'also invented another melody which they used in the hospitals, at the break of day, and which had the virtue of assuaging pain due to the infirmities and ills suffered by the patient, alleviating their violence and even curing certain sicknesses and infirmities' (Shiloah 1978: 16-7 n.6). Since the term *laḥn* (melody) is used in this context as the equivalent of mode (melody types), we can safely assume that there is a concrete association between modes and healing procedures. More particularly, the Brethren maintain that, in order to be effective, the influence of mode must rest on the knowledge of racial, environmental and individual differences, which are functions of the variegated mixtures of the humours and the diversity of temperaments.

2. Medicine and Music: The Physician's Point of View

Thus far, we have become acquainted with the philosopher's viewpoint regarding the relations between music, modes and medicine. Let us now consider the physician's view of the same question.

2.1. Ibn Hindū: Old and Modern Medicine

Ibn Hindū (d. 1019), one of the earliest Arab authorities in medicine, wrote an important and sizable medical encyclopedia in ten chapters, called *miftāḥ al-ṭibb* (*The Key to Medicine*), of which the eighth chapter is entitled 'The enumeration of those aspects of the sciences the physician must know in order to be perfect in his profession'.[4] The sciences referred to in this chapter, by order of their appearance, are philosophy, physics, astrology, arithmetic, music, theology and logic. In treating the science of music, ibn Hindū begins with a report, purportedly by Hippocrates, regarding the method practised by the ancient philosophers—that is to say, the Pythagoreans—of healing patients with melodies and by playing the *luwār* (lyre) and *zamr* (probably aulos).[5] This type of medicine, he adds, has ceased and disappeared. He also maintains that, although Hippocrates was the true father of medicine, he did not actually practise musico-therapy but only referred to the practice of ancients who preceded him. Hence, ibn Hindū supposes that he and his contemporaries rely only on Hippocratic medicine.

Despite this supposition ibn Hindū argues that, although the subtleties and esoterics of the ancient healing musical science are no longer entirely comprehensible, there is evidence of their existence and effectiveness. For example, physicians know that certain kinds of melody, rhythm and instrumental music are meant to arouse sorrow or joy, to tranquilize or excite passions and so on. Moreover, in treating cholerics, physicians 'often prescribe recourse to musical modes' (*ṭarā'iq*—a designation used for the modes practised between 226 and 651, the Sassanide era[6]) which correspond to the condition of patients and, so, contribute to healing. Nevertheless, this does not imply that the physician himself is expected to blow a trumpet or reed-pipe or get up and dance; rather, he should use the services of an expert musician, just as he uses the services of other experts, assistants and practitioners. The same holds true for other sciences.

Ibn Hindū's approach to ancient medicine mirrors the rationalistic attitude in the science of medicine that already prevailed in a much earlier period.[7] But it also stems from his need to defend medicine against the attacks of two kinds of opponents. On the one hand, there were theologians who accused physicians of trying to contravene the omniscience and omnipotence of God. On the other hand, there were the 'faddists', who, according to Rosenthal, 'were hardly intentional opponents of medicine. Rather they were people unable to dissociate themselves from old-fashioned beliefs in the efficacy of certain practices which made medicine superfluous and, by implication, deprived it of its *raison d'être*' (1969: 525-6).

In his long argument against the allegations of the faddists, ibn Hindū uses the comparison of medicine with other arts:

Disciplines such as astrology and music are not rejected out of hand, and they are more obscure than medicine and deal with more difficult subjects. Astronomy attempts to understand the remote and majestic celestial bodies. Music affects not only man's body but also his soul. According to the musician's skill and intention, music can produce laughter or tears, joy or sadness, and disarm enemies. If the human intellect can encompass the heavens and manage something as mysterious as the human soul, it certainly should possess the courage and ability to discover and cultivate a science such as medicine (Shiloah 1979: 60-2).

This passage emphasizes the professional and intellectual aspect of music therapy as against the incantative and magical character of old practices. By placing first the effects of music on man's body, we have further confirmation of ibn Hindū's statement that physicians 'often prescribe recourse to musical modes'.

2.2. Ibn Sīna: The Pulse and The Musical Proportions

Ibn Hindū's even more famous contemporary, ibn Sīna, Latinized as Avicenna (d. 1037), was a philosopher and physician. The Latin translation of his *kitāb al-qānūn fi'l ṭibb*, the Canon on Medicine, was known and respected in Europe and was still being edited and re-edited in the seventeenth century (*see* Shiloah 1979: 60-2). Ibn Sīna refuted and rejected as nonsense all the theories linking music with astrology and cosmology; but in his *Canon* we find a special relationship between music and medicine that recurs in Arabic and European writings even as late as the nineteenth century. This relationship combines rhythm, consonances and pulse as chief indicators of good health or illness.

Ibn Sīna writes:

I cannot say which are the three consonances: octave, 5th and 4th, just by feeling, but this may be easily obtained by one to whom the paths of rhythm and musical proportion are clear and who is also versed in the science of music and able, therefore, to compare that which exists to what is known. Such a man, if he examines the question of the pulse in depth, will be able to understand these proportions by feeling.

Ibn Sina continues to discuss the comparison between music and pulse in greater detail and tries to define in musical terms the phenomenon of regular and irregular pulse. Beyond this, however, it is clear from all of ibn Sina's writings that he is not interested merely in the practical aspects of these comparisons but sees in music an outstanding example of the order which must also exist in the human body.[8]

2.3. al-Anṭaki̅: The Healing Effect of Rhythmical Modes

The third viewpoint of a physician is presented by a sixteenth-century writer, Dāhūd al-Anṭāki̅ (lit., from Antioch), a blind doctor who by his own testimony travelled in the territories of Asia Minor in search of Greek sources on medicine (see Shiloah 1979: 60-2). In his medical encyclopedia, al-Tadhkira (Memorial for Wise Men), al-Anṭāki̅ not only included many of the ideas encountered in the previous examples but also drew extensively from the important tract on music that appeared in the encyclopedia of the Brethren of Purity. Yet, his treatise includes some new facets on music therapy, for he introduces the notion of specific modes associated with their particular medical properties.

Al-Anṭāki̅'s treatise has the odd title, al-mūsqiri, probably derived from mūsiqār (musician), a term used by the Brethren of Purity in their 'Epistle on Music'. Following the Brethren, al-Anṭāki̅ defines music as a manual craft whose object is the exploration of sounds comprising specific melodies. He ascribes the invention of the science of music to the Arab philosopher, al-Fārābi̅ (d. 950), but claims that al-Fārābi̅ omitted certain ideas of a Greek scholar (probably Pythagoras) which al-Anṭāki̅ found suitable for his own purposes.[9] According to al-Anṭāki̅, the Greek scholar arranged melodies (alḥān[10]) in accordance with the illnesses and the condition of patients' bodies, applying them to astral musical proportions, rhythms and sounds. Previously, people had made music at random, inspired by bird song and other natural sounds such as wind, water and air passing through different bodies. But the Greek scholar used a definition of musical proportions which corresponded to astral movements as well as to sounds heard in nature. He then created the lute and provided its strings with measures designed to fit the proportions of the astral movements.

Before reaching the major point of his presentation, al-Anṭāki̅ enumerates the variety of modes and melodies in accordance with their characteristics and their proper correspondences. For example, modes arousing courage in battle fit those whose horoscope is Mars; modes stirring love, good manners and artistic creativity correspond to those whose horoscope is Venus. Therefore, concludes al-Anṭāki̅, the musician whose aim is to entertain his audience, to deal with a particular sickness, to stop a quarrel or to dissipate worries should be able to choose and administer the right melody for each case. If he fails in this task, it might be due to the instrument or the melody or the rhythm chosen; it might be due to a wrong horoscope or to pre-occupation on the part of the listener. In the last case, the musician should start by inducing his listener to concentrate better, after which he can proceed to modify the song and the type of instrument.

Al-Antākī goes on to explain the principles of rhythm and their relation and similarity to the action of the pulse. According to his account, the various degrees of rhythmic celerity correspond to pulse beats. Moreover, there is no doubt, he adds, that, when rhythms and melodies penetrate the ear, they provoke a change of heartbeat which in turn necessarily causes a change in pulse-rate and astral movements. He adds that, since the rhythms and instruments vary in accordance with times and places, the musician should comply with the circumstances—for example, by using instruments like the ķanūn in wintertime, since its multiple copper strings endow it with high, hot and dry sounds opposed to the cold surrounding atmosphere and, so, contribute to the creation of a harmonious balance.[11]

The importance the author attaches to rhythm is well-emphasized in the last part of the section on music. In his system rhythm, heartbeat and pulse-rate proceed according to the same principles and embody the same patterns. Their action is characterized by movement, acuity and quality. After a short presentation of the ten categories of rhythms considered under their rhythmical patterns (a theory developed in more detail by ibn Sina), comes a long paragraph on the 'ūd and its multiple cosmological associations. This paragraph, which is almost entirely taken from the Brethren's 'Epistle of Music', summarizes the totality of configurations confined in the system of association between music and other components. This is followed by an exposition of the eight rhythmical modes, also borrowed from the Brethren.

For our purposes, the concluding part of al-Antākī's chapter on music is the most significant, since the author introduces medical applications for the eight rhythmical modes, providing them with appellations suggesting their major effect.[12] The first mode is called misalli, derived from misalla— a sacking needle. This needle, which has a slender point at one end and is thick in the middle, indicates the concentration of humours in the chest, ribs and heart, the secretions of the glands and the place of bellyache; misalli, therefore, has the property of eliminating impurities from the elements. The second mode, 'inclined', is the opposite of the first in its form and effect. The third mode is 'undulated', since its parts vary gradually; it resembles the waves and indicates excessive moistness and hydropsie as well as most of the phlegmatic diseases. The fourth mode is namlī (ant-like), so-called because of its subtlety and weakness of its movements. It corresponds to the fourth stage of high fever and indicates death in the fifth. It might be assimilated with dūdī (worm-like), the mode that follows if the patient recovers his strength by absorbing a potion prepared in response to the symptoms shown by dūdī.

3. Musical Modes and Medical Treatment

From about the fifteenth century, the theory of music therapy found a prominent place in the literature on music. At this period both medical and musical writings provided detailed tables of correspondences in which the melodic modes under their specific names replace the rhythmical modes of al-Antākī and other authors. I propose to illustrate the linking of the melodic modes with medical treatment by describing a fragment in which the modes are listed with their medical properties and by quoting an excerpt from a longer treatise. Both works are by anonymous authors who certainly lived after the sixteenth century (*see* Anonymous 64 and Anonymous 66 in Shiloah 1979: 421-3).

The fragment offers a list of eight modes according to the classification accepted in the fifteenth century. This classification consists of four principal modes, eight derived secondary modes, six *awāzāt* and a variable number of branches (Shiloah 1981). The four principals and seven out of eight secondary modes occur in the fragment. The list undoubtedly continues in the same manner; but, alas, it has not come down to us. According to the fragment, *rast* is good for hemiplegy (paralysis of half the body); *'irāq* helps to cure acute conditions of the humours such as brain diseases, vertigo, pleurisy and suffocation; *isfāhān* stimulates the intelligence, increases the capacity for study and heals cold and dry illnesses; *zirafkand* is prescribed for headache, suffocation and blood illnesses; *rahāwī* is used for colitis, rheumatism, backache; and so on.

The other text also mentions specific *maqāmāt* (modes) with their medical properties, but they are treated generally in the spirit of what we have encountered previously. The anonymous author first gives a lengthy explanation of the principles of the diverse correspondences and then enumerates the modes with their appropriate associations. The following passages are representative of the nature of this text:

Know thee that the modes (*anghām*[13]) are parallel to four qualities: hot, cold, dry and humid; corresponding to the humours: choler, black bile, blood and phlegm as well as day and night time. Therefore, the musician ought to know all this in order to perform the mode that is appropriate to a given circumstance. Thus, he will intone hot modes for a hot humoured person in his normal state and cold modes in a state of sickness. He will do the same with the other humours: a corresponding mode for a normal state, a mode of an opposite quality in case of sickness. He will do the same in playing the modes pertaining to the male Zodiacal signs for men and those belonging to female Zodiacal signs for women. Nocturnal modes should be heard at night and diurnals at daytime. He should see that a diurnal mode corresponds to the Zodiacal sign of the given day and even to each hour of it, since each hour has its own sign. . . . If the musician wishes to achieve perfect equilibrium and harmony, he should moderate each thing by its opposite when it is in a

state of excess and reinforce it with its analogue when it is in a normal
state . . . .

The author goes on to describe how to deal with different cases by applying
what he calls simple and compound modes.[14] The units that compose a
compound mode, he says, can be opposites or concordants; those that are
opposite can be so in all attributes or only in some of them. Thus, one of
the compound modes can be hot and dry and the other, cold and humid;
as, for instance, in the combination of the *maqāmāt rast* and *'ussāq* from
which the *maqām sīkā* is derived. The latter ensures a balanced mixture of
the hot and the cold qualities; in the same way the combination of *rast*,
masculine, with *'ussāq*, feminine, gives birth in the *sīkā* to a harmonious
blend of masculine and feminine elements. Consequently, the *sīkā* is
harmonious from all aspects. That is why it is the most pleasurable of all
the well-balanced modes. The author pursues the analysis of other modes
in the same way, indicating their affective or medical properties.

Conclusion

The approach characterizing the anonymous treatise, as well as some
others like it, represents the culmination of music therapy in Arabic
musical sources. Thereafter, no further development took place. Although
al-Anṭākī and the two anonymous writers elaborate in detail the musical
and medical dimension, it is noteworthy that al-Anṭākī, despite being an
authoritative physician, refers to the musician rather than to the doctor as
the appropriate agent for fulfilling healing tasks. At the same time, his
discussion implies a medical proficiency that becomes more evident in the
two anonymous texts. Thus, we are confronted with two questions: (1) was
it because al-Anṭākī and other physicians who wrote on music were
proficient musicians themselves? or (2) should we admit that contemporary musicians were versed in medicine to an extent enabling them to
fulfill the healing tasks incumbent to them? It is not easy to answer these
questions with certainty, yet it seems that the prevailing opinion comes
close to that of ibn Hindū, who wrote that music therapy belongs more to
the realm of the musician, whose art should be regarded as an auxiliary to
medicine. This conclusion does not exclude the possibility that physicians
well-versed in the art of music would have played a double role of
physician and musician. Indeed, that prolific writer, ibn Ṭulūn (d. 1546),
asserted: 'every physician ought to know some music, and the musician
some medicine and astrology' (Shiloah 1979: 224).

Notes

[1] This article is based on Arabic sources, of which many are still in
    manuscript. A detailed description of the cited manuscripts is included
    in Shiloah (1979).

2   The Biblical *kinnor* is a type of lyre. A specimen occurs on a coin of the
    second Temple period.

3   *Laḥn*, singular of *alḥān* or, occasionally, *luḥūn*, signifies melody.
    Yet, like many other technical terms in ancient Arabic sources, it
    embodies other meanings. We deduce from the context that *laḥn* here is
    used as the equivalent of mode with its Greek connotations. The
    term 'mode' is designated, as we shall see, by other Arabic denomina-
    tions.

4   A French annotated translation of this chapter, with commentary on
    the relationships between music and medicine, is included in Shiloah
    (1972: 447-62).

5   The first name is clearly related to the Greek lyra. The second, *zamr*, is
    an Arabic term that probably stands here for *mizmār* or *zummāra*,
    words which designate usually a reed-pipe instrument.

6   The word, *ṭarīqā*, singular of *ṭarā'iq*, means 'way, manner, rule of life'; it
    is thus very close to the signification of the term 'mode'.

7   For example, the rationalist, Soranus, who practised medicine in Rome
    in the first decades of the second century, tells us that some physicians
    charmed away the pains of sciatica by using a piper who played over the
    affected parts. This mode of treatment, he adds, was among the many
    innovations and discoveries attributed in antiquity to Pythagoras. But
    in modern time, according to Soranus, some consider it a survival of
    magic and incantation, whereas others look upon it as an instance of
    musico-therapy completely divorced from magic and incantation (*see*
    Drabkin 1951).

8   Similar ideas may be found, for example, in *De musica* by the monk and
    music theorist, Remi d'Auxerre (d. 908). After defining musical rhythm,
    he writes:

    This rhythm is perceived in three manners: by sight, by audition and
    by touch (palpation). The eye discerns the rhythm in gestures and
    movements of the dance, the ear hears it in the sound of instruments
    or the human voice, the touch feels it in the physiological phenomena.
    Let us leave the biological and tactile rhythm to the physicians who
    draw from it certain practical conclusions (quoted in Bruyne 1946:
    tom. I, libre 2, 321).

9   This legendary ascription appears frequently in literary sources up to the
    nineteenth century. However, the tribute paid here to al-Fārābī is
    followed by criticism concerning his hostile attitude against the opinions
    linking music with cosmological, astrological and medical consid-
    erations. Al-Fārābī's views, therefore, were in conflict with the
    supposedly Pythagorean doctrine alluded to in this passage.

10 Here again, *alḥān* is used as the equivalent of the Greek modes (*see
    supra*, note 3).

11 The *kānūn* is a trapezoidal zither provided with twenty-six triple strings,
    traditionally made of gut. The strings are plucked with two plectra. In al-

Antākī's account, an interesting detail is the indication that, in wintertime, the strings should be made of copper.

[12] This is the number of rhythmic modes (*iqā'āt*) usually dealt with in the
musical sources of the Golden Age era (*i.e.*, eighth to ninth centuries). In
later periods, including the author's time, the number and denomi-
nations of the rhythmic modes were significantly different.

[13] *See supra*, note 3.

[14] For a detailed description of this classification, *see* Shiloah (1981).

Glossary

alḥān: see *lahn*
anghām: see *naghm*
awāzāt (*pl.* of *awāz*): generic name for secondary modes
dūdī (*lit.* worm-like): name of a rhythmic mode
iqā'āt: (*pl.* of *iqā*): rhythmic modes
'irāq: name of a melodic mode
iṣfahān: name of a melodic mode
ḳānūn: a trapezoidal zither
kinnor: Biblical name for lyre
lahn (*pl. alḥan* or *luḥūn*) melody, tune, melodic and rhythmic mode
luḥūn: see *lahn*
luwār: Greek lyre
maqām (*pl. maqāmāt*): generic name for mode
maqāmāt: see *maqām*
misalla: a sacking needle
misallī (derives from *misalla*): name of a rhythmic mode
mizmār: a reed-pipe instrument
mūsiqār: musician
al-mūsqirī: unusual name for the science of music
naghm or *nagham* (*pl. anghām*) mode, sound, melody
namlī (*lit.* ant-like) name of a rhythmic mode
rahāwī: name of a melodic mode
rast: name of a melodic mode
sīkā: name of a melodic mode
tarīqā, *tarā'iq*: generic name for old Persian modes
'ūd: short-necked lute
'ussāq: name of a melodic mode
zamr: a reed-pipe instrument
zīrafkand: name of a melodic mode
zummāra: a reed-pipe instrument

References

BRUYNE, E. de
   1946 *Études d'esthétique mediévale*, 3 tom., Bruges
DRABKIN, I. E.
   1951 'Soranus and his System of Medicine', *Bulletin of the History of Medicine*, 25: 503-18
HALL, T. S.
   1969 *Ideas of Life and Matter: Studies in the History of General Physiology 600 B.C.-1900 A.D.*, 2 vols., Chicago and London
ROSENTHAL, F.
   1969 'The Defense of Medicine in the Medieval Muslim World', *Bulletin of the History of Medicine*, 43: 525-8
SHILOAH, A.
   1972 'Ibn Hindū le médécin et la musique', *Israel Oriental Studies*, 2: 447-62
   1978 *The Epistle of Music of the Ikhwān al-Ṣafā*, Tel-Aviv
   1979 *The Theory of Music in Arabic Writings (c. 900-1900): Descriptive Catalogue of Manuscripts of Europe and the USA*, RISM B, Munich
   1981 'The Arabic Concept of Mode', *Journal of the American Musicological Society*, 34: 34-9

Man a la Mode: or, Reinterpreting the Book of Nature from a Musical Point of View

Jamie C. Kassler

Abstract

In this paper the 'book of nature' is human nature, and the interpreter of the 'book' is Roger North (1651?-1734). North's problematic is Cartesian mind/body dualism which introduced an element of doubt that the 'book' of human nature could be read. To solve this problem, North adopted two main tenets of Stoicism—tension and goodness; he then extended these tenets by means of a pioneering theory of musical air which unites external manner (mode) with internal character (mode). By drawing on a number of his writings, many of which are still unpublished, the author provides a general account of North's musical solution to the mind/body problem.

Introduction

There is a venerable hermeneutic tradition which regards the entire world as a text written by God and through which His purposes are manifest in the things that are. From time to time, this tradition has undergone revision by means of sceptical currents of thought. The most notable of these revisionist periods dates from the sixteenth century, when scholars began to question whether the interpretations of Plato, Aristotle and other authorities corresponded to the 'live book' of nature that God had written. By the end of that century, there were increasing attempts to compare the writings of the authorities with the primordial book itself in order to recognize from the original, written in God's own hand, where they had copied right and where wrong. The resulting intellectual ferment led, in the seventeenth century, to modern critical methods which, in turn, contributed to the emergence not only of modern natural science but also other modern subjects.[1]

The conception of God as an author and the world as a text is a literary metaphor, of course. For its completion, the metaphor requires a reader as well as a language in which the text is written. The language need not be restricted to natural languages such as English but may include paralanguages such as music or mathematics. If the book in question is *human* nature, the chief problem becomes how to read the text. This problem was addressed by the Hon. Roger North (1651?-1734), who is known chiefly for his contributions to life writing. These contributions include a theory of biography, lives of three of his brothers and an autobiography covering his early years to about 1698.[2] In striving to understand the 'springs' of human thought and action, North focused on bodily motions as signs of intention. Hence, he had to confront a problem bequeathed by René Descartes.

As is well known, Descartes distinguished material body from mind by defining the latter as a spiritual substance that thinks. Even though he asserted that mind uses body as an instrument, his dualist approach seemed to deny any interaction between body and mind. Accordingly, Cartesian mind-body dualism left the visible face of human nature as a tantalizing illusion, for 'if the ego was hidden, if mind was but a ghost in the machine, how could inspecting the outside of the machine tell you about the ghost?'.[3] In short, Cartesian ontology introduced an element of doubt that the book of human nature could be read.

To solve this problem, North adopted two main tenets of Stoicism, a tradition that has yet to be fully analyzed for its contributions to early modern science and scientific method.[4] According to Stoic philosophy, nature is a world spirit, immanent in everything and directing events by expansion and contraction to achieve worthy ends. The two Stoic tenets, therefore, are tension and goodness. North extended these tenets by recourse to a book-of-nature metaphor. In his version, the book of nature is written in acoustical signals, and nature itself is a large-scale model of musical activity as shown in Figure 1.

Body: A Consort of Musical Instruments
Mind ('Soul'): The Conductor of the Instruments
Spirit: The Composer and the Musical Score

Figure 1: Roger North's Book-of-Nature Metaphor

Body is a consort of musical instruments that has the potential to play together harmoniously. Mind is the conductor of the consort, for it has the potential to read the musical score and direct which instrument, or group of instruments, is to play at appropriate times. The potential of body and mind is made actual by spirit, which is the composer as well as the musical score that the unity of body and mind expresses.

In what follows I shall show how North solved the mind- body problem by examining separately the three aspects of his book-of- nature metaphor: body, mind and spirit. By the term 'body', North denotes the knowing subject, that is, the whole personality consisting of thoughts as well as actions. By the term 'mind', he signifies the knowing process. And by the term 'spirit', he means life or animating principle. To explain living creatures, North adopts a functional approach to body, whereby the instruments or nerves and muscles, the conductor or central processing unit, and the creator and regulator or spirit must all cooperate else there is no knowledge and, indeed, no life. North's conception of nature, therefore, proceeds from the assumption of the immanence of life and function in organized matter. Neither of these can exist independently of each other, since, as he himself states: spirit makes the difference between a living and a dead corpse.[5]

1. Body as a Consort of Musical Instruments

In his treatment of body as knowing subject, North follows Thomas Hobbes, for he posits one substance: matter. He then argues that 'all the varietys of sense, may be produced by simple matter onely moved'.[6] According to Hobbes's hypothesis, if motion is the natural state of matter, human individuals may be reduced to the effects of a mechanical apparatus consisting of sense organs, nerves, muscles, memory, imagination and reason, which apparatus moves in response to the impact (or imagined impact) of external bodies on it. The human apparatus is not, strictly speaking, self-moving; but it is always in motion, because other things are always impinging on it. In a less strict sense, it is self-moving, because it has built into it an endeavour to maintain its motion. Our most complex and refined actions can be explained as effects of the operation of this mechanical system, not by treating them all as mere reflex actions but by treating voluntary or willed actions (intentions) as a process of deliberation or calculation which calls into play the external as well as internal senses and puts them all to work in service of the in-built endeavour.[7]

North's in-built endeavour is tension, for he regards every body as a tensional field made up of inward and outward action, contraction and expansion; through this two-way motion, the utility and existence of body is preserved. Thus he writes: 'the body is a mobile engin like a compage of springs, that on the least percussion, will fall to shaking and vibrating a long time, which is from an interne principle, and not [from] the force that occasions it'.[8] In conceiving expansion and contraction as vibratory motion, North has recourse to the pendulum condition, that is, the isochrony of 'springs' such as taut strings and other systems having equilibrium configurations along axes, although he is fully aware that, physically, no pendulum is truly isochronous. According to North, people and musical instruments exemplify the pendulum condition.[9]

But people and musical instruments share another attribute, for both have the potential to sound. In order to do so, such bodies, or parts of them, must first become agitated so as to shake all the contiguous air.[10] When the agitation is equal-timed, the pulses occasion the simple harmonic motion of air particles, the particles then acting on each other according to the laws of impact. By means of the air, an invisible and impalpable body, sound spreads around the spot where it has been produced by a vibratory motion which is passed on successively from one part of the air to another. The spreading of this motion, taking place equally rapidly on all sides, forms spherical surfaces or waves. These waves, ever enlarging, strike our ears. Sound, therefore, is transmitted by pulses.[11]

For immediate knowing to take place, sensible presence, by itself, is insufficient, for there also must be attention. Hence, pulses must be notable, that is, they must engage the attention and lead to sustained reflection and thought.[12] In North's theory notable pulses consist of indistinguishable ('insensible') moments of time, because they are so swift. When pulses meet this condition, they excite the tympanum of the ear, the chain of events taking place internally in human bodies being the same as that which happened externally. The vibrating tympanum transmits the pulses to the nervous system.[13] The nervous system, in turn, vibrates and transmits the pulses to the brain, which coordinates the various pulses and elevates them into consciousness as images. The mind, by its presence to the brain, then 'reads' the images in the act of perception.

The images represented to, and seen by, the mind are the rules of vibrations, which North exemplifies in a series of 'punctations' (L. *punctum*, pl. *puncta*), one of which is illustrated in Figure 2.

In this punctation the parallel vertical lines represent the flow of time, and the points represent the pulses. The lowest row represents the pulses that correspond to the fundamental tone ('key'); the pulses above correspond to the intervals of the octave, 12th, 15th, 17th, 19th and 22d. These intervals form what North calls the 'full accord' (he never uses the terms 'harmonic' or 'overtone series'), which, with some octave transposition, is represented in current common musical notation above the punctation.

From this punctation alone, it is clear that sounds co-exist and do not obliterate each other, because they are dynamic processes in the air, of which each of them is a certain modification. Such modifications can undergo what now is called 'superposition' without losing their identity, whereas a superposition of static states does away with them. We may conclude, therefore, that the brain is not a wax tablet on which images are impressed or a piece of paper on which creases are made.[14] North himself suggests that the brain or 'residence of thought' is like the reflecting telescope invented by Isaac Newton. According to this comparison, the

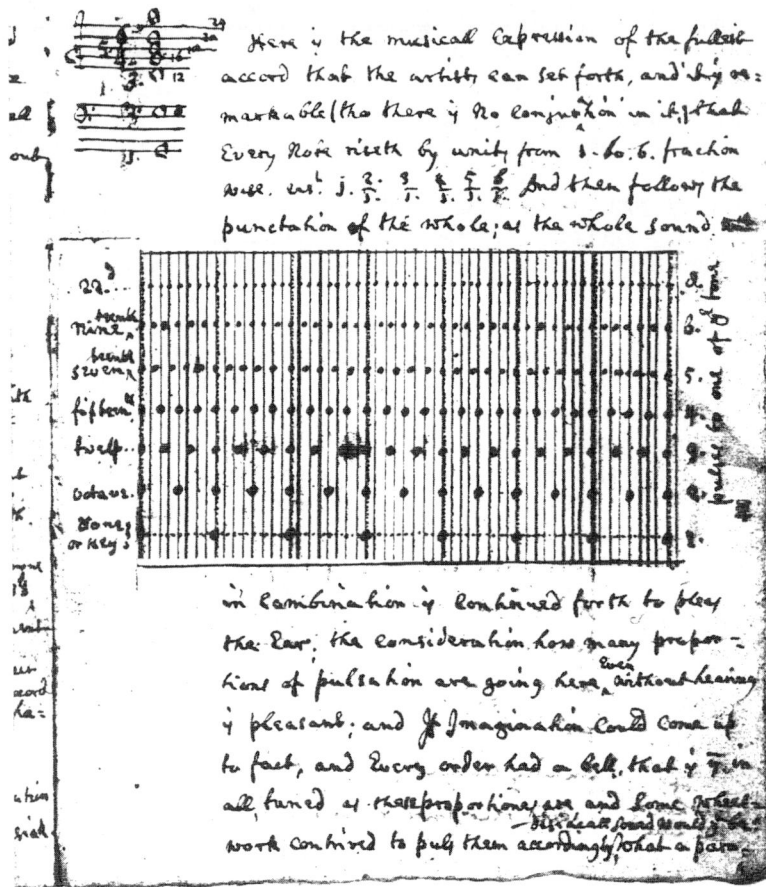

Figure 2: 'Punctation' of the Full Accord (BL Add MS 32535: f.113)

concave mirror or speculum is the cerebellum ('sensorium'); the eyepiece or combination of lenses for magnifying an image is the cerebrum ('brain'); and the eye is the mind.[15] But North insists: 'I doe not argue extention, or locality of the mind otherwise then it hath power over this particular matter, to which in every humane body it is affix't.' Mind, therefore, differs from the instruments of body only in its function as 'a president to determine among the capacitys of the body, which shall be imployed, and which not'.[16]

2. Mind as Conductor of the Instruments

To fulfill its function as president, the mind scans the images transmitted to the brain. Despite the rapidity with which it performs this action, the mind can attend to only one image at a time, because in the act of perception the mind must perform various computations on the data represented to it.[17] In performing these computations, the mind employs three powers: the ear, the memory and the imagination. These powers are not separate faculties; rather, they are different functions of mind. The first power, the ear, processes data communicated as notable or indistinguishable pulses, the computation of which occurs subconsciously ('without science', 'incogitanter') and involves counting. The method may be illustrated in the Key to Figure 2, showing North's punctation in numbers, followed by the mechanical derivation on the monochord.

```
                    1
                  1 2
                1 2 3
              1 2 3 4
            1 2 3 4 5
          1 2 3 4 5 6
```

Monochord Divided	Intervals Produced	Ratios of Frequencies	Order of Perfection
1	Unison	1:1	(Most perfect)
2	Octave	2:1	
3	Fifth	3:2	
4	Fourth	4:3	
5	Third #	5:4	
6	Third ♭	6:5	(Least perfect)

Key to Figure 2

In the punctation and its computational model, the bass or fundamental tone (1 in the computational model) is the normative sound in determining the character of harmonic sonorities, all the upper parts being more or less perfect as they have more or fewer pulses that coincide with pulses of the bass.

In the computational model and in the mechanical derivation shown in the Key, the ratios of simple consonances stop at 6:5, because North holds that we know only the numbers 1 to 6 by forming ideas of so many bodies. Beyond this, he writes, we know only hypothetically and 'by names where of the signification is granted'.[18] Hence, the mind's power of distinguishing natural things is limited; and the measure, according to North,

    . . . is given from our faculty of moving some part of our bodys which is done, actually or mentally, when ever wee mark or number things passing by us. And if the transits are so quick wee cannot attend them with our reall action, then the idea of a continuation emergeth. And in like manner the waves of pulses that follow so swift, that we have no corporeall means to distinguish them, become a continued sound, and we call it noise.[19]

When pulses strike us faster than we can count, the mind is unable to separate them in conscious thought into preceding and succeeding moments of time. In processing such pulses, memory, the second power of mind, gathers them into larger units, which North regards as appearances or mental fictions.[20] Appearances consist of distinguishable pulses, the computation of which occurs consciously and involves comparison. Pitches, for example, do not merely exist at the moment they are heard, they also endure in the memory and relate to what came before and what follows after. The memory accepts or rejects a pitch as harmonically functional by a process of comparison, as North insists when he writes:

Experience tells us . . . that some tones are proper, and others very improper, to succeed each other. And this is discovered by certein mutuall relations or habitudes. As if two tones are made to sound together the compound effect, to our sence may be gratefull, or harsh and offensive: and thereupon it must be concluded that tones which accompany well, are best qualifyed to succeed one and other, for so near as immediate succession, memory doth as it were joyne them.[21]

The names by which we designate these appearances are conventional, for North acknowledges that 'wee have litle else, but names, to be concerned with in this theory . . . [and] it must be no surprise if some termes occurr, without a sufficient vocabulary, but I shall take care, whatever names are assumed, the things shall be clear enough'.[22] Accordingly, names such as 'noise' and 'tone', 'accord' and 'discord', 'high' and 'low', 'harsh' and 'smooth' are common terms for various combinations of vibrations that are impressed on our organ of hearing and transmitted to the mind to read. That is, high and low are not intrinsic to bodies. Nevertheless, there is a correspondence between reality and appearances, for, as North states:

It is very remarkable that altho the mind hath no distinction of the elements of continued sounds, yet there is a resentment of the reall propertys that attend them, but yet in different ideas, whereby every alteration or variety amongst them is vertually perceived and one composition is distinguish't from another . . . .[23]

Once the mind is stocked with data from sensation and memory, it forms new ideas by means of its third computational power, imagination, which combines the data in order to yield new ideas. North explains this computational process by recourse to a logical calculus of ideas conceived as a combination of simple into complex concepts. In his version ideas are like pitches: we all employ the same musical lexicon, and musical thinking is merely the concatenation of pitches according to a rudimentary probabilistic mechanics—the art of combinations and permutations. Simple ideas consist of single pitches, as well as pitches in relation, for, as North insists, it is the scale 'out of which all variety of harmony and melody is derived'.[24] Complex ideas consist of larger levels of structure, starting with the formation of chords, whereby the notes may 'counterchange' their 'scituations' by means of the combinatorial procedure we now call 'chord inversion'.

In the knowing processes just described, the imagination plays a major role, for it serves to represent the images received from the external senses; to bring the images back into consciousness from memory in the absence of the sensed object; and to combine the images in order to yield new ideas.[25] In each of these roles the imagination provides images for the mind to read. Nature, therefore, is a visible language, for it can be seen by the mind. But to exist as a sign, nature must be interpreted. In North's account, reading involves interpreting, for although he holds that sense representations are necessary for knowledge in that they form the raw material in which the knowing power exercises itself, his emphasis is on the way the sense material is handled and articulated, for he details how the mind follows certain patterns in action. Forms are automatically imposed on sense input by the person receiving, thus enabling the knowing subject to order reality.

The forms imposed are judgments, for they concern relations between things. Indeed, counting, comparing and combining all involve different kinds of relation. The tendency to perform judgments is active from the first moment of contact between people and their environment. But what are the criteria of such judgments? According to North, the criteria derive from our ability to feel pleasure and pain, for he holds that nature constituted all creatures with an instinctive attraction towards those things which promote their own well-being and a complementary aversion towards their opposites.[26] Hence, pleasure is motivational, for it is analysed in terms of realization of the good—the object of striving. On this view, the affections and passions of the mind can be defined in terms of endeavour. Although the foetus has the capacity to feel pleasure and pain, experience alone brings on endeavour, for, as North writes:

. . . wee bring onely the instruments of motion, a litle determined by instinct. But wee have not power to move any member or part to the porposes of life or arts, but by slow degrees and tryalls . . . so that all that wee doe in life, is acquired, as musick is.[27]

Since knowledge is entirely empirical, the truth of what people apprehend depends upon external impressions of a sufficiently clear and distinct kind. But people are prone to err, and there are two principal sources of error. One source is from the mind itself as subjective delusions occasioned by disorders in the body.[28] The other source is from hasty or excited inference.[29] Hence, judgments made in response to our environment provide us with an understanding of what is only apparently good and apparently evil. What, then, are the criteria for judging what is really good and really evil? According to North, the basis of moral choice is a causal understanding of events and the consequences which follow from them.

By a causal understanding, North signifies analysis ('resolution'); and he conceives analysis as an exercise of the imagination, whereby simple motions or forces are imagined which, when logically compounded, provide a causal explanation of complex phenomena. What, for example, makes a person tick? One cannot find the answers as a watch repairer can do, by taking the watch apart. But one can take a person apart in imagination, that is, hypothetically. In so doing, North writes, the power of the human understanding 'is magnifyed, and proved by algebra',[30] which is like the watch repairer's art—a taking apart in order to show the pieces. Accordingly, he describes algebra as

> . . . a method of working a proposition, without ideas of the subject matter, . . . wherein the demonstration and the method of working it, is rather, as the word imports, a shewing things in peices, like explaining a watch, then proving. For it deals altogether in present existent certein quantity.[31]

Hence, North consistently explains all stages of the knowing process as computations.

3. Spirit as the Composer and the Musical Score

In North's interpretation of body in motion, there are two kinds of cause: primary and secondary. When, for example, he writes of 'mechanicall causes of all agencys that usually affect us by means of hearing',[32] North denotes secondary causes ('occasions'), for he holds: 'As to the operations of the mind, I look upon the action of things sensible to be occasions onely, and not causes of those ideas that are framed in the imagination'.[33] An account of nature based on secondary causality leaves us in the realm of what is only apparently good and apparently evil. To understand what is really good and really evil, recourse must be had to primary causality.

North's conception of primary causality is a cosmic one, for he adopts a thoroughgoing monism: the world is a plenum filled with particles of matter. But matter has two principles, a passive and an active principle. The manifold variety in the world is explained by reference to these two features of matter. The passive principle is unqualified body; the active principle is subtle matter, which North also calls 'the spirit of the world'.[34] Spirit is responsible for all activity, change and variety and, therefore, for knowing.

To explain how spirit accomplishes its creative and regulative functions, North has recourse to the Stoic tenets of tension and goodness. He describes spirit as a very tenuous, invisible, elastic medium extended throughout the universe,[35] for he writes:

> Body is extended, and of that nature no one is more perfect then another, but the least have the same pretensions as the greatest; but if we would consider the perfection of that nature [body], it consists in extension or space in infinitum, as philosofers now hold: and the other nature[,] spirit[,] which consists in power, may be all alike as to essence [*i.e.*, extended in space], yet is spirit or (as the most wee can say) non body. The advances are in power and the perfection is in the Almighty.[36]

The assumption of its extreme tenuity is in strict accordance with North's hypothesis that spirit is omnipresent not only within body but also within the apparent emptiness of the space between bodies.

As the active principle of matter, spirit functions 'like a spark firing the powder in a mine: it is not the spark that heaves the bastion, but some other mechanicall power derived from the latent energie of matter at large in the world. And if the globe of earth were of like composition as gunpowder is, it were the same thing.'[37] Hence, spirit works 'just at the incoation of the power of body, and then in the way of explosion is disperst over the whole, by the machination of the organs and parts of it'.[38] But body is not merely a passive recipient: it actively and vitally collaborates with spirit in that it undergoes certain dispositions, for, North writes:

> What signifies the matter of nitre sulfur, and charcoal, without a disposition, whereby it may explode, and such are humane bodys which from very insensible touches are made to move an immense weight, whereof the opperations are manifestly mechanick in all respects but the occasion, which is lodged like a spark of steel till it exerts itself, and produceth a spacious effect.[39]

Body's potential, then, is made actual by spirit.

In addition to creating life and motion, spirit regulates the world by pneumatic action, for its component particles endeavour—that is, have a tendency to vibratory motion—by pressing inward from the surfaces of ordinary bodies or by pressing outward from the interspaces of those bodies. By means of these two opposing tendencies, spirit maintains ordinary bodies in a dynamic state of equilibrium ('balance', 'posture of rest'). Thus North writes: 'By the ballance of impulses, I mean when the force imprest by the subtile matter tends to drive the body one way as much as another, . . . so long it must needs rest'.[40] When ordinary bodies are displaced from their positions of equilibrium by some additional or external force, the particles of spirit behave like the restoring forces acting on a bent spring or oscillating pendulum.

By these same pneumatic actions, spirit mediates between the properties of external objects and the consciousness of the perceiving mind. In North's account of the knowing process, every stimulus from the outside is conducted from the specific sense organ excited by it to a central processing unit which coordinates the various impressions, elevates them into consciousness and then releases the impulse reacting to the sensation. The mind ('soul'), North writes, 'gives the inception that occasions the whole [body] to work with its proper forces; and the externall incidents of the body, or sense, administers objects to affect the soul, and so returnes are reciprocally made'.[41] The vital function of the central processing unit, unifying all the activities of body and maintaining and regulating its contact with the external world, clearly defines a dual direction of communication. But it is only through the incessant movement of spirit that this two-way communication is established.

To prove the universal law of causality, it is necessary to look for observational sources of evidence. North relies on inferences based on signs and events in his physical surroundings. Since, in his philosophy, modifications of spirit take place in body as modifications of tension or 'tone', nerves and muscles may be either tense or relaxed, just as the mind may be 'nerved up' or 'enervated'.[42] The effect of tonicity and flaccidity, therefore, is visible not only in objects such as pendulums, springs and musical strings but also in the external movements of the human body, including the countenance of the face. Internal and external movements together result in an 'air' or sign of a particular passion or affection. The word 'air' here means external manner, appearance or mien, but it is the result of an internal character: a tense or relaxed spirit. Thus North solves the problem of the ghost in the machine.

Conclusion

North's solution to the mind/body problem arises from his theory of music and also informs that theory, for North is the first writer in the history of music to bring together the concepts of external manner and internal character to form an original conception of musical air.[43] In his writings the term air (or 'ayre') is an omnibus word. It may mean melody, song or tune; but this usage is rare. More often, it may mean the 'complexion' or 'ayre' of a key, that is, its tonality; or it may refer to the 'character' of a key, that is, its mode, major or minor; or it may refer to the various 'manners' of a piece, that is, its tempi, slow to fast. North also uses ayre to signify 'common measure', that is, harmonic rhythm, which maintains the interaction (sympathy) between the different parts (melody and harmony) of a composition. In this usage ayre is analogous to spirit, which mediates between mind and body and animates the mass, which would be dead without it.

North also uses the term 'air' to refer to the external manifestation of a composer's 'wit' or '*anima*'. By these latter terms, he means the internal 'spark' or 'spirit' of a composer, which, North hints, is imagination, for he holds that 'our ideas are not in the object but in our imagination'.[44] But ideas, or internal music, become manifest in the air of a musical composition, because spirit is imprinted on a work, thereby giving that work its air, that is, its external style or excellence of expression. North's conception of musical air, therefore, forms the basis of his semiotic theory, for he argues that music is the invention of humans and a representation of their changing history and habits. Accordingly, he holds that through music we may read the book of human nature.

Acknowledgments

Thanks are due to Pierre Laszlo for opening the world of chemical analogies and to Warren D. Anderson for his helpful comments on an earlier draft of this paper.

Notes

[1] This article draws material from, and recasts part of my introduction to, *Roger North's The Musicall Grammarian 1728* edited with Introductions and Notes by Mary Chan and Jamie C. Kassler (Cambridge, 1990). All quotations from unpublished texts are taken from the British Library Additional Manuscripts (referred to hereafter as BL Add. MS). These texts are detailed in Mary Chan and Jamie C. Kassler, *Roger North: Materials for a Chronology of his Writings . . .* (Kensington, N. S. W. 1989). For the metaphor of the 'text' in musical scholarship, *see* Jamie C. Kassler, 'Interpretive Strategies in Australian Musical Scholarship', *Musicology Australia* (1988-89) 11/12: 24-26.

[2] *Roger North: General Preface and Life of Dr John North* edited by Peter Millard, (Toronto, 1984); *The Lives of the Norths* edited by Augustus Jessopp, 3 vols., (London, 1890); and *The Autobiography of the Hon. Roger North* edited by Augustus Jessopp, (London and Norwich, 1887). The last item is a bowdlerized version of North's text, *Notes of Me*, the title of which is reminiscent of the meditations, *On Himself*, of the Stoic philosopher, Marcus Aurelius, which North's great-great uncle, Thomas North, had freely translated.

[3] Roy Porter, 'Making Faces: Physiognomy and Fashion in Eighteenth-Century England', *Études Anglaises* (1985) 38: 385-96, p. 386.

[4] Only two attempts at analysis have come to my attention, the most important of which is by Peter Barker and B. R. Goldstein, 'Is Seventeenth-Century Physics indebted to the Stoics?', *Centaurus* (1984) 27: 148-64. *See also* B.J.T. Dobbs, 'Newton and Stoicism', *The Southern Journal of Philosophy*, supplement (1985) 23: 109-23. Dobbs argues that Newton was not only familiar with Stoic doctrines but also found some of them useful upon occasion. Her approach consists chiefly of structural parallels that still require historical and philosophical analysis.

[5] *The Autobiography of the Hon. Roger North*, p. 86.

[6] *Prejudices*, BL Add. MS 32526: f.4v.

7   This summary of Hobbes's hypothesis is from *Leviathan* edited with an
    Introduction by C.B. Macpherson (Harmondsworth, 1986). Although
    North's physics is derived from, or close to that of, Christiaan Huygens,
    his metaphysics is from Hobbes's treatise on optics of 1644. For details
    about this work, which began the kinematic tradition in optics, *see* Alan
    E. Shapiro, 'Kinematic Optics: A Study of the Wave Theory of Light in
    the Seventeenth Century', *Archive for History of Exact Science* (1973)
    11: 134- 266. *See also* Jamie C. Kassler, 'The Paradox of Power: Hobbes
    and Stoic Naturalism', in Stephen Gaukroger (ed.), *The Uses of
    Antiquity: The Scientific Revolution and The Classical Tradition*
    (Dordrecht, forthcoming) and *Roger North's Cursory Notes of
    Musicke (c.1698-c.1703). . .*edited with Introduction, Notes and
    Appendices by Mary Chan and Jamie C. Kassler, (Kensington, N.S.W.
    1986), pp. [47]-[51].

8   *Of Humane Capacity* [*i.e.*, on human movement], BL Add. MS 32526:
    44v.

9   *Roger North's Cursory Notes of Musicke (c.1698-c.1703)*, pp. 27-8, 32-4
    et passim, and *Roger North's The Musicall Grammarian 1728*, [f. 1v *et
    passim*] detail and exemplify the pendulum condition.

10 In the case of the voice and wind instruments, it is not the instrument but
    an enclosed quantity of air which vibrates [*Roger North's Cursory
    Notes of Musicke (c.1698-c.1703)*, pp. 97-8 *et passim*].

11 *Ibid.*

12 According to North [*Untitled Essay*, BL Add. MS 32546: f.262v], our
    perception is
        . . . a notice of pulses, or remarkable alterations of body. And these
        things cannot be all observed at once, but successively one after
        another, which gives the idea of time. And as all are not of equall
        circumstance, but some more eclattant then others, so wee are
        attentive to some, and let others pass, with litle or no notice. And
        often the pulses from memory, shall have force to prevail and be
        attended to rather then others without us, which is called not minding.
        And there is no sleep or moment of life without attention to (that is
        perception of) one thing or other.

13 North has little to say about the external senses, leaving details to the
    'anatomists'. In one of his last writings on music [*Theory of Sounds . . .
    1728*, BL Add. MS 32535: f.95], he simply remarks that
        The fabrick of the ear is very considerable, with regard, not onely to
        the perceiving, but judging of sounds. The place of the sensible touch,
        is reputed to be the drum membrane, for by the modes of attaque
        upon that, wee judg the modes of the percussion, as quik, dull,
        continued, or otherwise as the case is.

14 Both images were used by Descartes, who regarded the brain as a soft
    substance in which animal spirits leave traces. These traces are
    preserved, the animal spirits passing through them again and again,

thereby endowing the living creature not only with sensory perception but also with memory. The conception of cerebral traces of impressions of ideas became known as *engrams*, which until the nineteenth century were conceived as static imprints. The implication of such models is that function is localizable in some portion of the brain. North does not hold this view. *See* Jamie C. Kassler, 'Man—A Musical Instrument: Models of the Brain and Mental Functioning before the Computer', *History of Science* (1984) 22: 59-82.

[15] *Some Essays, concerning the Manner of our Sence, or Perception of Things*, BL Add. MS 32526: ff.13-15.

[16] *Ibid.*: f.15. In *Change of Philosoficall Methods*, BL Add. MS 32549: f.97v, he writes: 'an organized body shall be like a windoe to the whole world'.

[17] In *Power of Humane Understanding*, BL Add. MS 32526: f.89, North explicitly states that 'the mind is not capable of observing more then one thing at a time'; it 'seems to observe more onely by a swift passage of the attention from one thing to another, and so passing and repassing seems to dilate the observation'. *See also* n.12 above.

[18] *Roger North's Cursory Notes of Musicke* (c.1698-c.1703), p. 152.

[19] *Theory of Sounds. . .1728*, BL Add. MS 32535: ff.99-99v. Before North, numerous writers attempted to explain why the ratios of simple consonances stop after 6:5. Starting with the scenario of Gioseffo Zarlino, the various explanations are detailed and critically examined by H. Floris Cohen, *Quantifying Music: The Science of Music at the First Stage of the Scientific Revolution, 1580-1650* (Dordrecht, 1984). None of the writers surveyed by Cohen seem to offer North's explanation, which is based on the 'dullness of our materiall engin' [*Untitled Essay*, BL Add. MS 32546: f.254v].

[20] This conception is similar to that of Helmholtz, who argued that when we listen to a series of four or more consecutive harmonic vibrations we do not hear a series of partial tones. Our hearing faculty blends the partial tones into a compound whole (whence their name, *s.v.* 'Tone', *OED I. 2.*) and perceives a single musical tone of definite pitch. Phenomena such as musical tones, therefore, are the products of sensory perception. *See* Hermann von Helmholtz, *On the Sensations of Tone as a Physiological Basis for the Theory of Music*, 2d English edition, translated. . .and. . .adapted. . .by Alexander J. Ellis (New York, 1954).

[21] *Roger North's The Musicall Grammarian 1728*, [f.15v]. Memory enables the mind to compare pitches, and it is by comparison that the scale is formed.

[22] *Theory of Sounds. . .1728*, BL Add. MS 32535: f.105v.

[23] *Ibid.*: ff.99v-100.

[24] *Roger North's The Musicall Grammarian 1728*, [f.15v].

[25] North's solution to the problem of whether matter can think, feel or

judge seems to be found in the important role assigned to imagination. In a text from the middle period of writings, he indicates the lines along which this problem might be solved. According to him, only the mind can create new ideas which are not found in objects. That is, North ascribes all 'sensible formes' to the 'workings' of the imagination rather than to the nature of objects [*Change of Philosoficall Methods*, BL Add. MS 32549: ff.94-102v, especially f.95v].

26 North asserts that 'certeinly nature calls for that which is good for itself. And setting aside wantonness, which is easy to be perceived and may be as easily checked in children, their appetites are the best Indications of what is good for them' [*The Autobiography of the Hon. Roger North*, p. 3].

27 *Of Humane Capacity*, BL Add. MS 32526: ff.42-42v. The foetus does not come into the world with innate knowledge. Indeed, before people can govern their own 'economy', they must first know and be acquainted with their members. Accordingly, North writes:

It is a comon fancy, that wee bring into the world with us, as innate, the knowledg of our hands, fingers, etc. and that a child new borne can tell which finger is pricked, and the like. But I thinck otherwise, and that naturally and originally we have no knowledge of our selves and our parts, and that wee learne it all by experience; all that wee bring is to know wee are well, or ill. I need not appeal to nurses, to declare how long it is before an infant can make both ey[e]s point to a candle, or ceas to wonder at its litle hand, or to point at any thing. And much of this sort of philosofy would be had from children's processes, if men had as much to doe with them, as weomen have. But the state they are in at first is no more or other than this: they have members which from occasions of nature move, without order or government of them; and those being touched makes them sensible [*ibid.*: f.37].

Hence,

. . . the more children are tost[,] danc't and playd with, the faster they come on, and have more knowledg and spirits. [But] . . . if they always ly dull . . . they grow up to be more stiff and inept, and almost uncapable of learning the infant skill of it self, and so it becomes dull, and approaching to that, they call changeling [*ibid.*: f.37v].

28 North recommends that we avoid pleasures that destroy health, for once our nature is weakened, we cannot form adequate images of reality. Disease occasions false images, which, North remarks, 'are strange things and few that are sick observe them, but think the reality is according to their sense'. Instead of choosing pleasures that lead to sickness, therefore, we should gratify our inclinations by pursuing pleasures such as music that preserve health [*The Autobiography of the Hon. Roger North*, p. 147].

[29] 'Our sences, or imagination doth not deceiv us, but our hasty and immature unweighed conclusions from them are so fallacious that we have scar[c]e a just opinion of any thing without us' [*Untitled Essay*, BL Add. MS 32546: f.250v].

[30] *Power of Humane Understanding*, BL Add. MS 32526: f.88v.

[31] *The World Part I* [my title], BL Add. MS 32546: f.9; *Roger North's The Musicall Grammarian 1728*, [f.40v]. At least two writers propounded such a notion: Hobbes and Gottfried Wilhelm Leibnitz. Hobbes, who held that ideas have their origin in sensation, attempted to differentiate between understanding and imagination. In so doing, he identified understanding with formal logical reasoning, which in turn is reduced to a pure combination of names established by rules of agreement. But the influence of the algebraic calculus is clear in Hobbes's conception of definition based on the definition of a quantity by means of a formula, whereby definition is 'the resolution of a compound into parts' [William Molesworth (ed.), *The English Works of Thomas Hobbes*, 11 vols., London 1839-45, reprinted 1962, Vol. I, pp. 83, 85-86]. Leibnitz attempted to extend the language of algebra to all rational sciences by his 'combinatory art' or 'general characteristic', that is, by universal symbolism. He regarded definitions as being similar to an expression of a quantity by means of an algebraic formula; and he also conceived the decomposition or analysis of a complex concept into simple ones after the fashion of the decomposition of a whole number into its prime factors. North's conception is closer to that of Hobbes's. For some background relating to these issues, insofar as they relate to music, *see* Jamie C. Kassler, 'The Emergence of Probability reconsidered', *Archives Internationales d'Histoire des Science* (1986) 36: 17-44.

[32] *Theory of Sounds. . .1728*, BL Add. MS 32535: f.74v.

[33] *Change of Philosoficall Methods*, BL Add. MS 32549: f.95.

[34] *Roger North's Cursory Notes of Musicke (c.1698-c.1703)*, pp. 1-25. After c.1703 North tends to omit explanations of subtle matter, a primary cause, and to focus on secondary causes. Thus, in *Theory of Sounds. . .1728* [BL Add MS 32535], he makes only passing reference to subtle matter, which he obliquely terms 'interstitiall' or 'finer' matter. But it would be a mistake to conclude that at the end of his life North relinquished the subtle-matter hypothesis, for in the final summary of his philosophy, written c.1726, he clearly states that 'subtle matter is no figment' [*Physica*, Rougham MS; the statement occurs only in North's own holograph and not in his son's copy now held by the British Library]. For this information I am indebted to Mary Chan, who visited Rougham and made notes of the headings in the manuscript.

[35] Although the word 'gas' had been coined in the first part of the seventeenth century by J. B. van Helmont, the chemical nature of the air was not understood. The work of Robert Boyle is regarded as the starting point for the development of pneumatics or gas chemistry and

for the discovery of particular gases. In North's day this incipient science was still part of physico-mechanics.

[36] *Change of Philosoficall Methods*, BL Add. MS 32549: f.97. North's spirit is not to be confused with the 'animal spirits' of the physiologists and physicians, for he writes that Thomas Willis 'and others that use the terme, animal spirits, seem to intend the same as I doe, but yet I subtileize more' [*Some Essays, concerning the Manner of our Sence, or Perception of Things*, BL Add. MS 32526: f.14]. Willis, an English physician and contributor to anatomy, provided the most extensive treatment of the nervous system to his day.

[37] *Essay on the Reciprocall Forces of Body and Spirit influencing each Other*, BL Add. MS 32549: f.81.

[38] *Change of Philosoficall Methods*, BL Add. MS 32549: f.97v.

[39] *Ibid.*

[40] *Roger North's Cursory Notes of Musicke* (c.1698-c.1703), p. 8.

[41] *Essay on the Reciprocall Forces of Body and Spirit influencing each Other*, BL Add. MS 32549: f.81.

[42] For example, *Roger North's The Musicall Grammarian 1728*, [f.12 and n.2; f.82]. Even today, the word 'tone' (*tonus*), in physiology, denotes the tension (contraction) of the muscles as the condition by which health and vigor are maintained. More specifically, it refers to the usually moderate physiological activity of a tissue or organ, for example, the striated muscle, which, as a result of continuous nervous stimulation, is normally in a state of moderate contraction by which posture is maintained.

[43] *Roger North's Writings on Music to c.1703: A Set of Analytical Indexes* prepared by Janet D. Hine with Digests of the Manuscripts by Mary Chan and Jamie C. Kassler (Kensington, N.S.W. 1987); *Roger North's The Musicall Grammarian and Theory of Sounds*: Digests of the Manuscripts by Mary Chan and Jamie C. Kassler with an Analytical Index of 1726 and 1728 *Theory of Sounds* by Janet D. Hine (Kensington, N.S.W. 1988).

[44] *Change of Philosoficall Methods*, BL Add. MS 32549: f.94; *see also* n.25 above. North hints that his notions are heterodox, for he writes: 'Those who ascribe all sensible formes to the nature of the objects, and not to the working of the imagination, charge us with supplanting what all the world hath agreed upon to be the incontestable proof of the Deity vizt., the order and beauty of the universe' [*ibid.*: f.95v].

Analogy in Leonard B. Meyer's Theory of Musical Meaning

Naomi Cumming

Abstract

Leonard B. Meyer's first book, Emotion and Meaning in Music, *has stimulated wide discussion and analysis since its publication in 1956. This paper seeks to elucidate the function of analogy in Meyer's thinking, showing its fundamental importance in the construction of his 1956 argument, and its ramifications for his later work. This leads to some generalizations about the place of analogy in music theory and aesthetics. After an introduction defining analogy in its relation to metaphor, the paper is divided into four sections. The first deals with the influence of selected texts by American Pragmatic thinkers on Meyer's understanding of semiotic relationships, which are the basis for his analogy between meaningful interactions in social and musical contexts. The second discusses the manner in which Meyer appropriates these texts in the construction of his own theory of musical meaning. A third section looks at the problem of semiotic failure, how the occurrence of error in interpreting musical implication calls into question the assumed correlation between musical style and a perceiver's 'competence'. Finally, the post-structuralist or 'deconstructive' thinking of Derrida is used to give a different perspective on the problem cited in section three. It is shown that Meyer represses the connotations of his analogy in his later writings, while retaining the structures built on it as an analytical tool.*

Introduction

I want to start with two related questions: first, is it possible to construct a general model of 'meaning' which applies to actions, utterances, texts and musical gestures? and, second, can we explain in general terms what it is for a musical passage to have meaning?

These are the questions which occupied Leonard B. Meyer in his Chicago Ph.D., *Emotion and Meaning in Music* (1956), a seminal work both for his own thinking and for the aesthetic branch of musicology. In forming his conception of music's meaning and affective content, Meyer drew primarily upon the approach to questions of meaning advocated by the American Pragmatists, John Dewey and George Herbert Mead. Meyer chose texts which are incipiently semiotic in their approach to the signification of actions or words, responding above all to extracts which ratified his intuition that a listener's expectancy was essential to the perception of musical meaning. His treatment of the cited texts does not indicate a rigorous or systematic study of their sources in Mead's social psychology or Dewey's instrumental logic. The focus of attention in *Emotion and Meaning in Music* is on the musical exemplification of reference and expectancy, rather than on its epistemological foundation. The ideas put forward cannot be set up as a systematic aesthetic theory. They must rather be accepted as the initial working out in musical terms of an analogy which had already been found fruitful by the pragmatic thinkers. This article looks at the nature of analogy, its place in the formative period of Meyer's thinking and its ramifications for his later work.

An analogy is an explanatory device in which a pattern of relation-ships postulated for one realm of thought or activity is transferred in its essential aspects to another realm, whose attributes are believed to be similar. Stephen Pepper describes the formation of an analogy as fol-lows:

A man desiring to understand the world looks about for a clue to its comprehension. He pitches upon some area of commonsense fact and tries if he cannot understand other areas in terms of this one. This original area becomes then his basic analogy or root metaphor. He describes as best he can the characteristics of this area, or, if you will, discriminates its structure. A list of its structural characteristics becomes his basic concepts of explanation and description (1957: 91).

The value of analogies is in their power to illustrate a perceived pattern which cannot be adequately described using the normal vocabulary of a given experiential realm or academic discipline. To describe the experience of meaning in music is clearly an aesthetic problem beyond the grasp of the theoretical vocabulary used in describing the functions of pitch, duration and simultaneity which are the literal properties of sound. Yet if meaningful interactions follow a certain pattern in one area of human activity, this pattern may be taken as a constant, applicable to the explanation of musical signification. It is on this postulate that Meyer bases his argument. The presence of meaning in a musical passage is a judgement made by the listener on his or her experience of listening. Meyer elucidates the basis for this judgement by forming an analogy with other circumstances in which meaning is found. As patterns for the description of meaning are offered by the American Pragmatists, he transfers them to the description of (primarily tonal) music.

In Pepper's discussion, the terms 'analogy' and 'metaphor' are virtually synonymous. An analogy becomes the root-metaphor for a world hypothesis when it generates general categories for explanation. The term 'metaphor' is used in a non-poetic sense to refer to this philosophical device. The analogical thinking found in Meyer's work is consistent with that in his sources and reflects their root-metaphor. Most potent in the pragmatic theory is the metaphor of an adaptive action. The explanation adopted by Meyer is accordingly founded upon observations of the function of signs in behavioural interactions. Meyer's version is derived from a number of texts, in which significant relationships and interactions are variously described.

While the use of analogy proves very fruitful in Meyer's discussion of musical meaning, a fundamental problem for his theory is created by not examining the epistemological stance assumed by Dewey and Mead in developing a semiotic pattern from their root-metaphor. As Meyer did not explore pragmatic views on the relationship between the subject and object of experience, his own writing slips without announcement from one direction of reference to the other as if they were entirely equivalent, until that point when he recognizes a potential dislocation between the perceiver and perceived, born of a failure of reference and interpretation. The adopted theory of signs begins to demand a more secure framework in the theory of knowledge, but no attempt is made by Meyer to systematize the relationship of subject and object in perception. This problem has been commented on by a number of authors (Dipert 1983: 4, Hansen 1967: 203).

To point out that *Emotion and Meaning in Music* does not present a systematic semiotic theory is not to dismiss the work. The more systematic development of semiotic theory has been undertaken by later writers (*cf.* Hatten 1982). Meyer's ideas point to an understanding which remains unclosed and unresolved in the text. It is, appropriately, his approach to conflict, uncertainty and incompleteness in life and music that presents a pertinent challenge to any assumption that organicism (Pepper 1957: 280) is a root-metaphor with inalienable superiority in either the analysis or aesthetics of music. His pragmatic sources offered an alternative analogy, which Pepper identifies as 'contextualism' (1957: 232).

1. Meyer, Meaning and the Pragmatists

Meyer's knowledge of the writings of Charles Sanders Peirce was limited and indirect, coming through a brief excerpt in a work on logic by Morris Cohen (Cohen 1946: 59, Meyer 1956: 34). Peirce's seminal influence on the later development of pragmatic thought is however essential to the development of the root-metaphor held in common by its proponents. His influence on William James is evident in James's functional psychology. This offered an understanding of behavioural processes adopted by both Dewey and Mead. Each of the texts cited by Meyer, although written forty years apart, reflect James's pragmatic approach to meaning. These are Mead's *Mind, Self and Society* (1934) and two articles by Dewey on the conflict theory of emotion (1894, 1895). The contextualistic root-metaphor held in common by these writers is 'a transitory historical situation and its biological tensions' (Pepper 1973: 198). More specifically, the transitory situation is that of an adaptive action taking place between an organism and some element in its environment.

Mead's theory of the social act is built on three basic terms, which have their source in Peirce's semiotic theory: (1) the gesture (or sign), (2) the object (or signatum) and (3) the interpretant. Mead elaborates the idea of positing a hypothetical consequence for a given event as the basis of its meaning. A gesture performed by an organism indicates the action which will follow. This sign is perceived by another organism, who modifies his action in accordance with it, and the consequent action of the first organism (signatum) then occurs. Mead says that this relationship 'constitutes the matrix within which meaning arises, or which develops into the field of meaning' (1934: 75-82, Meyer 1956: 34). He believes the signification of a gesture to be socially encoded when the mutual adjustment occurring between organisms in several related acts leads to an agreement on the appropriate response. The meaning is confirmed in any individual act if the gesture activates this response in another organism (1934: 78). An act of pointing, for example, leads to a turning of the head in the indicated direction. The kind of reference embodied in a gesture may be described as 'linear' in so far as it involves a 'transition from an initiation to a satisfaction' which is intelligible to interpretation (Pepper 1957: 253).

In his much earlier articles on emotion, Dewey is concerned with what happens when the significance of an object or gesture is misinterpreted by an acting organism, whether man or animal. As in Mead's theory, a given pattern of response is said to be activated when a gesture is classed by an organism as being similar to one previously encountered. The gesture may, however, deviate in such a way as to conflict with the organism's expectations, and so demand some adjustment in his interpretation and response. Irrelevant aspects of the learned patterns of behaviour must be aborted and replaced by ones which take account of the new information. The gesture's signification (its 'pointing') is mentally reconstituted during the process of forming a more successful adaptive response (Angier 1927: 395, Meyer 1956: 14). Dewey contends that it is at this point, during the organism's adjustment to a deviant or ambiguous sign, that conflict is experienced as the condition for a subjective emotion. He nevertheless maintains that the object and response are not distinguished from one another in experience (1895: 25-6; in referring to 'that terrible bear' a person implicitly says 'how frightened I am' 1894: 20-1). By absorbing this account into his own account of an individual's interaction with significant gestures, Meyer opens himself unintentionally to the use of intentional terms—those which refer to a subjective state by describing an aspect of its object (Scruton 1982: 75).

The idea of conflict, derived from Dewey, is most important to Meyer. The basis for Meyer's analogy between behavioural and aesthetic spheres is actually found in Dewey's work, as the outlines of Dewey's conflict theory form the structure for both his instrumentalist theory of logic and his aesthetics. In these later theories the point of conflict is presented by Dewey as the point when reflective thought is initiated and meaning achieved (Thayer 1968: 184). In *Art as Experience* (1934) the emotive patterns found in an organism's response to conflict becomes a metaphor for artistic self-expression. The organism's activity is presented as an equivalent of impulsive thinking or creativity. A creative thought points to fulfillment, but conflict is posited as essential to its true expression:

> The impulsion . . . meets many things on its outbound course that deflect and oppose it. In the process of converting these obstacles and neutral conditions into favoring agencies, the live creature becomes aware of the intent implicit in the impulsion. The self . . . does not merely restore itself to its former state. Blind surge has been changed into a purpose; instinctive tendencies are transformed into contrived undertakings. The attitudes of the self are informed with meaning (Dewey 1934: 59, Meyer 1956: 31).

Dewey here extends the pattern of adaptation put forward in his articles on the conflict theory of emotion (1894, 1895), creating an analogy between an organism's undisturbed action and an artist's mental activity. In both life and art inhibition is believed to initiate some form of reflection, differing according to the realm of activity, and affect is seen to be its by-product. The patterns of a transitory situation, an adaptive act, are thus demonstrated to have a general explanatory application. Dewey's analogy between perceived references and their obstruction in biological adaptation and similar patterns of reference and blocking in artistic activity has the status of a root-metaphor, because the analogy is used to form categories of explanation which are transferable to new contexts in which reference and blocking occur. An incipient semiotic theory is thus enriched. In addition to the basic linear reference found in Mead's account of behavioural gestures, Dewey's discussion provides for the blocking of a reference, a factor of disorder and novelty (Pepper 1957: 255).

Meyer takes Dewey's model for the formation of analogies between biological adaptation and artistic activity and, in doing so, participates in the use of his contextualistic root-metaphor. Like Dewey, he generalizes the situation of conflict, seeing it as essential to both cognitive and affective responses. When a listener's stylistic competencies are challenged by an unexpected event, so that the activity of unselfconscious but purposeful listening is disturbed, he or she responds by seeking to objectify the meaning of the foregoing musical gestures (their 'hypothetical meaning') in the light of the perceived consequent event. The conflict acts to promote a reconstitution of the sign and leads to a new 'evident meaning'. Blocking is seen as essential to the conscious consideration of the sign.

> Reflection is . . . brought into play where some tendency is delayed, some pattern of habitual behavior disturbed. So long as behavior is automatic and habitual there is no urge for it to become self-conscious, though it may become so. If meaning is to become objectified at all, it will as a rule become so when difficulties are encountered that make normal, automatic behavior impossible (Meyer 1956: 39).

Where the listener does not possess the theoretical knowledge to reassess an event, Meyer believes that an affective response is experienced as a product of the conflict but not objectified as a form of meaning.

2. Meyer's Theory of Meaning

Meyer's explanation of musical meaning and affect involves a conflation of Mead's and Dewey's ideas. As a result of this conflation two different types of meaning are recognized, the basis of both types being in the semiotic reference of one event to another. Meyer affirms, first, that 'if, on the basis of past experience, a present stimulus leads us to expect a more or less definite consequent musical event, then that stimulus has meaning' (1956: 35). In this statement he adapts James's and Mead's pragmatic equation of meaning with the perceived consequence of an event, acknowledging the validity of a basic linear reference. Later, he refines the definition to say that meaning is only objectified by the listener when some form of conflict occurs, either by a deviation from an expected course of events, or through the occurrence of an ambiguous gesture which inhibits the forming of a clear expectation (1956: 39). In these statements he assimilates Dewey's conflict theory, as seen above, and affirms the importance of blocking to the conscious interpretation of a sign.

Meyer's thought on these types of signification is further developed in an article of 1957, where the use of analogy is complicated by reference to information theory. The type of meaning found in a direct linear reference is now rejected in favour of that produced by blocking. The sign is seen as a piece of information, and the later event to which it points (the signatum) arrives in the form of 'feed-back' to confirm or deny the perceiver's interpretation. Meyer says that 'if an antecedent event arouses no uncertainty and the consequent comes precisely as expected then meaning will be neutral, information nil, and feedback is superfluous' (1957, in 1967: 13). What was identified by Dewey as a situation of conflict has now been made analogous to a position of uncertainty in communication, which maximizes the informative value of later elements in the sequence. Under the influence of this further analogical leap, Meyer after 1957 identifies meaning exclusively with occurrences of deviation, ambiguity or stylistically improbable events. In *Emotion and Meaning in Music* he does recognize unmediated signification, emphasizing that the import attached by the listener to the processes of signification is changed by the mental conflict induced by uncertainty. He gives greater importance to the listener's perception of the music's failure to fulfil an implied reference, or to make an initial reference clear, since conflict in a perceived gesture is deemed essential to the objectification of meaning.

Clarification of the basis upon which a listener becomes competent to interpret musical signification is clearly essential to the coherence of a theory which assumes the presence of a listener as mediator of the sign. Even 'embodied' musical meaning requires interpretation by a perceiver to whom its components are intelligible. In describing how a perceiver might gain musical competence, Meyer relies on Mead's argument for the social encoding of signs and posits style (or culture) as the social context in which musical meanings are defined:

> Without a set of gestures common to the social group, and without common habit responses to those gestures, no communication whatsoever would be possible. Communication depends upon, presupposes, and arises out of the universe of discourse which in the aesthetics of music is called style (1956: 42).

A listener demonstrates competence in the perception of a style when a musical gesture prompts expectations in him or her of a stylistically probable form of continuation. The attitude of expectancy makes it evident that the musical gesture has 'meaning' for that listener at a particular point in time. Such an attitude signifies an involvement in the semiotic processes of the piece, so demonstrating an internalized and tacit knowledge of the probabilities inherent in the style being exemplified. Meyer recognizes the constant development of styles, but nevertheless affirms a correlation of known stylistic probabilities with the attributes of perceptual competence possessed by a practised listener. He does not attempt a detailed account of the actual components of such a listener's knowledge.

The according of even a defective synonymity between mental structures, stylistic systems and musical reality is problematic but nonetheless essential to an understanding of how linear references are interpreted. Meyer assumes that when a system of signification has been fully internalized, perception can take place without the mediation of conscious thought. It is an habitual response to familiar stimuli, similar to that found in the adaptive contexts described by Dewey. The perceptual psychologist, James Gibson, gives an example which supports the kind of situation Meyer is thinking of in describing the type of meaning found in linear reference where conflict is absent. He argues that in a natural environment 'the senses can obtain information about objects in the world without the intervention of an intellectual process, if they are operating as systems in a given way' (Gibson 1968: 2). When an invariable motion has, for example, been detected, the organism conducts an exploratory search to confirm his perception. The affinity of this form of perceiving with the activities of expecting or predicting is suggested by the organism's active response of intercepting the moving object (as a runner intercepts a ball), but the thought content of the expectation is not separated by the runner from the perception itself (*ibid.*: 280). In a musical analogue the listener might identify continuity in a progression, mentally projecting its probable extension and resolution. His or her mental involvement with the progression is not the subject of selfconscious reflection. Listening is rather a direct, unmediated activity in which the listener is aware only of the object of his perception. Thought in the form of expectancy is thus seen to be intrinsic to the perceptual act, although perceptual thought remains distinct from abstract reasoning (*see* Scruton 1982: 180-1). Like Dewey, Gibson allows an absorption of the perceiver in the act of responding which does not necessitate a distinction of the object from the self. This description does not, however, address the problem of conflict (such as might be induced if the moving object turns out to be the projection of an electric light and, thus, incapable of interception).

3. Divergent Events

The kind of adjustment recognized by Gibson can only be known in responses which are informed by unchallenged competencies. Even if we accept the possibility of such an unreflective perceptual response completely attuned to the implications of the music, and suspend any judgement on the idea of competence itself, the occurrence of disruptive events which contradict a listener's expectation must challenge the extent of his or her competency. The first type of meaning is predicated upon the existence of orderly and predictable patterns, which arise out of an understood system: diatonic progressions; linear continuity; regular metric patterns; standardized forms and archetypal gestures such as the cadence. In the second type, produced by the blocking of reference, it is precisely the disruptive, centrifugal forces which are said to promote the objectification of meaning and to elicit an affective content (or response). In his analytical examples Meyer cites various forms of chromaticism; a cycle of fifths which fails to close at the predicted point due to a change in the position of diminished fifths; indecisive harmonic progressions; deviation from an established melodic line and a texture in which the theme is indistinct. He emphasizes those facets of the music which subvert the authority of a closed structure on a higher level, focusing detailed attention on anomalous minutiae of the surface. Even in this early work, when he was not yet familiar with the writings of Heinrich Schenker, he opposes the standpoint on modulation expressed in Salzer's (1952) adaptation of Schenker. The wish to uncover a hierarchical organization within which surface conflicts can be absorbed at a higher level, is uncongenial (1956: 53), since it is in these very conflicts that he finds the music's power to involve and move the listener.

It is at this point that the assumptions of Dewey's epistemology, unexamined or commented upon by Meyer, appear to disturb the consistency of his argument. If there is, indeed, a correlation between mental structures and style, how can uncertainty or perceptual error be accounted for? Disruptive events must engender a separation of the subject and object of perceptual experience in order for the reflection posited by Meyer to take place. Those factors which affront competency also subvert the existence of style as a stable entity capable of being internalized. Meyer has appealed both to the authority of style and to its failure as sources of meaning.

Some aspects of this problem are addressed by Meyer in a more recent article (1983) which embraces the same aesthetic viewpoint as that put forward in 1956. Meyer here distinguishes between changes which take place in the underlying systems which govern the operation of tonal music (the 'rules') and changes in the method of realizing these rules in particular structures ('strategies'). The degree of any affective response is seen to be determined by the level at which competencies are threatened. Of the first form of innovation he says: 'Such systemic change seriously threatens our sense of psychic security and competent control. Far from being welcome, the insecurity and uncertainty thus engendered is at least as antipathetic, disturbing, and unpleasant as stimulus privation' (1983: 519). By contrast, he finds the introduction of new strategies less threatening to competencies and hence less disturbing:

> Though they may initially seem to threaten existing competencies, the function and significance of novel strategies within the larger set of stylistic constraints can usually be grasped without too much delay or difficulty. For a while the tensions produced by strategic innovation may seem disturbing. But in the end, when our grasp of the principles ordering events is confirmed and our sense of competency is reestablished and control is reinforced, tension is resolved into an elation that is both stimulating and enjoyable (1983: 519).

At each of these levels the likening of perceptual thought to action is made evident in a strong correlation between the affirmation of existing competencies and a sense of control. The listener cannot literally control the unfolding of the musical structure; but when competency in the style permits correct predictions to be made, a sense of control is the predominant subjective state. This is analogous to the making of a correct choice on the basis of well understood behavioural conventions in other realms of activity.

This refinement in Meyer's thinking allows there to be a correlation between mental structures and style at a general level (that of rules) while permitting variation or conflict in how stylistic features are realized. A tacit grasp of compositional rules is quite compatible with perceptual error in the positing of specific implications for a musical phrase. The listener's expectancies, being determined by his or her experience with a given style, are distinct from the objective implications of the particular music being heard. Thus, the problem of subject and object is also clarified. Expectancy and implication may be one to the perceiver, before conflict has induced objectification, but they are distinct in the analysis of perceptual experience.

4. Deconstruction

The post-structuralist ideas put forward by Jacques Derrida under the name of Deconstruction throw a different light on the conflicts found in dealing with the correlation of style and competency. Three facets of his attack on structuralist thought are particularly relevant and may be summarized under the terms 'competence', 'structure' and 'presence'. First, competence. In the words of Christopher Norris, deconstruction 'starts out by rigorously suspending [the] . . . assumed correspondence between mind, meaning and the concept of method which claims to unite them' (1982: 3). Derrida criticizes the habit of seeking a truth in philosophical or literary writing which is somehow to be authenticated by the critic's competence. By analogy, a listener's competence cannot be taken to authenticate the structure which he or she finds in the auditory text, as the music's various significations exist quite apart from the presence of any perceiver.

Second, structure. Any approach which has a prior commitment to a standard of truth or structural unity is classed by Derrida as 'logocentric'. Meyer's theory escapes the allegation of being logocentric to the extent that it emphasizes subversive features and rejects any notion of a determinate high-level structure applicable to all tonal works. Meyer does, however, adopt a theory which posits an underlying unity of structure between various meaningful interactions. Although the assumption of such commonality is essential to the semiotic project, and its problems are not unique to Meyer's treatment, challenges to it must be considered. George Pitcher has commented that no essence can be extracted from the contexts in which meaning is used in ordinary language, saying that the attempt to find it 'is just another instance of the craving for unity, and in particular, of the desire to find essences' (1964: 261). This challenge may apply also to attempts at codifying the experience of musical meaning.

Third, presence. Derrida shows that a metaphysic of presence cannot be effectively maintained in the interpretation of linguistic signs. The repressed metaphors of language betray the writer by contradicting his asserted truths, thus undermining a reader's belief in the sincere presence conveyed by his literary voice. This is in part true of Meyer's text. In *Emotion and Meaning in Music* he seeks to maintain the essential function of expectancy; but in describing a theme as an analytical object, he slips into the use of terms which deny immediacy to the listener's presence. Given a complex structure, it is simpler to identify an area of deviation and specify the differing functions which contribute to its formation, than to attempt an analysis in terms of expectations and hypotheses, inhibitions and rationalizations (*see* Narmour 1977: 137). The listener's expectant identification with a line is most easily asserted in the description of an isolated melody. But even here there are problems, as a melody may contain multiple conflicting lines, and a single purposive direction for listening cannot be maintained if it is dependent on directional continuity. Meyer therefore assumes an objective language with implicit intentional content when undertaking an analysis.

A good example of this is found in Meyer's analysis of the theme from Hindemith's symphony *Mathis der Maler* as a compilation of three implicative lines (1956: 140, Ex. 46). An exclusive identification with any one of them cannot be maintained, and their mutual deflection cannot be said to create a series of points of rationalization. The lines are not retained in memory as individual entities; but their operation is a constitutive factor in the perception of the melody; and were their conflicts absent, the listener would be less active in looking for an integrated whole.

The impossibility of maintaining a listener's attentive presence to the fulfilment of every linear implication in Hindemith's melody indicates the limitations of Meyer's behavioural analogy as a means of understanding the processes of signification in music. An analogy between the meanings found in the encoded responses of social or adaptive interaction, and those found in music, is built on the essential features of patterned learning, memory and prediction. The Pragmatists' descriptions of sign functions are, however, relatively simple. Mead reflects on isolated gestural interactions, and Dewey on adaptive responses to a situation of conflict. The levels of signification and conflict possible in the hierarchical system of tonal music are considerably more complex than those represented here. In dealing with music, a language which refers constantly to the reactions of the perceiver becomes cumbersome, and references to perception are dropped in the interests of analytical clarity. The analogy between perceptual expectancy and an active response to some element in the environment thus recedes into the background, and an appearance of objectivity is assumed.

Aspects of the analogy which deal with levels of consciousness or affective response are discarded by Meyer in his later analytical work, *Explaining Music* (1973); but this work retains the structural features suggested in *Emotion and Meaning in Music* and transforms them into more objective terms. 'Expectancy' becomes 'implication', as Meyer recognizes the problem of referring constantly to a listener's presence. He nevertheless maintains that his aesthetic standpoint has not changed (1973: 114 n.1). The continuity of the theory of melody found in *Explaining*

Music with the earlier aesthetic theory is indeed supported by a description of the methodology employed by a 'critical' analyst. A close relationship between critical methodology and the structure of the aesthetic theory is demonstrated by the practice of introducing an artificial interruption into a melody in order to force an awareness of the implications suggested by it. Meyer's account of the critic's introspective methodology forms a surprisingly authentic application of the pragmatic test for meaning advocated by Peirce: 'the critic will often perform a kind of mental "experiment." He will stop the melodic flow and try to imagine what continuations seem probable' (*ibid*.: 116). An artificial interruption is an induced conflict, permitting the critic to objectify the expectations which he or she has unconsciously entertained in hearing a melodic segment (*ibid*.). After interrupting a notated progression, the critic thus ascertains its implications, consciously seeks out their realization, and reassesses them. A close correlation between the critic's expectations and objective linear implication is still assumed, but rules for the analytical reduction of an implicative line are posited as a test of objectivity (*ibid*.: 121-3). These are presumed to approximate the selective criteria intuitively applied in perception.

Having given this methodological explanation, Meyer employs objective language in his analyses. Conflict between perceptual expectancy and the actual realizations of implicative lines remains a central concern, but the affective and meaningful connotations of such conflict are repressed in the interests of linguistic objectivity. The question of how perceptual activity is related to analysis remains open, as the degree of listener 'presence' which is being asserted is undefined.

In Meyer's most recent work (1989), the analogy between musical and behavioural conventions, as the basis for semiotic explanation, is replaced by an exploration of those aspects of cognitive psychology which deal with the formation of cognitive schemata (*see* Meyer and Rosner 1982). Meaning is still predicated upon a listener's expectancy, but the processes by which expectancy is formed and the mental structures which it entails are now much more precisely formulated. An investigation of musical meaning is directed toward the identification of specific musical structures (schemata) which have demonstrated constancy over time, thus establishing concrete entities as the vehicles for stylistic continuity and as the constituents of a listener's competency and expectation (Meyer 1980, Gjerdingen 1984, 1986). Analogy is apparent once more, as the identification of cognitive schemata was initiated in disciplines other than music. This analogy might prove more fruitful in being more scientifically based.

Conclusion

The structure contained in the pragmatic definition of meaning as interpreted by Meyer is very general. The identity observable between meaningful events is limited to two categories: (1) events forming a linear reference by pointing to a consequent, and (2) those inducing conscious interpretive activity by blocking reference in various ways. Even the basis of this semiotic has been questioned, since the presence of a listener, interpreting each individual sign, cannot be maintained; and the objective language of music analysis represses the listener's presence altogether. Yet deconstructive criticisms are not sufficiently cogent to undermine the heuristic value of Meyer's analogy between the functions of behavioural and musical signs. The scepticism of post-structuralist thought might suggest the demise of both 'competence' and 'style' as terms denoting real and definable entities, but vagueness of meaning does not justify an entire disinheritance of the concept of style, given that patterns of commonality do exist between works and provide the basis for a listener's predictive capacity. Not even the event of perceptual error can in itself discredit the notion of style, since a play with uncertainty is predicated upon the existence of some recognized norms.

A valuable outcome of Meyer's work is in offering an alternative root-metaphor as the basis for musical analysis. In reflecting the American Pragmatists' contextualism, Meyer's use of analogy is quite distinct from that found in theories influenced by organicism. Although the root-metaphors of these world hypotheses are related, their divergent emphases upon the processes of reference on the one hand, and the emergent unity of completed reference on the other, lead to quite different consequences in the interpretation of real events. Organicism contains both progressive and ideal categories, but an insistence on the primacy of the latter in defining 'Reality' may lead a dogmatic adherent to dismiss progressive tendencies as mere 'Appearance' (Pepper 1957: 282). That organicism is inherent in Schenker's thought is quite apparent from the analogies he uses (Kassler 1983, Solie 1980), but Schenker's emphasis on distance hearing attests to the importance of the progressive unfolding of structure in his system. Some applications of his thought are nevertheless susceptible to an over-emphasis on the ideal categories. Greater reality is then attributed to the background structure, once unfolded, than to the elaboration of linear structures in foreground events which may display ambiguity in their deflection of the longer-term goal. One example of this problem is found in the work of Bruce Campbell, who states that 'ambiguity in music does not really exist', justifying this denial by pointing to the higher contextual levels in which it is resolved (1985: 193). Local ambiguity is judged an ephemeral state which cannot contribute to the formation of the real musical object.

By adopting a different metaphorical foundation, Meyer's approach emphasizes that the building of contexts takes place in time and that the impression of ambiguity may be manipulated even when a long-term goal is envisaged by the composer and performer. It affirms the value of the disruptive, ambiguous and unclosed, stressing that meaning may arise out of uncertainty, an affront to perceptual competency. Meyer's analytical method does not offer a fully-developed alternative to Schenkerian theory. It does, however, suggest a re-assessment of how progressive and ideal categories are viewed. The root-metaphor of contextualism may also be fruitful in suggesting alternative approaches to musical signification. Its emphasis on diversity of reference is particularly relevant to the description of surface features which are not necessarily embraced by tonal processes. Finally, the difficulties found in Meyer's embryonic semiotics are relevant to current thought. An on-going problem is that of how the perceiver, as an actively involved individual, is implicated in analytical statements about a musical structure. This question remains an epistemological challenge for music theory and analysis.

Acknowledgments

I would like to express my sincere gratitude to Leonard B. Meyer for the generosity he has shown me in spending time talking about his theories during January and February 1984, giving me access to his unpublished manuscripts and maintaining a correspondence and interest in my work. I am greatly indebted to him for opening up to me the rich area of discourse on musical meaning. I would also like to thank Jamie Kassler for her helpful comments and suggestions.

References

ANGIER, Roswell
    1927   'The Conflict Theory of Emotion', *The American Journal of Psychology*, 38: 390-401
CAMPBELL, Bruce
    1985   Review of Janet Levy, *Beethoven's Compositional Choices: The Two Versions of Op. 18 No. 1, First Movement* (1982), *Journal of Music Theory*, 29: 187-97
COHEN, Morris
    1946   *A Preface to Logic*, London: Routledge
DEWEY, John
    1894   'The Theory of Emotion I: Emotional Attitudes', *The Psychological Review*, 1: 553-69
    1895   'The Theory of Emotion II: The Significance of Emotions', *The Psychological Review*, 2: 13-32
    1934   *Art as Experience*, New York: Perigree, 1980
DIPERT, Randall
    1983   'Meyer's *Emotion and Meaning in Music:* A Sympathetic Critique of its Central Claims', *In Theory Only*, 6: 3-17
GIBSON, James
    1968   *The Senses Considered as Perceptual Systems*, London: George Allen & Unwin

GJERDINGEN, Robert
 1984 'A Musical Schema: Structure and Style Change 1720-1900',
  Ph.D. dissertation, University of Pennsylvania, Philadelphia
  (UM # 8505072)
 1986 'The Formation and Deformation of Classic/Romantic
  Phrase Schemata: A Theoretical Model and Historical Study',
  Music Theory Spectrum, 8: 25-43
HANSEN, Forest
 1967 'Music, Feeling and Meaning: A Study of Four Theories',
  Ph.D. dissertation, Johns Hopkins University, Baltimore
  (UM # 7014814)
HATTEN, Robert
 1982 'Toward a Semiotic Model of Style in Music: Epistemological
  and Methodological Bases', Ph.D. dissertation, Indiana
  University, Bloomington (UM # 8300851)
KASSLER, Jamie C.
 1983 'Heinrich Schenker's Epistemology and Philosophy of Music:
  An Essay on the Relations between Evolutionary Theory and
  Music Theory', *The Wider Domain of Evolutionary Thought*,
  ed. David Oldroyd and Ian Langham, Dordrecht: D. Reidel
  Publishing Co., 221-260
MEAD, George Herbert
 1934 *Mind, Self and Society*, Chicago: University of Chicago Press
MEYER, Leonard B.
 1956 *Emotion and Meaning in Music*, Chicago: University of
  Chicago Press
 1957 'Meaning in Music and Information Theory', *Journal of
  Aesthetics and Art Criticism*, 15: 412-24 (reprinted in Meyer
  1967: 5-21)
 1967 *Music, the Arts, and Ideas: Patterns and Predictions in
  Twentieth Century Culture*, Chicago: University of Chicago
  Press
 1973 *Explaining Music: Essays and Explorations*, Berkeley:
  University of California Press
 1980 'Exploiting Limits: Creation, Archetypes and Style Change',
  Daedelus, 109: 177-205
 1983 'Innovation, Choice, and the History of Music', *Critical
  Inquiry*, 9: 517-44
 1984 'Music and Ideology in the Nineteenth Century', unpublished
  Tanner Lectures on Human Values, Stanford University, 17
  and 21 May: 23-51
 1989 *Style in Music: Theory, History and Ideology*, Philadelphia:
  University of Pennsylvania Press
MEYER, Leonard B. and ROSNER, Burton S.
 1982 'Melodic Processes and the Perception of Music', *The*

Psychology of Music, ed. Diana Deutsch, New York: Academic Press: 316-41

NARMOUR, Eugene
  1977 *Beyond Schenkerism: The Need for Alternatives in Music Analysis*, Chicago: University of Chicago Press

NORRIS, Christopher
  1982 *Deconstruction: Theory and Practice*, London: Methuen

PEPPER, Stephen C.
  1957 *World Hypotheses: A Study in Evidence*, Berkeley: University of California Press (1st edn. 1942)
  1973 'Metaphor', *Dictionary of the History of Ideas*, ed. P.P. Wiener, New York: Scribner's Sons, vol. 3: 196-201

PITCHER, George
  1964 *The Philosophy of Wittgenstein*, Englewood Cliffs, New Jersey: Prentice Hall

SCRUTON, Roger
  1982 *Art and Imagination: A Study in the Philosophy of Mind*, London: Routledge and Kegan Paul

SALZER, Felix
  1952 *Structural Hearing: Tonal Coherence in Music*, New York: Dover

SOLIE, Ruth
  1980 'The Living Work: Organicism and Musical Analysis', *Nineteenth Century Music*, 4: 147-56

THAYER, H. S.
  1968 *Meaning and Action: A Critical History of Pragmatism*, Indianapolis: Bobbs-Merrill

Analogy in Music: Origins, Uses, Limitations

Graham Pont

Abstract

Most metaphors depend on a perception of analogy, real or imagined. But analogy itself is a very broad and diffuse concept, embracing relationships that actually exist among things of this world as well as resemblances, close and remote, that have been created, imposed, conceived or suggested by human beings. Analogy plays an important role in music, as in all the arts and sciences; but its true significance in human culture is not generally appreciated. As there is no adequate history of musical analogy, the author's aim is to indicate some of the origins, uses and abuses of this diverse concept, through a brief survey of the theory and practice of music and related arts, across the history and prehistory of civilisation.

Introduction

The concept of *analogia* comes from Greek mathematics, but the use of analogies or proportions is much older. The musical use of analogy is seen in the modular construction of scales and metres as well as the Pythagorean-Platonic world-view, which was modelled on the integral ratios and, possibly also, on the irrational temperaments of musical tuning. The limitations of analogy are revealed by the existence of anomalies, such as the impossibility of tuning an entirely regular scale by integral ratios. Ancient grammarians recognised linguistic analogies, *e.g.*, regularities of construction and etymology; but the 'analogists' were opposed by the 'anomalists' who accepted the existence of natural irregularities of idiom. Although the argument from analogy is strictly invalid, analogising remains a useful mode of popular and scientific reasoning.

The argument from analogy was adopted into modern musicology from

Germanic philology (the Grimm brothers, Georg Friedrich Benecke and Karl Lachmann), where the comparison of similar passages in literary texts had been used as a way of correlating and correcting divergent sources. From c.1850 this method was improperly applied to the editing of autograph scores, causing massive falsification in the collected editions of Bach, Handel and many other composers. Recent trends in editorial procedure and performance practice show an increasing recognition of musical anomaly or variety as opposed to the analogy or uniformity assumed by older interpreters.

Thus, while analogy remains an essential part of musicology and all the other arts and sciences, allowance must always be made for the existence of anomaly or variety, a natural phenomenon as well as an artistic licence, whose occurrence is more easily overlooked in the age of standardisation, mass-production and mechanised data-processing.

1. Origins

We owe the term 'analogy' to the ancient Greek mathematicians who developed the first known theory of exact proportions. Starting from the concept of *logos* as number and ratio, they defined *analogia* as similarity or identity of ratio, as in A:B=B:C (continuous proportion) or A:B=C:D (discontinuous proportion). The theory of proportion or analogy was elaborated between the times of Pythagoras and Plato, when arithmetic and geometry were closely aligned with cosmological speculation and music theory; but the practical use of proportion is much older than the Greeks. The monumental art of the Egyptians and Babylonians was clearly controlled by some system of proportions; and evidence of proportional design, evidently based on the canons of the human hand and foot, has been found at Çatal Hüyük (in modern Turkey), one of the oldest towns in the world. Here the rooms of houses dating from the seventh and sixth millennia B.C. have been reported as 'commonly averaging 20 by 15 feet'—though it might be somewhat premature to describe this harmonious proportion as *diatessaron*![1]

The Greeks showed their exquisite sense of proportion not only in architecture, sculpture and painting but also in music and dance, which they regarded as a single, fundamental art. Árpád Szabó is probably right in supposing that the terminology of proportional mathematics was derived from the theory and practice of the monochord, for with this precise instrument the first musical theorists laid the foundations of mathematical order and symmetry that still hold today.[2] In the science of harmonics the Greeks established the numerical principles of tonal order and symmetrical scale construction, deriving them from an archetypal module or *analogia*, 6:8:9:12. This module encodes the interlocking proportions of the structural intervals in the octave system, the frame of the ancient and modern scales. In the science of rhythmics the Greek theorists measured the movements of the dance and the periods of poetry and song, establishing the symmetries of long and short duration and classifying the various feet that are still recognised in our musical and poetical metres. With the aid of these measures, they identified the various harmonic and rhythmic modes and created a scientific taxonomy of melodic and rhythmic forms whose value has long outlasted the phenomena originally classified. Over a period of centuries the Greek theorists and their less exact Roman successors made intensive investigations of analogies, not only within and among the arts but also between the human microcosm and the macrocosm of the universal system.

It is well known that Plato postulated a musical analogy as the bond of the cosmic elements in the World Soul of the *Timaeus*; but Ernest G. McClain has now identified this bond as the *analogia* or proportion of 6:8:9:12 and the three means it encodes, arithmetic, geometric and harmonic. In a *tour de force* of harmonic and numerological exegesis, McClain has revealed how Plato applied the precise mathematics of tuning and temperament to the quantitative modelling of political systems and the fine attunement of the ideal city-state.[3]

Long before the Greeks it was discovered that the pursuit of analogy often ends with the recognition of anomaly. The observation of diurnal, monthly and annual analogies made the calendar possible; but the anomalous cycles of the sun and moon made it impossible to construct an harmonious calendar: our tempered calendar of twelve notional months is a musical approximation. Perhaps the most famous anomaly to be discovered by the ancients was the lack of 'symmetry' or common measure between the equal sides and the hypotenuse of the right-angled isosceles triangle. Pythagoras did not discover 'Pythagoras's theorem'; nor could he conceivably have wished to prove it; for the proof of incommensurability in this and other geometric figures meant the downfall of the old Pythagorean world-view. It showed by the most rigorous logic that the world could not be entirely reduced to a common arithmetical measure and that analogies did not always involve rational numbers. The proof of irrational magnitudes was one of the great achievements of Plato's day— much of the research was done by members of the Academy. This fact lends credence to McClain's sensational finding that Plato knew of equal temperament (the octave-scale divided into twelve equal semitones) and used it as a political analogy in the *Republic* and the *Laws*.[4] In such a climate of opinion, one would not be surprised to find contemporary artists and architects employing systems of irrational proportions, such as the golden section. Whether or not such systems were actually applied to the design of the Parthenon and other monuments of the day must remain a speculative question, in the absence of any contemporary literature on architectural theory.

The extant classical writings on music, however, reveal a persistent concern with the proportions of tuning and temperament, particularly with the anomalous fact that a perfectly tuned scale cannot be constructed solely from simple numbers or small-number ratios. Because of a natural discrepancy between the series of octaves generated by the ratio of 1:2 and the series of fifths generated by the ratio of 2:3, the cycle of twelve fifths does not quite return to its starting point at the seventh octave. The difference, ironically named the 'Pythagorean comma', is the subtly irrational interval of 531,441:524,288. Similarly, there is a more comprehensible *diesis* of 125:128 between three pure thirds in the exact ratio of 5:4 and the true octave of 1:2. Having tried to create a musical world view—one of the oldest metaphysics—based on the proportions generated by the first ten integers, the Greeks were forced to recognise these and other embarrassing anomalies, such as the *diaschisma* of 2025:2048 and the *schisma* of 32,768:32,805. Thus the simple, harmonious analogies of the 'fixed' notes of the scale—octave, fifth and fourth—led inexorably, by the same mathematics, to the anomalies of the 'moveable' notes, those smaller intervals whose proportions cannot be entirely rational. It was dissatisfaction, presumably, with the philosophical failure of arithmetical Pythagoreanism that led Aristoxenus to attempt an alternative theory of harmonics without recourse to the old numerical canon.

Despite his belated recognition of incommensurability, Plato remained a Pythagorean to the end: 'To the man who pursues his studies in the proper way, all geometric constructions, all systems of numbers, all duly constituted melodic progressions, the single ordered scheme of all celestial revolutions, should disclose themselves . . . [by] the revelation of a single bond of natural interconnection.'[5] This grand Pythagorean vision irradiates the *Epinomis*, a final Platonic pronouncement whose authorship but not authenticity has been disputed. This invaluable document contains Plato's only explicit reference to the musical analogy 6:8:9:12 which he thought could provide the cosmic bond in a proportional system of arithmetic, geometric and harmonic means (as previously set out in the cosmology of the *Timaeus*).[6] There is no denying the grandeur of the world-view which sought to trace the same musical analogy from the highest level of the macrocosm, in a rational harmony of planetary movements, to the full spectrum of the human microcosm throughout the musical and constructive arts. All the arts, according to Plato, should imitate the universal harmony in reflecting the archetypal form or *schema*, the musical analogy of 6:8:9:12. What is so remarkable here is the sublime faith in a world-view which had conspicuously failed to discover a plausible explanation of the observed planetary motions and which did not really take account of incommensurable magnitudes in geometry or the impossibility of obtaining simple and consistent integral ratios in musical scales. The Pythagorean Plato never lost his faith in the musical cosmology; but the full impact of these dissonant anomalies becomes evident in the thought of Aristotle, who shows none of his teacher's profoundly musical enchantment. For the pupil, pythagoreanism is a myth; yet even the less musical Stagirite retains a theory of proportional justice based on the harmonic concept of analogy.[7]

Despite the Aristotelians and other critics, Plato's Pythagorean ideas remained influential throughout antiquity. His cosmic vision of the musical analogy was kept alive principally through the *Timaeus*, which was always known to the West, at least in the part-translation and commentary of Chalcidius. But Plato's influence alone does not explain the enormous popularity of *analogia* and related terms in Greek writings. A measure of this popularity is now provided by the computer-based *Thesaurus Linguae Graecae*, at the University of California, Irvine—a data-base which contains over 60 million words of Greek texts from Homer until the 6th century A.D. A recent automated search revealed about 14,000 occurrences of *analogia* in all its declined forms, a figure one would hardly anticipate from the available literature on the subject. For the antithetical concept of *anomalia*, the comparable number of occurrences in the data-base is only 1,400.[8] Thus, the bibliometrical comparison confirms the general point I wish to make in this paper. My contention is that we belong to a civilisation that prefers analogy to anomaly: We show a characteristic prejudice in favour of modular forms, regular rhythms, uniform repetitions and standardisation generally, a prejudice that has been greatly reinforced by the advent of industrial technology and mass-production with machines like the printing press.

2. Uses

This preference for analogy or regular proportion, evidently a universal characteristic of civilised societies, dominates our music, architecture, urban design, social manners and most of the other arts, crafts and technologies. Its evidence can be traced back to the earliest forms of agricultural society and considerably earlier. At the extraordinary Terra Amata site, near modern Nice, are the remains of huts built by a community that intermittently hunted and gathered food there about 30,000 years ago. All twenty-one of the huts were found to have the same elongated oval shape in plan and regular tent-like form.[9] Even at this remote period, then, human beings showed a marked preference for regular or analogical forms, which probably informed their musical and other behaviour as well. The human sense of rhythm and form is extremely ancient, certainly much older than the material remains of tools and artifacts would indicate. Lewis Mumford has argued persuasively that the era of human tool technics must have been preceded by an immeasurably longer period of purely 'biotechnical' or bodily development during which man acquired the mental and physical coordination necessary for the formation and manipulation of tools.[10] Since bodily rhythm—that is, the regular repetition of analogical patterns in human behaviour—is necessary for any kind of efficient labour, dance might well have been what Curt Sachs called it, 'the mother of the arts'.[11]

The historian's preoccupation with the literary and mathematical remains of proportional theory, particularly with the suggestive but imperfectly documented traditions of the Pythagoreans, can easily overlook a fundamental point: that the origins of proportionate art and of the analogical world-view in general are much older than philosophy and mathematics—older, probably, than writing itself. In the Egyptian hieroglyph for 'town', a circle enclosing a centrally located cross, we already find the essential geometry of urban form concisely expressed in the symbol or *mandala* which traditionally encoded the analogy of the macrocosm and the microcosm, and the idea of the city or temple as an *imago mundi*. The cosmic associations of the circle (symbolising heaven) and the square (symbolising earth) are found in all the old Eurasian civilisations, which must therefore be presumed to have shared this formative world-view. The high antiquity of these ideas is confirmed by the etymology of key technical terms, some of which take us back to the oldest root-stock of the Indo-European languages. For example, the root, (h)ar, is common to the Greek *harmonia*, the Sanscrit *rta* (world order) and the Latin *ritus* (whence the English terms, rite and ritual): these and many other related terms convey the notion of fitting together opposites, at all cosmic levels, into a balanced whole. The same world-view connects the root, tem, with *temenos* (the sacred circular space), *templum* (the divine house within the sacred space), *tempus* (perhaps expressing the image of time as circular) and apparently also *template* (which preserves the idea of an outline or analogical form).[12] Closely related is the extensive vocabulary of tuning, words such as temper, temperance, temperament, which, as Leo Spitzer has shown, is employed throughout the cosmic hierarchy and widely diffused among the European languages.[13] The distribution of this terminology alone demonstrates the cultural significance of analogy or proportion, especially *due proportion*, a concept deployed in most areas of human regulation and control, including ethics, law, politics, medicine, architecture and the polite and ornamental arts generally. The unifying principle here is music, whether in the concrete forms of human song and dance or in the more intellectual abstractions and cosmic associations of the vibrating string.

For thousands of years, then, analogy has been part of the civilised world-view, informing the beliefs, customs, ideas and arts of urbanised, agricultural society. The conception of proportional form and modular organisation was so deeply embedded in the civilised consciousness that it even survived the 'untuning of the sky', the decline of the old cosmic mythology with the rise of modern science in the seventeenth century.[14] The prejudice in favour of the analogical still remains, however, in the modern mentality where it enjoys almost the status of a Kantian category of thought and understanding. Here we are still virtually at one with the ancient Greeks who delighted in analogical argument so much that they omitted to include its logical limitations and typical forms of abuse in their classification of sophisms. Aristotle's list of fallacies does not include the *argument from false analogy*, which was first named by the Elizabethan lawyer and logician, Abraham Fraunce, in 1588.[15] But the principle of the fallacy is easy enough to state: if things resemble each other in some respects, it is never valid to infer that they will resemble each other in further respects. Very often, however, additional resemblances are discovered by analogical reasoning, whose convenience, utility and success-rate sometimes outweigh the dangers of fallacious inference and false analogy.

The ancients obviously found great utility and convenience in the analogical conception of nature and art; but, to our eyes, their analogies often seem far-fetched and ridiculous. For example, there was an admirable balance and wholeness in the philosophy which saw the quaternary of the four elements (earth, air, fire and water) imitated analogically in the four seasons, the four winds, the four corners of the world, the four quarters of the city (and their four resident castes), the four strings of the tetrachord, the four ages of man, the four humours and the four cardinal virtues.[16] But the scientific revolution finally produced too many anomalies for the four-fold cosmology. After that profound transformation of human consciousness which gave rise to the modern world, how much was left of the old system of cosmic order beyond the mechanical convenience of orthogonal design and the vague feeling that the decent person or place was still somehow *four-square*?

But the Age of Science was not entirely destructive of analogical thought. Indeed, it actually produced some new forms, including the clockwork model of the universe (and its corresponding microcosms, mechanistic medicine and the industrial production-line); empiricist psychology and the behaviourist techniques of education, persuasion and management; the uniformitarian (or non-catastrophic) theory of organic evolution; the logical machine and the simulation of thought in the technology of artificial intelligence. We are now entering a post-scientific, post-mechanist age—one more akin, in some respects, to the spirit of the ancient vitalist or animist world—but we are still too much imbued with the mechanistic models of Isaac Newton, John Locke, Charles Darwin and Norbert Wiener to be able to recognise the true strengths and weaknesses of their potent analogies.

3. Limitations

Among the creations of modern science was the editorial technique of the influential philologian and Germanist, Karl Lachmann (1793-1851). The non-mathematical or fallacious kind of analogy was an important part of his linguistic methodology, which included the classification of sources, the comparison of variant spellings and passages, the establishing of the *stemmata codicum*, and the final 'normalisation' of the text in a definitive *Urtext*.[17] These procedures are immediately recognised by a musicologist because they were adopted wholesale into the new discipline of *Musikwissenschaft* to become the editorial methods for the collected works of the great composers, such as the German edition of Bach which began to appear in the year of Lachmann's death.[18] The old Bach-Gesellschaft edition and most of the subsequent *Gesamtausgaben* are full of normalisations in the Lachmann manner, particularly of passages which are melodically analogous but notated in the original sources with inconsistencies of rhythm, articulation, ornamentation, dynamics and so on.[19] For well over a century the scores of most early (that is, pre-twentieth-century) composers have been systematically 'regularised by analogy' and the details of the additions and alterations laboriously recorded in critical commentaries.[20]

Until the 1960s hardly anyone paused to question the systematic regularisation of early music according to the principle of analogy or to consider the possibility that the extensive alterations of the original scores were not always justifiable corrections but sometimes outright falsifications. Signs of dissatisfaction with editorial standardisation go back to the 1840s;[21] yet even today there would be very few professional musicologists who would be prepared to admit that the editorial argument from analogy might after all be fallacious and to entertain the anomalous and inconsistent notations as the old composers so often left them.

Once raised, however, these doubts are hard to dispel. Linguists no longer wholeheartedly endorse Lachmann's methods, which, as Paul Oskar Kristeller reminds us, are inappropriate for certain kinds of texts and sources, for example, autograph manuscripts.[22] There is now a growing awareness of their impropriety in musicological editing. Australian musicologists, I am proud to say, have been at the forefront of this new movement from analogy to anomaly. It is more than thirty years since the Australian conductor, Denis Vaughan, began his long campaign for the recognition and protection of the original texts of Verdi and Puccini, in all their amazing variety of detail.[23] In 1962 Dene Barnett edited the *St Matthew Passion*, preserving its original inconsistencies of articulation, for a performance in Sydney under Charles Mackerras; and in 1977 he published a rigorous authentication of Haydn's irregular slurs.[24] In 1979 I published a general analysis of the 'revolution' that is now occurring in editorial procedures and performance practices, as more and more of the original anomalies and irregularities are accepted as authentic nuances and deliberate variations.[25] My views on Handel's notorious inconsistencies, especially of note-length and rhythm, have now been fully confirmed in a computer analysis of the incipits to his operas and oratorios: the results, which leave no room for doubt as to where his intentions lay, should be ready for publication soon.[26] I am also proud to recall that my methodological 'paradigm of inconsistency' was endorsed by the late Professor Gordon Anderson who, before his untimely death, was our most distinguished student of medieval music. Professor Anderson published an important article on irregularities in the rhythmic modes of medieval music,[27] and he also agreed with my opinion that the accidentals of this music were not always meant to be notated or performed consistently.[28]

Conclusion

When the European colonists came to this southern land, they found the climate and many other aspects of life to be the reverse of what they had been used to in the northern hemisphere; and so it would not be surprising to discover a new view of music emerging (actually, an old view re-emerging) from the topsy-turvey Antipodes. It may be that the effort of coming to terms with an anomalous landscape has made Australians more alive to the irregular beauties of nature and less susceptible to the rationalistic mythologies of the Old World. But, whatever the geographical lines of the dispute might turn out to be, there is now a fundamental debate about the uses and limitations of analogy in music, recalling in some respects the dispute between the analogists and the anomalists of classical grammar.[29]

The key issue here is the balance of uniformity as against variety in music; and the outcome, which I expect to favour increased variety, will affect not only editorial procedures and performance practices in early music but also aesthetics, the history of taste and our understanding of the art and nature of music as a whole. The result, I predict, will be a heightened appreciation of how ingeniously the old masters managed to represent, in the same system of notation, the rigid modules of measured pitch and rhythm together with the free or irregular nuances of a natural, living music. In so doing, they demonstrated that art could imitate nature not only in the contrived analogies of rational geometry but also in the unpredictable anomalies of irrational expression and spontaneous behaviour.

Notes

[1] W. A. Fairservis, Jr., *The Threshold of Civilization: An Experiment in Prehistory* (New York, 1975), pp. 143-4.
[2] Árpád Szabó, *The Beginnings of Greek Mathematics* (Dordrecht and Boston, 1978), pp. 132ff.
[3] Ernest G. McClain, *The Pythagorean Plato: Prelude to the Song Itself* (New York, 1978), pp. 8ff. and Chapters 6-8.
[4] McClain, *ibid.*, pp. 5, 14, 55, 99-101, 127-9.

5 *Epinomis* 991e-992a; see also McClain, *op. cit.*, p. 7.

6 *Epinomis* 990e-991b. *Cf.* McClain *op. cit.*, pp. 8ff. and A. E. Taylor, *Plato: The Man and His Work*, 3d edn. (London, 1929), p. 501.

7 Aristotle, *Ethica Nicomachea* 1131a-1134b.

8 I thank the Director of the Text Search Service of *Thesaurus Linguae Graecae*, Professor Theodore F. Brunner, for kindly providing this information and other help. It is surprising to discover that this huge data-base preserves only one instance where a Greek author (Posidonius) has mentioned *analogia* and *anomalia* in the same passage.

9 Fairservis, *op. cit.*, p. 61.

10 Lewis Mumford, 'Technics and the Nature of Man', in Paul H. Oehser (ed.), *Knowledge Among Men* (New York, 1966), pp. 126-42.

11 Curt Sachs, *World History of the Dance* (New York, 1937), p. 3.

12 *Cf.* Marco M. Olivetti, *Il tempio simbolo cosmico* (Rome, 1967), pp. 26ff., 41ff.

13 Leo Spitzer, *Classical and Christian Ideas of World Harmony: Prolegomena to an Interpretation of the Word 'Stimmung'* (Baltimore, 1963).

14 John Hollander, *The Untuning of the Sky: Ideas of Music in English Poetry* (New York, 1970).

15 C. L. Hamblin, *Fallacies* (London, 1970), p. 142.

16 Spitzer, *op. cit.,* pp. 64ff. The general principle is stated by M. T. Varro, *De Lingua Latina*, Book V, 12-13.

17 On the philological use of normalisation, *see* Magdalene Lutz-Hensel, *Prinzipien der ersten textkritischen Editionen mittelhochdeutscher Dichtung . . . Eine methodenkritische Analyse* (Berlin, 1975), a study of the editorial methods developed by the Grimm brothers, Benecke and Lachmann. On the use of analogy by these influential philologians, see the references under 'Analogie' in Lutz-Hensel's subject index, p. 519.

18 For evidence of Lachmann's influence in musicology, *see* Friedrich Blume, 'Probleme musikalischer Gesamtausgaben', in A. A. Abert and M. Ruhnke (eds.), *Syntagma Musicologicum II* (Kassel, 1973), pp. 79-87.

19 Lutz-Hensel, *op. cit.*, pp. 192ff. (*cf.* 360ff.), who throws much light on the origins of procedures that became standard in musicological editing.

20 Graham Pont, 'A Revolution in the Science and Practice of Music', *Musicology V,* (1979), pp. 1-66; *see especially* pp. 2-22.

21 Pont, *op. cit.*, pp. 27-33.

22 Paul Oskar Kristeller, 'The Lachmann Method: Merits and Limitations', *Text: Transactions of the Society for Textual Scholarship*, 1 (1981), pp. 11-20; *see especially* p. 16. I thank Richard D'Avigdor for his help in locating this very useful review of Lachmann's methods by a distinguished representative of the German philological tradition. Philip Brett has recently provided a valuable analysis of this tradition and its influence on the editing of early music: *see* 'Text, Context and the Early

Music Editor', in Nicholas Kenyon (ed.), *Authenticity and Early Music* (Oxford, 1988), pp. 83-114.

23 For a list of Vaughan's relevant publications, *see* Pont, *op. cit.*, p. 66. A representative statement of his views is found in 'The Inner Language of Verdi's Manuscripts', *Musicology V*, (1979), pp. 67-153.

24 Dene Barnett, 'Non-uniform Slurring in 18th Century Music: Accident or Design?', *Haydn Yearbook*, 10 (1977), pp. 179-99.

25 Pont, *op. cit.*

26 A brief preliminary announcement of results from the computer analysis of Handel's incipits is found in 'Handel's "Inconsistencies"', *The University of New South Wales Annual Report 1987* (Kensington, 1988), p. 58.

27 Gordon Anderson, 'Johannes de Garlandia and the Simultaneous Use of Mixed Rhythmic Modes', *Miscellanea Musicologica*, 8 (1975), pp. 11-31.

28 *See* Pont, *op. cit.*, pp. 31-2. My discussion of *musica ficta* was written with Anderson's advice and approval. *See* his citation in *Journal of the American Musicological Society*, 31 (1978), p. 480.

29 The argument from analogy was used in classical times to amend natural irregularities in language, including those of Homer. *See* F. H. Colson, 'The Analogist and Anomalist Controversy', *The Classical Quarterly*, 13 (1919), pp. 24-36, especially p. 25. The issue between analogists and anomalists is precisely stated by Varro, *De Lingua Latina*, Book VIII, 23; and the continuity between ancient and modern regularisation by analogy is noted by R. G. Kent, the translator of the Loeb edition, *On the Latin Language* (London, 1938), vol. II, p. 389. It is not difficult to foresee that the present musical controversy will find a resolution like the ancient linguistic controversy, in the 'ultimate recognition of the fact that in the realm of language, as in the world of nature, uniformity and variety are inextricably intermingled with one another'. *See* Sir John Edwin Sandys, *A History of Classical Scholarship* (Cambridge, 1903), vol. I, pp. 179-81.

Contributors

CAROL K. BARON is writing a theoretical study of Charles Ives's music for Yale University Press. Her article, 'Dating the Music of Charles Ives: Facts and Fictions', appeared in *Perspectives of New Music* (Winter issue, 1990). Address: 321 Melbourne Road, Great Neck, NY 10021, USA.

JUDITH BECKER has published *Traditional Music in Modern Java* (1980) and, with A. Feinstein, *Karawitan: Source Readings in Javanese Gamelan and Vocal Music* (3 vols., 1984–88). She is now writing a book entitled *In the Presence of the Past: Aesthetics and Tantrism in Central Java.* Address: School of Music, University of Michigan, 804 Burton Tower, Ann Arbor, MI 48109-1270, USA.

NAOMI CUMMING holds a Rothman's Foundation Post-doctoral Fellowship for 1990–91, during which period she has pursued studies in the philosophy of music theory, particularly as related to concepts of melody. Address: Elder Conservatorium of Music, University of Adelaide, P.O. Box 498, Adelaide, SA 5022, Australia

PATRICIA DEBLY has published articles in *Musick* (1988) and *Studies on Voltaire and the Eighteenth-Century* (1989). Her main area of research has been the Italian operas of Joseph Haydn. Address: Department of Music, Brock University, St Catharines, Ontario L2S 3A1, Canada.

MARION A. GUCK is a member of the Society for Music Theory's Executive Board and an Associate Editor of *Perspectives of New Music*. Her work focuses on questions of the nature of musical discourse, in particular the part played by metaphoric description, and on twentieth-century music. Address: Department of Music, Washington University in St Louis, Campus Box 1032, One Brookings Drive, St Louis, MO 63130-4899, USA.

JAMIE C. KASSLER was a founder of the North Papers project at the University of New South Wales, the purpose of which is to produce editions and bibliographical tools relating to the unpublished and published writings of Roger North and his milieu. She is now investigating the role of music in understanding internal character. Address: School of Science and Technology Studies, University of New South Wales, P.O. Box 1, Kensington, NSW 2033, Australia.

RICHARD LEPPERT has co-edited with Susan McClary *Music and Society: The Politics of Composition, Performance and Reception* (1987) and is now writing a book provisionally entitled *The Sight of Sound: Visual Constructions of Meaning in Western Musical Practices.* Address: Humanities Department, University of Minnesota, 314 Ford Hall, 224 Church Street S.E., Minneapolis, MN 55455, USA.

GRAHAM PONT teaches historical aspects of the philosophy of technology (including music) and is writing a book on *The Handel Tradition*, while developing a computer-based taxonomy of baroque musical notation. Between 1975 and 1977 he was President of the Musicological Society of Australia. Address: School of Liberal and General Studies, University of New South Wales, P.O. Box 1, Kensington, NSW 2033, Australia.

GEOFFREY SAMUEL is an anthropologist and ethnomusicologist, whose publications include 'Songs of Lhasa' (*Ethnomusicology*, vol. 20), *Mind, Body and Culture* (in press, Cambridge University Press) and *Shamanic and Clerical Buddhism in Tibet* (in press, Smithsonian Institution). Address: Department of Sociology, University of Newcastle, Rankin Drive, Newcastle, NSW 2308, Australia.

AMNON SHILOAH received the Jerusalem Prize for contributions to ethnomusicology. He has written extensively on Near Eastern music history and theory and on the living musical practice of Arabic and Jewish music. Address: The Hebrew University of Jerusalem, Rothberg School for Overseas Students, Goldsmith Building, Mount Scopus, 91905 Jerusalem, Israel.

MARTINA SICHARDT is a technical editor with the Arnold Schönberg Gesamtausgabe. Her doctoral thesis will soon appear as a book, *Die Entstehung der Zwölftonmethode Arnold Schönbergs* (Mainz: Schott). Address: Arnold Schönberg Gesamtausgabe, Forschungsstelle, D-1 Berlin 15, Bundesallee 1-12, Germany.

MORRIS TAYLOR teaches music history and research. A former student of Dame Myra Hess and Mme Rosinna Lhevinne, he also performs as soloist and duo-pianist. Address: Andrews University, Berrien Springs, MI 49104, USA.

ASHLEY TURNER is completing his dissertation on the music of the Petalangan Malay people of Riau, Sumatra, where, and in Nias, he has conducted fieldwork. Currently, he is a consultant for the Ford Foundation in the Ethnomusicology Department, University of North Sumatra, Medan. Contact address: Department of Music, Monash University, Clayton, VIC 3168, Australia.

Index

compiled by Janet D. Hine

Page numbers in **bold face** under names of persons refer to their contributions to this work